Entente Cordiale

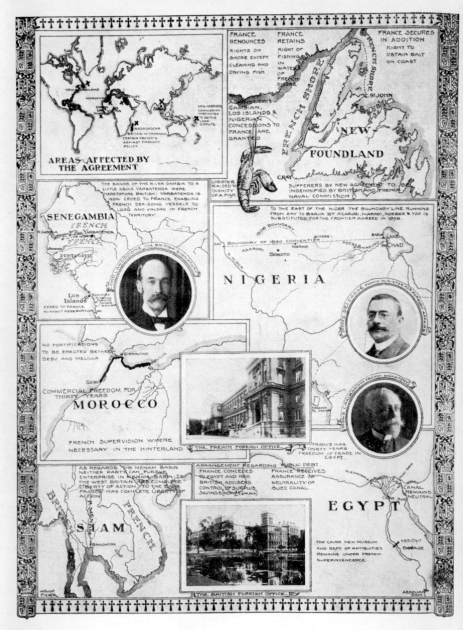

A great guarantee of European peace: The Anglo-French agreement

Entente Cordiale

THE ORIGINS AND NEGOTIATION OF THE ANGLO-FRENCH AGREEMENTS OF 8 APRIL 1904

P. J. V. Rolo

MACMILLAN
ST MARTIN'S PRESS

© P. J. V. Rolo 1969

First published 1969 by
MACMILLAN AND CO LTD
Little Essex Street London W C 2
and also at Bombay Calcutta and Madras
Macmillan South Africa (Publishers) Pty Ltd Johannesburg
The Macmillan Company of Australia Pty Ltd Melbourne
The Macmillan Company of Canada Ltd Toronto
St Martin's Press Inc New York
Gill and Macmillan Ltd Dublin

Library of Congress catalog card no. 77-86588

Printed in Great Britain by
ROBERT MACLEHOSE AND CO LTD
The University Press, Glasgow

*To my mother
and in memory of my father*

Contents

LIST OF ILLUSTRATIONS

MAPS

ABBREVIATIONS

BD   *British Documents on the Origins of War, 1898–
1914*

DDF i   *Documents Diplomatiques Français, 1871–1900,
1ère Serie*

DDF   *Documents Diplomatiques Français, 1901–1911,
2ème Serie*

CC i   *Paul Cambon Correspondence, 1870–1924,* vol. i

CC ii   vol. ii

Introduction

'WHEN dealing with the English', wrote Cambon[1] on 30 July 1899, 'it is much easier to reach an understanding on concrete and practical questions than on general principles.' The Convention between the United Kingdom and France about Newfoundland and West and Central Africa and the mutual Declarations about Egypt, Morocco, Siam, Madagascar and the New Hebrides, all signed on 8 April 1904, were clearly concerned with 'practical and concrete questions'. And yet, throughout the course of the negotiations, the prospective settlement was described as an *Entente Cordiale*. The term, suggestive of agreement on 'general principles', had previously been applied to a spell of Anglo-French co-operation during the reign of Louis-Philippe[2] and had from henceforth slipped easily into use on both sides of the channel whenever any kind of *rapprochement* was being canvassed. There was, therefore, not necessarily any new significance in the naming of the specific bargains concluded in 1904 as *Entente Cordiale*. Friendly understanding, quite apart from its previous currency in the vocabulary of Anglo-French relations, is a normal objective in diplomacy. It can be based equally well on 'general principles' as on 'concrete and practical questions'. In this case, however, the term *Entente Cordiale* was to achieve dramatic fame.

During the years after signature of the agreements of 1904 and before the outbreak of the First World War, *Entente Cordiale* assumed the character of a close, if unwritten, alliance. In that war it was cemented by blood. Thus strengthened it survived the frustrations and quarrels which followed the peace. It rallied, however uneasily, to resist Hitler. It was invoked by Winston Churchill at the nadir of Anglo-French fortunes when he offered common citizenship to the French. It proved a beacon in the dark days of Vichy. It was triumphantly proclaimed at the liberation of

---

[1] Ambassador in London. See pp. 92–5.
[2] See p. 19.

France. Its emotive force as a symbol of 'general principles' is even now not yet spent.

On the other hand the 'concrete and practical questions' settled in 1904 have proved of far more ephemeral significance. The last traces of the British occupation of Egypt were painfully obliterated in the Suez fiasco. French Morocco, won at such human and financial cost, is French no more. The two great colonial rivals have ceased to be colonial powers. The practical basis of the bargains of 1904 has vanished with the wind of change. But the image of *Entente Cordiale*, in spite of passing shadows, survives. It may yet have a part to play, not only in the development of Anglo-French relations, but perhaps in the eventual achievement of European unity.

But the *Entente Cordiale* legend, however potent for the future, can easily throw a distorting light on the significance of the agreements made in 1904. The purpose of this study is to trace the origins of those agreements, to examine the negotiations in their contemporary setting and to investigate what wider considerations, if any, lay behind the bargains then concluded.

I cannot understand why a book on this particular theme has not already been written. Perhaps it is because, with the publication of the British and French Diplomatic Documents, such a book seemed unnecessary. But, after using these documents as the basis for teaching a history special subject on the making of the *Entente* for the past twenty years, I cannot help feeling that the story, as there revealed, is of sufficient interest to be made readily available to those who do not habitually read diplomatic documents. My object, therefore, is to present a topic which might otherwise only be approached by specialists, so that it may be pursued by a wider range of history students and by general readers interested in recent history. For the convenience of those who are not fluent in French I have rendered all French quotations into my own English translation.

In my study of the *Entente* negotiations I have relied mainly on original printed sources. I am quite sure that there is much unpublished material demanding attention but I am equally sure that justice has not yet been done to the material which is available in print. That task, as a first step, seemed to me worth attempting. In giving some account of the general background I have, of course, relied a great deal on secondary sources. My references and bibliography will, I hope, indicate acknowledgement of these debts. But here I would like particularly to mention J. Gallagher and R. Robinson, *Africa and the Victorians*; J. D. Hargreaves, *Prelude to the Partition of West Africa*; G. N. Sanderson, *England, Europe and the Upper Nile*; J. L. Miège, *Le Maroc et l'Europe*, vol. 4: *Vers la Crise*; J. A. S. Grenville, *Lord Salisbury and Foreign Policy*; and G. Monger, *The End of Isolation*.

In my last chapter I have tried to indicate how the *Entente* was transformed into a war-time alliance and to consider how far this result was a consequence of the existence of the *Entente* itself. These problems touch the nerve centres of power politics during the decade before the war. To tackle them in any kind of depth would require another volume. I have therefore confined myself to a summary of my own conclusions. In so doing I hope at least to have been able to add one awkward question concerning the origins of the First World War to those which still attract the belligerent attention of scholars.

While writing about the *Entente Cordiale* I have throughout been conscious of the gratitude which I owe to Keele students whose work on the subject has provided a constant and illuminating stimulus. Among them I should particularly mention Mr H. J. Koch, now a lecturer at York, who did his best, not only to sharpen my wits, but to bring to my notice a number of relevant secondary sources which would otherwise most probably have escaped me. To Professor W. M. Simon of the University of Keele I am grateful for permission to make use of an unpublished thesis prepared in 1947 and entitled 'Spain and the Morocco policy of the Powers: a decade of diplomacy (1902–1912)'. I also wish to thank Squadron-Leader Chivers for permission to make use of an unfinished thesis entitled 'The Committee of Imperial Defence and the Defence of India 1900–1907', which he is preparing to submit for a Ph.D. under my supervision. To Dr Andrew I am especially indebted for letting me see the galley proofs of his *Théophile Delcassé and the Making of the Entente Cordiale* (1968), which in fact constitutes the first major study to have been attempted of Delcassé's foreign policy and which includes much hitherto unpublished material mainly from Delcassé's private papers.

Finally I would like to thank my stepdaughter Margaret Gordon

Walker for her help in the making of maps and Dr Field of the University of Keele for proof-reading and consequent advice.

I

Rivalry and Rapprochement

THE French, like the Irish and the Scots, live with their history. The English, although they may now be living on it, are far less emotionally involved. In spite of the efforts of nineteenth-century romanticists English attitudes to France at the beginning of the twentieth century were not tinged by bitter memories of 1066 and Lansdowne[1] was never even tempted to evoke the spirit of Hereward the Wake. Delcassé,[2] however, readily confessed to a cult for Joan of Arc. There was no doubt that the springs of French patriotism were deeply embedded in the Hundred Years War against England. The memory of that struggle remained carefully cherished down the centuries.

Nevertheless, once fighting in France had ceased to provide a regular occupation for the barons of England, relations between the two nations improved. The religious, economic and dynastic conflicts of the sixteenth century were too complex to perpetuate an Anglo-French dual. On the contrary, English fears of Spain and French ambitions in Europe promoted occasional alliance and a basic understanding which survived almost throughout the seventeenth century. While England turned against her Dutch commercial rivals France harassed the Hapsburgs. Their interests on the whole coincided.

It was not until Louis XIV sought to establish what English statesmen could only interpret as a European hegemony that France became *the* enemy. English money and the military genius of Marlborough eventually turned the scales against Louis XIV's bid for European mastery. At the Treaty of Utrecht, which ended

---

[1] Henry Charles Keith Petty-Fitzmaurice, 5th Marquess of Landsdowne (1845–1927), British Foreign Secretary 1900–5.

[2] Théophile Delcassé (1852–1923), French Foreign Minister 1898–1905.

the long series of wars, English statesmen tried to make their compromise European settlement more palatable at home by insisting on colonial gains. Among these was recognition in Article XIII of British sovereignty over all the islands of Newfoundland with the exception of the two small islands of St-Pierre and Miquelon. Certain important fishing rights were however reserved to the French. These rights were to become the source of much future friction and a main topic in the *Entente* negotiations. Their association with the Treaty of Utrecht gave them a status which time had by then hallowed. By the same treaty French possessions in North America were also reduced by the loss of Acadia and Hudson Bay. Thus, on a pattern which was to become familiar, France was made to pay heavily overseas for the compromises salvaged from defeat in Europe.

In the meanwhile, with the collapse of Louis XIV's wider European ambitions, the statesmen who governed French policy during the regency which followed his death sought and established good understanding with England. They also turned with some enthusiasm to colonial ventures. But the colonial rivalries, which inevitably developed, gradually eroded the good understanding. In the War of the Austrian Succession (1741–8) and again in the Seven Years War (1756–63) this rivalry played a main part in determining England's involvement and European alignment. In spite of military defeat in the Seven Years War, France survived as a great power in Europe. But she lost most of her overseas empire. Her challenge to Britain in India was virtually spent while Canada and a lion's share of the West Indies became British prizes. One small consolation, upon which the French successfully insisted, was a reaffirmation, at the Treaty of Paris, of Newfoundland fishing rights. In 1761 Pitt's[1] endeavour to swallow these rights and Choiseul's[2] obstinacy in their defence proved important factors in the failure of peace negotiations then attempted.

The revolt of England's American colonies offered France an opportunity for some kind of revenge. At the price of a very costly war this was achieved. The colonial gains secured at the Treaty of Versailles were small in comparison. Tobago in the

---

[1] William Pitt, 1st Earl of Chatham (1708–78).
[2] Étienne-François, Duc de Choiseul (1719–85), French Foreign Minister.

West Indies, and Senegal in Africa, both lost in 1763, were recovered. The islands of St-Pierre and Miquelon, which the British had seized during the war, were restored and French fishing rights in Newfoundland were reaffirmed with some revision in favour of France.

In 1786 the younger Pitt[1] concluded a Treaty of Commerce with France. As a disciple of Adam Smith[2] he was more interested in trade than in colonial disputes. The French Government, in cautious pursuit of limited ambitions in Europe, was anxious to cultivate English friendship; an era of *rapprochement* seemed to be at hand.

It was interrupted by the French Revolution. The success of the revolutionary armies against Austria and Prussia, with Belgium as the immediate prize, led almost inevitably to war between England and France. French possession of all the channel ports was regarded as a direct threat to England's security. When war became the business of revolutionary governments and the road to power was opened to Napoleon, Pitt's essay in preventive war developed into an epic struggle for national survival. To Napoleon, England was not only the paymaster of European resistance but also the mistress of empires overseas which France had lost and which he dreamed of recovering. His expedition to Egypt,[3] fortuitously undertaken at a critical juncture in his own career, had led him to speculate on a hegemony which stretched beyond Europe through the Near East to India. After his own return to France he was loth to sever the Egyptian contacts which had been so spectacularly established. One of the reasons for the failure of the compromise peace achieved by the Treaty of Amiens in 1802 was Napoleon's reluctance to sacrifice the last remaining links with Egypt and England's consequent unwillingness to abandon Malta. French involvement in Egypt was to prove one of the least ephemeral of random Napoleonic legacies.

In the face of British naval superiority, as illustrated at Trafalgar, Napoleon was obliged to conclude that neither Great Britain nor her overseas empire could be taken by assault. This led him to a

---

[1] William Pitt (1759–1806).

[2] Adam Smith (1723–90), Glasgow professor whose *Wealth of Nations*, published in 1776, became the handbook of the Free Trade movement.

[3] Nelson's annihilation of his fleet at the battle of the Nile on 1 Aug 1798 effectively blockaded Napoleon in Egypt.

clumsy and complicated experiment in economic warfare. The Continental System, designed to deny all European markets to English trade, was to have ruined England by glut of goods. It implied complete French mastery of the whole of Europe. Partly in pursuit of this objective Napoleon was led to the invasion of Spain. The Spanish ulcer proved England's first opportunity to strike back on the continent. From then on England became an active participant, and not merely a paymaster, in the fight on land. It was not until Waterloo that the full significance of this fact was forced upon Napoleon.

With hindsight 1815 has proved the great dividing line in Anglo-French relations. Waterloo has remained the last important occasion on which Englishmen and Frenchmen have fought on opposite sides in battle. The scars of that conflict healed with rapidity on both sides of the Channel. There were several reasons for this. As far as England was concerned the war had developed into a war against Napoleon rather than against France. Pitt in 1790 had seen Russia, rather than France, as representing a future threat to Britain. Provided France was not seeking the kind of hegemony which Napoleon had attempted, she could be regarded, not only as a very valuable customer, but as a useful guarantor of power balance in Europe. The dismemberment of France was no part of Castlereagh's[1] peace programme. On the contrary, at the Congress of Vienna Castlereagh made a secret treaty of alliance with Talleyrand[2] and with Metternich[3] in an endeavour to conjure Russian dangers. Although precautions must be taken to insure against a recrudescence of French aggression in Europe, good understanding with Bourbon-restored France was an immediate objective. In France the revolution rather than the wars represented reality. The wars originally seemed to have been fought in defence of the revolution and against the rulers of Europe. But Napoleon's European Empire, however gratifying to many Frenchmen's pride and to some Frenchmen's pockets, damaged the character of those wars. They became less popular. Divergence between the interests of France and the will of Napoleon

---

[1] Robert Stewart, Viscount Castlereagh and afterwards 2nd Marquess of Londonderry (1769–1822), British Foreign Secretary 1812–22.

[2] Charles-Maurice de Talleyrand-Périgord, Prince of Benevento (1754–1838). French Foreign Minister and Plenipotentiary at the Congress of Vienna.

[3] Clemens, Prince Metternich (1773–1859), Austrian Chancellor.

was increasingly apparent. The argument that the revolution was being defended against the rulers of Europe grew threadbare. On the contrary it was more plausible to believe that battle was engaged against and not for the peoples of Europe. Furthermore the diversity of the enemies encountered prevented the emergence of one identifiable enemy. Even though England, a traditional rival, had proved the most consistent opponent, there was no concentration of bitterness. The memory of Napoleon's victories was cherished and yet his final defeat was accepted almost with relief. Rancour against the agents of that defeat was inevitably somewhat blunted. Talleyrand, who considered himself the residuary legatee of French patriotic purpose, was concerned above all else to cultivate England's friendship, which he regarded as the cornerstone of any immediately viable foreign policy.

This assumption survived his own fall from grace in the euphoric atmosphere of ultra-royalism which bedevilled the Bourbon restoration. In 1823, however, events in the Iberian Peninsula caused serious strain on Anglo-French relations. The French decision to impose a counter-revolution by military force in Spain seemed like a major challenge to British interests. Not only Spain but Portugal and Latin America could be considered at stake. British warnings over Latin America and British action in Portugal brought diplomatic triumphs to Canning.[1] But in fact the French ministers, with the possible exception of Chateaubriand,[2] had no grand design and knowledge of their desire to avoid any serious clash with England gave Canning the confidence to assume aggressive attitudes.

When French troops were eventually withdrawn from Spain, Canning was able to turn to the problem which was to dominate British foreign policy in the nineteenth century: the Eastern Question. He followed a policy already outlined by Pitt and endorsed by Castlereagh of trying to protect Turkey against Russia. His method was ingenious in that, by working with Russia over the question of Greek independence, he sought to contain Russia. France he regarded as a natural ally, and thanks

---

[1] George Canning (1770–1827), British Foreign Secretary 1822–7.
[2] François-René, Vicomte de Chateaubriand (1768–1848), French writer and statesman; Foreign Minister 1822–4.

partly to the philhellenism of Charles X,[1] he succeeded in associating the French with his objective. This first essay in Anglo-French co-operation in the Mediterranean, illustrated by the Anglo-French naval action at Navarino,[2] foundered after Canning's death.

The calculations were too subtle for his successors. Russia was allowed to drift into war with Turkey. The ministers of Charles X, anticipating a Near Eastern landslide for Russia and eager to bolster up a tottering régime by spectacular foreign policy, dreamed of exacting rewards in Europe as the price of compliance. They also prepared an Algerian expedition, ostensibly against the Barbary pirates. The Algerian expedition proved to be the beginning of the French conquest of Algeria, but plans for aggression in Europe were rudely and fortunately interrupted by the July Revolution in 1830.

With Talleyrand again in favour and quickly installed as ambassador in London, where he remained until 1834, avoidance of adventures and close co-operation with England were re-established as principles of French foreign policy. This, in the light of the Belgian revolution,[3] was a factor of major importance. France was presented with an easy opportunity to annex Belgium. There could have been no clearer case for Anglo-French conflict. The self-denying ordinance which Talleyrand imposed eventually enabled Palmerston[4] to find a solution to the Belgian question which French arms finally imposed on the reluctant Dutch.

The consequent cordiality of Anglo-French relations gradually came to grief over the Eastern Question. Though Russia occupied a position of dominant influence at Constantinople she had not destroyed the Turkish Empire. On the contrary, at a price[5] which filled England with foreboding, Russia had rescued Turkey from destruction at the hands of her Sultan's vassal, Mohammed Ali

[1] Charles X (1757–1836), King of France 1824–30.

[2] Battle of Navarino, 20 Oct 1827. French, Russian and British squadrons under Vice-Admiral Codrington's command destroyed the Turco-Egyptian fleet.

[3] Against the Union with Holland imposed by the 1815 Vienna peace settlement.

[4] Henry John Temple, 3rd Viscount Palmerston (1784–1865), British Foreign Secretary 1830–4, 1835–41, 1846–51; Home Secretary 1852–5; Prime Minister 1855–8, and 1859–65.

[5] By the Treaty of Unkiar Skelessi (1833) Russia committed herself to come to the aid of Turkey, if attacked, and Turkey agreed, in those circumstances, to open the straits to Russian warships. In England the treaty was interpreted as implying a virtual Russian protectorate over Turkey.

of Egypt.[1] Mohammed Ali, halted in his hopes of wider conquest, was turning for aid and expert advice to France. French enterprise was engaged in a 'civilising' mission in Egypt. Palmerston viewed this with increasing mistrust. Mohammed Ali's power still remained a threat to Turkey and the preservation of Turkey remained a paramount British interest. When Sultan Mahmud,[2] against British advice, decided on a trial of strength with Mohammed Ali, Palmerston reverted to Canning's tactics of seeking, by co-operation, to draw the sting from Russian ambitions. An Anglo-Russian pact to defend Turkey was concluded. British naval and military action effectively robbed Mohammed Ali not only of his Constantinople prize, but of his previous Syrian conquests. France was forced to choose between watching the humiliation of her Egyptian client or once again trying to meet the challenge of British naval power. It was an unpleasant but not a difficult decision. There was, on the whole, less resentment against England than criticism of the policy which had led to confrontation. By the Straits settlement of 1841 Palmerston hoped that he had solved the Eastern Question. The closing of the Dardanelles to all ships of war was a formula which gave comfort both to Russia and to England. Palmerston could claim that he had guaranteed the security of British Mediterranean trade and of routes to India. As safeguards against future contingencies he had successfully opposed French-backed plans to dig a Suez Canal and he had also occupied Aden. The typical Palmerstonian bluster which accompanied his successful policy probably offended the French Government even more than the incidental damage to French credit in Egypt. A residue of tension in Anglo-French relations was inevitable.

Changes of government in England and France, however, soon helped to ease the strain. Peel[3] and Guizot[4] were equally determined on close co-operation. Even though in Greece and in Egypt local jealousies could not be curbed, incidents, far from being exploited by either government, were deliberately played down and patched over. *Entente Cordiale*, eagerly fostered by

---

[1] Mohammed Ali Pasha (Mehemet Ali), ruler of Egypt 1805–49.

[2] Mahmud II, Sultan of Turkey 1808–39.

[3] Sir Robert Peel, 2nd Bt (1788–1850), Prime Minister 1834–5 and 1841–6.

[4] François Guizot (1787–1874), French Foreign Minister 1841–7, Prime Minister 1847–8.

Princess Lieven,[1] was an established fact. *Enrichissez-vous* was a motto which appealed as much to Peel as to Guizot.

In both countries there were, of course, critics of so much sweet reasonableness, but it was not until the question of Spanish marriages revived an echo of old Iberian rivalries that any serious tension developed. Once again it fell to Palmerston to administer the snub which Louis-Philippe[2] had rather foolishly invited.

The overthrow of the Bourgeois Monarchy in 1848 and the advent of Louis Napoleon[3] posed a new series of problems. Critics of Guizot's cautious foreign policy were not least among the supporters of the new régime. Napoleon III might insist that 'the Empire means peace' but he also owed his place to a very different kind of legend. Inevitably French diplomacy spoke in louder tones. Greater encouragement was forthcoming to French capitalists and educationalists in Egypt and in Syria and to French merchants, adventurers and explorers in West Africa. The risks of Anglo-French friction were multiplied. In West Africa, however, British interest in her Gambia, Sierra Leone and Lagos possessions had declined steadily with the virtual disappearance of the slave trade while growing financial commitments were increasingly resented. British governments, therefore, were on the whole more anxious to avoid clashes with France than to espouse local British causes against the French. In these circumstances local rivalries were not capable of generating any dangerous heat. French activities in Egypt and in Syria might, however, have been expected to provoke livelier reactions particularly when in November 1854 de Lesseps[4] obtained a concession from Egypt's

---

[1] Princess Dorothea Lieven (1795–1857), wife of Prince Lieven, Russian Ambassador in London from 1812 to 1834; widowed in 1839, she was now settled in Paris and on intimate terms with Guizot. Dedicated at this time to the cause of Anglo-French understanding she acted as a link between Guizot and her old friend Lord Aberdeen, the British Foreign Secretary with whom she maintained a voluminous correspondence (see *The Correspondence of Lord Aberdeen and Princess Lieven 1832–54*, 2 vols, ed. E. J. Parry).

[2] Louis-Philippe (1773–1850), King of the French 1830–48.

[3] Charles-Louis-Napoléon Bonaparte (1808–73), President of the Second Republic 1848–52, Emperor of the French 1852–70.

[4] Ferdinand de Lesseps (1805–94). As a French Consular official in Egypt de Lesseps had for several years past been associated with French efforts to obtain a concession for building a Suez Canal. All these had failed because Mohammed Ali and his successor, Abbas Hilmi I, did not dare to risk British displeasure. See J. Marlowe, *Anglo-Egyptian Relations*, p. 62.

new ruler[1] for the construction of a canal from the Red Sea to the Mediterranean. But the attention of the British Government was at that time concentrated on reviving fears of Russian domination at Constantinople. While British influence remained predominant in Turkey, Britain was loth to admit the failure of reform and the growing decay of Turkey. Russia, on the other hand, stressed the signs of disintegration and adopted bullying attitudes at Constantinople. For various and perhaps mainly hypothetical reasons England and France assumed that Turkey was under threat from Russia and that they had a common interest in combating that threat. In the Crimean War the two powers fought as allies for the first time since the seventeenth century in a major war. Though victory was popular in France, critics of the Emperor could argue, with some justification, that Russia's defeat had been more in Britain's interest than in France's. The prestige role which Louis Napoleon played at the Treaty of Paris was, on the other hand, not relished in England. When the Emperor became embroiled in war against Austria in support of Italian reunification, with Nice and Savoy as his own rewards, fear that he might seek to emulate his uncle in Europe began to gain some ground in England.[2] In France there was irritation because the Italians seemed to be more grateful to the British than to the French.

In spite of these misunderstandings Cobden's[3] treaty of commerce with France in 1860 was a renewed sign of Anglo-French solidarity. Furthermore Cobden's general views of foreign policy were meeting with increasing favour in England. His criticisms of Palmerston's meddlesome and costly diplomacy were beginning to make sense. Trade, not empire, was the real source of England's strength. While England's security was not threatened by any other power there was no need for elaborate calculation in the conduct of foreign affairs. It might be necessary to continue to maintain a powerful navy but otherwise retrenchment in military expenditure and in diplomatic activity must be the order

[1] Mohammed Said Pasha (1822–63), youngest son of Mohammed Ali and uncle of Abbas Hilmi I, whom he succeeded in 1854. His friendship had been successfully cultivated by de Lesseps. Work on the canal project did not begin until 1859 and was not completed until ten years later.

[2] In 1860 there was even an invasion scare.

[3] Richard Cobden (1804–65); leading Free Trader and generally critical, particularly during Crimean War, of Palmerston's Foreign Policy, he was nevertheless offered but refused Cabinet Office by Palmerston in 1859.

of the day. One of the results of this conclusion was that when Louis Napoleon looked to Britain for support over Poland in 1863[1] there was no response from Palmerston. In his turn Louis Napoleon turned a deaf ear to Palmerston when he appealed for French backing over the Schleswig-Holstein question in 1864.[2] The diplomatic humiliation which Palmerston suffered was regarded in England as a product of his own mistaken values. European problems were of no concern to prospering Britain. With the disappearance of Palmerston[3] and of Earl Russell[4] from the political scene there was a virtual consensus of opinion among Liberals and Tories that diplomacy was a dying industry. The Foreign Office, once such a prized ministry, became difficult to fill. Indeed the Tories, returning to office in 1866, tried to persuade the Liberal Lord Clarendon[5] to remain as Foreign Secretary because no one in their own party was sufficiently interested.

It was in this atmosphere that Anglo-French negotiations for territorial exchange were opened in March 1866 when the French Ambassador offered ports at Grand Bassam, Dabon and Assinie on the Ivory Coast in return for Gambia.[6] In 1857 the French had surrendered their trading rights at Albreda on the river Gambia in exchange for British trading rights at Portendic in Senegal.[7] But since that time there had been a radical reappraisal of Britain's attitude to Gambia, the oldest and least popular of her West African possessions.[8] By 1865 the conclusion had been reached that Gambia was dispensable and that the best solution would be to give it to the French. As a precaution against possibly awkward questions in Parliament the gift ought at least to seem like an

[1] Louis Napoleon had hoped to be able to prevent the crushing of the Polish Revolution.

[2] Palmerston's virtual promises of support to the Danes had depended on French backing and therefore were not redeemed.

[3] He died in Oct 1865.

[4] Lord John Russell (1792–1878), created Earl Russell 1861. Foreign Secretary 1859–65, then succeeded Palmerston as Prime Minister, resigning in 1866 and afterwards retiring from active politics.

[5] George William Frederick Villiers, 4th Earl of Clarendon (1800–70), Foreign Secretary 1865–6, 1868–70.

[6] See N. A. Gailey Jr, *A History of Gambia*, p. 82.

[7] See J. D. Hargreaves, *Prelude to the Partition of Africa*, p. 109.

[8] For this and details of subsequent Anglo-French negotiations see J. D. Hargreaves, *Prelude to Partition of Africa*, pp. 136–64. See also N. A. Gailey Jr, *A History of Gambia*, pp. 82–9.

exchange. Hints to this effect were dropped and it was in response to these that the French offer was made in March 1866. But fears of assuming commitments on the Ivory Coast, the absence of any obvious alternative and changes of government in England caused delay. In 1870, however, in response to pressure from the Governor of the West African settlements, who by now was concerned about French advances[1] to the north of Freetown in Sierra Leone, Britain reverted to the Gambia exchange project; France was now invited to substitute, for Ivory Coast concessions, the claims which they had recently established on the Mellacourie River and which could be regarded as a threat to Sierra Leone. During the course of these negotiations, however, protests began to emerge from Gambia traders on the spot and Gambia trading interests at home. The Government showed little sign of being influenced by this small pressure group although Gladstone[2] did promise that no transfer of territory would take place without parliamentary approval. It seems most probable that, but for the outbreak of the Franco-Prussian War, the deal would have gone through.

The war, particularly after Bismarck had revealed Napoleon III's Belgian ambitions, confirmed dormant English suspicions of the Emperor but otherwise was hardly a challenge to England's new isolationary complacency. On the other hand France's defeat by Prussia in 1870 set the mould for a complete reshaping of French foreign policy. From henceforth the great majority of Frenchmen felt not only humiliated but directly threatened. The loss of Alsace-Lorraine was no mere symbol of wounded pride but a nagging reminder of basic insecurity. Fear of the hated new German Empire, rather than desire for revenge, gave some kind of unity to the mass of Frenchmen otherwise so hopelessly divided. Legitimists, Orléanists, unregenerate Bonapartists, Republicans as reluctant as Thiers,[3] as hopeful as Gambetta[4] or as

---

[1] For details see J. D. Hargreaves, *Prelude to Partition of Africa*, pp. 132–6.

[2] William Ewart Gladstone (1809–98), Prime Minister 1868–74, 1880–5, 1886, 1892–4.

[3] Adolphe Louis Thiers (1797–1877). A leading statesman during the July Monarchy and a leading critic of Napoleon III, he became head of the provisional government formed in 1871.

[4] Léon Gambetta (1838–82). Proclaimed a Republic in September 1870; organiser and hero of the later stages of the Franco-Prussian War.

uncompromising as Clemenceau,[1] all were agreed that France must cultivate every possible friendship abroad if she was to survive in any kind of comfort in the shade of Germany's power. Any other foreign policy considerations were secondary. In these circumstances the need for a good understanding with England gained new and urgent meaning; it was almost universally accepted as a main principle of policy.

In England reactions to Germany's triumph and the eclipse of France were slight. True enough Disraeli attempted to evoke the spectre of a German menace when he complained 'there is no balance'; but Disraeli was in opposition. Gladstone's government was not prepared to see any serious danger to British interests in the new situation, nor, after initial comment, was Disraeli. Cobden's now popular views on foreign policy were barely shaken. Although Russia's unilateral denunciation of the Black Sea clauses[2] of the Treaty of Paris recalled memories of Mediterranean dangers, even these, in 1870, seemed sufficiently remote to preclude the necessity of any drastic foreign policy reappraisal. Meanwhile, friendly co-operation with defeated and presumably chastened France seemed in every way desirable and feasible.

Once the revolutionary Commune in France had been defeated and regular government authority re-established, however precariously, prospects of reverting to the Gambian exchange proposals might have been presumed to be favourable. In fact, however, when Thiers's provisional government tentatively raised the question in August 1871 Kimberley,[3] then Colonial Secretary, replied that opposition within the Colony made it impossible to proceed. It was indeed true that the Gambia lobby had gained something in strength and that the growing difficulties of the Government now prompted postponement of any issues, however small, which might prove awkward. Furthermore the defeat of France had inevitably resulted in general French retrenchment in West Africa. With France quiescent, pressure to

---

[1] Georges Eugène Benjamin Clemenceau (1841–1929), at this time Mayor of Montmartre and regarded as an extreme radical.

[2] After defeat in the Crimean War Russia had been compelled to renounce the right to maintain any naval bases on the Black Sea.

[3] John Wodehouse, 1st Earl of Kimberley (1826–1902), Colonial Secretary 1870–4.

make a settlement based on the advantages of an exchange was reduced. So Kimberley, who constitutionally favoured inaction,[1] was able, without too much trouble, to avoid reopening the road towards a West African bargain.

When Gladstone's long administration finally crumbled to defeat the French made a new effort to revive the Gambia negotiations. Their ambassador called on Lord Derby[2] in April 1874 and, meeting with favourable response at a preliminary discussion, he submitted a memorandum offering both the Mellacourie, Grand Bassam and Assinie, and all claims to adjacent territory, in return for Britain's Gambia possessions.[3] These proposals were referred to the Colonial Office where the matter was slowly and laboriously investigated. Although Disraeli used the language of Imperialism his government was as little inclined as Gladstone's to consider African affairs as of other than secondary importance. Nevertheless by July 1875 the Cabinet was able to make counter-proposals to the French on the basis of Carnarvon's[4] recommendations. The terms were stiff; England would have gained a free hand to develop a unified coastal administration which would have linked the Gold Coast[5] to Lagos; in addition, and this was the only item which really irked the French, financial compensation must be paid for British interests in Gambia.[6] The French Foreign Minister, on general policy grounds, was so eager for a settlement that he was prepared to sweep aside the objections of the Colonial Director.[7] As French resistance was on the point of crumbling Disraeli intervened.[8] Trouble in the House over a Merchant Seaman's Bill made him anxious to postpone any possibly awkward questions over Gambia. On 28 July 1875 Carnarvon was persuaded to postpone making any statement in the House, and to let the matter lie until the next session. He explained his

---

[1] A more charitable interpretation is that he genuinely sympathised with what appeared to be the wishes of the Gambians.

[2] Edward Stanley, 15th Earl of Derby (1826–93), Foreign Secretary 1874–8.

[3] See H. A. Gailey Jr, *A History of Gambia*, p. 90.

[4] Henry Herbert, 4th Earl of Carnarvon (1831–90), Colonial Secretary, 1874–8.

[5] One of the results of the Ashanti wars 1872–4 was the annexation of the Gold Coast, formerly a Protectorate. See J. D. Hargreaves, *Prelude to the Partition of Africa*, pp. 168–72.

[6] For details of the British terms see ibid., pp. 177–9.

[7] See ibid., p. 181.

[8] For this intervention and its consequences see ibid., pp. 182–3.

difficulties to the French and expressed the hope that rumours of the proposed settlement could in the meanwhile be hushed. In fact an article in a French newspaper claiming that agreement had been reached appeared on 29 July. Carnarvon was obliged to deny the existence of any such agreement in the House.

The Gambia lobby took new courage. The French Government, with leisure now enforced, asked further questions. These then resulted in new dealings. Finally on 15 March 1876 Carnarvon advised the Foreign Office that it would be best to break off the negotiations.[1] This decision was reluctantly conveyed to the French who received it with surprise and regret. West Africa, where Anglo-French co-operation was ardently desired by French governments and where English and indeed African interests could only have benefited from the bargains proposed, was thus doomed to develop into a source of Anglo-French friction. Though that friction was eventually resolved the consequences, as far as West Africa is concerned, have proved incalculably unfortunate.

While these negotiations were in progress a train of events in Europe, in Persia, in Turkey and in Egypt revived British interest in foreign affairs and, on the whole, made France a far more significant factor in Disraeli's appreciations. The Franco-German war scare of 1875 was a reminder that Germany and not France was the next likely challenger for hegemony in Europe; in those circumstances support for France could be regarded as a future British interest. But of more immediate concern at this time was renewed suspicion and fear of Russia. Russian activity in 1875 on the borders of Persia touched England on a sensitive Indian nerve. This twinge seemed slight when compared to the problem posed by Turkey, where financial collapse and nationalist revolutions threatened total disintegration. The Eastern Question, in its most acute form, was reopened. Disraeli, with perhaps more haste than wisdom, assumed that the demise of Turkey in Europe must bring the Russians to Constantinople, with fearsome consequences to British commerce in the Mediterranean and, even worse, to the security of the Indian Empire. In defence of these vital interests he was prepared, if necessary, to go to war, and in any case

---

[1] See J. D. Hargreaves, *Prelude to the Partition of Africa*, p. 194.

to seek backing from Germany, Austria–Hungary and France. Against Russia, whether in diplomacy or war, England needed allies. French friendship, as on the eve of the Crimean War, was at a premium.

2

Dual Control in Egypt

THE value which Disraeli put on French friendship determined
his attitude to the crisis in Egypt which developed in 1876. Since
the action taken against Mohammed Ali in 1840 Britain had, as
far as possible, avoided interference in Egyptian internal affairs.
The restoration and growth of French influence had provoked
occasional resentment but little positive action. Even opposition
to the Suez Canal project, so frustrating to de Lesseps,[1] gradually
declined. Once the Canal was opened in 1869 British anxiety to
steer clear of involvement in Egypt was emphasised rather than
diminished. As chief user of the Canal, Britain was entirely satisfied with the Egyptian *status quo*. Provided the Khedive[2] remained
effective ruler of his country the advantages were manifest and
fully appreciated by Disraeli when he succeeded to the Premiership in 1874.

But, by 1875, the Khedive's position was already in some
jeopardy. His policy of rapid modernisation, which included the
building of the Suez Canal and a spectacular programme of public
works – combined with military adventures in the Sudan and
extravagant court expenditure designed to promote public relations – was sustained at the cost of ruinous borrowing.[3] Ismail

---

[1] See p. 20. Work on the project begun in 1859 was halted mainly because Said,
under British influence, refused de Lesseps concessions which would have provided
forced labour. Said's death in 1863, the advent of his successor Ismail and declining
interest on the part of the British Government enabled de Lesseps to surmount remaining obstacles, including the labour problem. See J. Marlowe, *Anglo-Egyptian
Relations 1800–1953*, pp. 63–70.

[2] Ismail (1830–95), son of Ibrahim and grandson of Mohammed Ali, succeeded
his uncle Said as ruler of Egypt in 1863. In 1867 he was given the title of Khedive by
the Sultan. Deposed in 1879.

[3] For a summary of the financial crisis which developed in Egypt and its consequences see J. Marlowe, *Anglo-Egyptian Relations 1800–1953*, pp. 90–109. See also
R. Robinson and J. Gallagher, *Africa and the Victorians*, pp. 80–6.

had the vision of a statesman but, in matter of finance, the myopia of an obsessive gambler. When he sold his Suez Canal shares to the British Government in 1875 it was a desperate effort to stave off bankruptcy. In purchasing them Disraeli's purpose, notwithstanding his boast to the Queen,[1] was to avoid rather than to assume commitments in Egypt. He hoped, while preventing further extension of French influence, to rescue the Khedive from insolvency. But Ismail's plight was beyond facile repair.

As panic among bondholders began to spread France pressed for drastic measures of security to protect Egypt's creditors. England reluctantly, and mainly out of deference to French wishes, followed. In response to this pressure the Khedive tried to restore confidence by promulgating a decree setting up an international *Caisse de la Dette publique*. It was to collect and distribute sums required for servicing the various debts. A subsequent decree made provision for the consolidation and funding of these debts, amounting to £91,000,000, at a rate of seven per cent interest. But this proposed settlement was rejected by the bondholders. With predominantly French support their representatives successfully insisted on dividing the debt into three categories: the Preferred Debt, the Daira (Estate) Debt and the Unified Debt which were to be respectively serviced from the revenue of State Railways, State Telegraphs and Alexandria Harbour, the private estates of the Khedive and the balance of general revenue. These arrangements were prejudiced from the start because no provision had been made in them for holders of what was known as the floating debt.[2]

Test cases brought to the Mixed Tribunals[3] successfully established their claims. Quite apart from this extra burden it emerged

---

[1] 'It is yours, Ma'am.'

[2] Estimated at about £16,000,000 and issued on the security of Egyptian Treasury Bills. It had been included in Ismail's original settlement plan.

[3] The Mixed Tribunals had been set up in 1875 as a result of an International Conference held in Cairo in 1869 to consider Egyptian proposals for juridical reform. In Egypt, as in other territories under Ottoman suzerainty, Europeans enjoyed extra-territorial privileges known as the Capitulations by virtue of Treaties with the Sultan dating back to the sixteenth century. The privilege which caused most difficulty to Egyptian governments was exemption from all local jurisdiction. But the powers rejected the far-reaching reforms proposed and the authority of the Mixed Courts, as eventually constituted, was limited to civil cases between Egyptians and foreigners or between foreigners of different nationalities. Other cases involving foreigners continued to be reserved for Consular Courts.

by 1878 that the settlement had in any case been based on a hopelessly over-optimistic estimate of Egyptian revenue resources. In
February 1878 Waddington[1] proposed concerted action and
Derby replied that the British Government would 'be happy to
co-operate with that of France in any measures not inconsistent
with the Khedive's independent administration of Egypt'.[2] In
response to Anglo-French pressure the Khedive set up a Commission of Enquiry which in fact soon assumed complete supervision
of Egyptian finances. Probably in order to shift responsibility
for inevitably unpopular retrenchment combined with increased
taxation the Khedive, in August 1878, recalled Nubar Pasha[3]
from exile and appointed an international government with
Nubar as Prime Minister, Rivers Wilson[4] as Minister of Finance
and de Blignières[5] as Minister of Public Works. To outward
appearances it seemed as if an Anglo-French Protectorate had
been created. The Khedive however, by dissociating himself
from the policy of his government, rendered their tasks more
difficult on the one hand and improved his own credit in Egyptian
nationalist circles on the other. In February 1879, after a day of
demonstrations, he dismissed Nubar. In May, again after popular
demonstrations which he had no doubt helped to organise, he
also dismissed Wilson and de Blignières. But although he was
thus able to reassert his own authority he failed, in spite of renewed
efforts, to pacify his creditors. The fact that some of them were
German nationals resulted in a warning from Bismarck that,
unless France and Great Britain could intervene effectively,
Germany might need to seek her own redress.

In these circumstances French and British representatives in
Egypt concluded that the replacement of Ismail as Khedive by his
son Tewfik[6] would be the best means of returning to a system
which would guarantee the kind of financial control required to
avert panic among the bondholders. But Ismail refused to abdi-

---

[1] William H. Waddington (1826–94), French Foreign Minister December 1877–9,
Ambassador in London 1883–93.

[2] Quoted J. Marlowe, *Anglo-Egyptian Relations 1800–1953*, p. 96.

[3] Nubar Pasha Boghos (1825–99), an Armenian and a Christian who had been
responsible for the original proposals which led to the setting up of the Mixed
Courts; he had subsequently been dismissed and exiled by Ismail.

[4] British representative on the international Debt Commission of Enquiry.

[5] French representative on the *Caisse de la Dette*.

[6] Mohammed Tewfik Pasha (1852–92), Khedive 1879–92.

cate. On the contrary he issued a decree raising the strength of the Army and he repudiated various categories of debt. On 25 June 1879 the Sultan of Turkey, whose support had been somewhat reluctantly solicited by England and France, declared him deposed and he was duly succeeded by his son Tewfik.

The British Government, still hoping to preserve shreds of Egyptian independence, would have wished to avoid imposing any strict surveillance on the new Khedive. But the French were adamant and Britain, as usual with reluctance, co-operated in requiring the appointment of Anglo-French Controllers. De Blignières was nominated by France and Major Baring[1] by Britain. As a concession to British opinion, and in supposed deference to Egyptian national susceptibilities, the title of Controller was chosen instead of Minister. But their functions, advisory in theory, were clearly intended to be executive. They had the right to be present at Cabinet meetings. They had access to the business of all departments. They could 'advise' on all matters and were empowered to report to their own diplomatic representatives any rejection of advice proffered. Thus was Dual Control firmly imposed.

The position of the Controllers was a difficult one. Although appointed to safeguard the interests of Egyptian creditors, they were, effectively if not ostensibly, responsible for the government of Egypt. These roles, at least in the short run, were bound to be conflicting. A preliminary examination of the financial situation revealed that the terms proposed for a settlement by the previous Commission of Enquiry were not compatible with the maintenance of even the most economic government. The Controllers therefore recommended amendment. Germany, Italy and Austria insisted on being consulted and, in deference to their wishes, a new International Commission of Liquidation was appointed to undertake the task. The Commission, inevitably, tried to secure the best possible bargain for Egypt's creditors; the Controllers, and particularly Cromer, were also concerned to husband Egypt's economy in the interest both of the Egyptians themselves and of viable government. In the compromise eventually thrashed out the bonded debt was refunded at £80,000,000[1] and a new issue of

---

[1] Evelyn Baring (1841–1917), cr. Earl of Cromer 1892 (but referred to as Cromer henceforth); British representative on the *Caisse de la Dette* from 1876.

£5,600,000 was made to pay off the floating debt. The great majority of Ismail's creditors thus obtained terms which promised security at rates of interest which, although reduced, were still substantial.[2] Of Egypt's total annual revenue – now estimated at £8,500,000 – £4,000,000 were reserved for service of the Debt and £4,500,000 allowed for government expenditure. It was, however, stipulated that any excess in the estimated annual revenue would be paid into a sinking fund under control of the *Caisse de la Dette* and would not, therefore, be available for use by the Government. This feature of the settlement was to prove by far the most irksome and frustrating to future Egyptian governments. In the meanwhile the Anglo-French Controllers were faced with the formidable task of implementing the settlement and of supervising government on a shoestring. England, together with France, was thoroughly involved in the domestic affairs of Egypt.

This unwelcome commitment was a consequence of a desire to secure French support against Russia and the Near East accompanied by unwillingness to allow France to establish a purely French Protectorate in Egypt. Both objectives stemmed from strategic considerations. Although Gladstone and Disraeli might differ over Bulgaria there was no difference either between or within the two major parties about the importance of safeguarding routes to India. The existence of the Suez Canal made Egyptian independence, once it seemed threatened – and it was threatened by France – a major British interest. But, even after the Congress of Berlin,[3] Russian designs on Constantinople were still suspect. In order that Britain might provide prompt aid to Turkey the bewildered Turks had been obliged to cede Cyprus

---

[1] It was divided into the following categories: (i) £14,000,000 Preferred Debt to be serviced by revenues from State Railways, State Telegraphs and Alexandria Harbour at 5% fixed interest. (ii) £9,500,000 Daira Debt to be serviced from profits of Anglo-French administered Khedival Estates at 4% fixed interest. (iii) £8,500,000 Domains Loan (a new loan raised on the security of the Khedive's remaining Estates under the auspices of the Commission of Enquiry to be serviced by profits from internationally administered Khedival Estates at 4% fixed interest. (iv) £48,000,000 Unified Debt to be serviced from specific taxation revenues (after any Preferred Debt deficit had been met) at 4% fixed interest.

[2] Even floating debt holders now were guaranteed a return. But the settlement took no account of certain other loans which the Khedive had raised from mainly Egyptian sources. This inevitably caused resentment and served to emphasise the privileges accorded to foreign interests.

[3] June–July 1878.

as a prospective base. Furthermore Britain had declared that, in the event of any future threat to Constantinople, she would feel free to send ships through the Straits. These declarations of intent depended, for their force, on the compliance of Germany and of France. It was important at least to keep France out of Russia's camp and at best to enjoy solid French backing. In these circumstances compliance with French wishes in Egypt, short of acquiescence in a French Protectorate, seemed mandatory.

From a French point of view England's friendship was certainly valuable. On the other hand the cost of incurring Russian displeasure was a high one. For any measure of complaisance at Constantinople the French, therefore, would expect to be amply rewarded. In addition to a large measure of British co-operation in Egypt, the French also required support for their ambitions in Tunisia. These had been deliberately prompted by Bismarck. England could not afford to be unsympathetic and, in spite of Italian anger and protest, the fate of Tunisia was quietly sealed.[1]

Great Britain's eagerness to accommodate France was also reflected in official policy towards West Africa. Local friction between English and French interests was deprecated. This feeling was reciprocated by the French Government and renewed enthusiasm for a comprehensive West African settlement resulted.[2] Waddington, the French Foreign Minister, had prepared the way with Salisbury[3] during the Congress of Berlin. There were further discussions during the autumn and winter of 1878. In the spring of 1879, however, news arrived of the French occupation of the island of Matacong, which was regarded as an eventual appendage of Sierra Leone. This provoked an outburst of agitation in the British Press. Waddington hastened to explain that the occupation had not been officially authorised and Salisbury ridiculed the notion of any serious quarrel over 'a desert island at the mouth of a pestilential river'.[4] Waddington, in return for Gambia, which still seemed a logical objective, was prepared to offer a wide selection of French holdings and claims in other parts of West

---

[1] By the Treaty of Bardo in May 1881 Tunisia became a French Protectorate.

[2] See J. D. Hargreaves, *Prelude to the Partition of West Africa*, p. 224.

[3] Robert Gascoyne-Cecil, 3rd Marquis of Salisbury (1830–1903), Foreign Secretary 1878–80; Prime Minister 1885–6, 1886–92, 1895–1902.

[4] Salisbury to Lyons, 4 Apr 1879. *Salisbury Papers*, quoted J. D. Hargreaves, *Prelude to the Partition of West Africa*, p. 226.

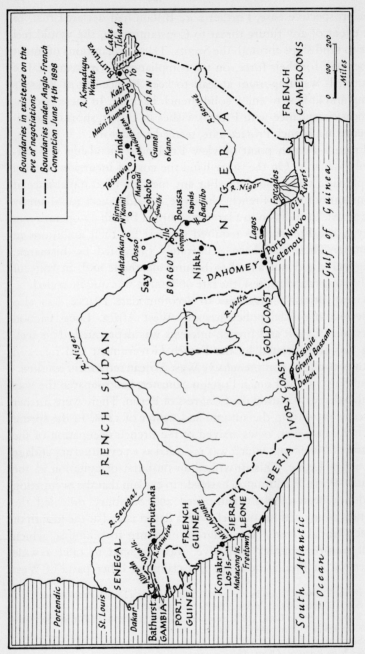

West Africa

Africa. As a declaration of intent he resisted pressures to renew a French protectorate over Porto Nuovo.[1] In Waddington's view a West African settlement would be part of a general series of Anglo-French agreements on questions in various parts of the world which had caused or might cause conflict. This policy was reflected in an inspired article in *Le Temps* on 9 April 1879 where a general settlement embracing Newfoundland fisheries, the frontier of Guiana, the French position in Tonkin and Cambodia, as well as the West African question, was advocated.[2] The exchange of Gambia, it was hinted, could now be profitably discussed. In London the Foreign Office was reluctant to reopen the Gambia exchange question; instead on 11 June 1879 proposals for a limited agreement on Anglo-French demarcation lines in the region of Sierra Leone were put forward.[3] Waddington indicated that he would have preferred to follow up the more comprehensive exchange plans but, finding no response, agreed on 30 June to study British suggestions. He was, however, in these circumstances inclined to drive a harder bargain particularly since French local interests were beginning to attract more powerful advocates in the French Chamber. Both Waddington and Salisbury found the dealings in which they had become involved frustrating.

In the hope of resolving difficulties Waddington visited Salisbury on 19 September at Puy near Dieppe where he was then on holiday.[4] Waddington underlined his desire for a close *entente* with Britain. The two Foreign Secretaries discussed co-operation in Egypt, the Newfoundland fisheries question and French plans to annex Raiatea and other Leeward islands north-west of Tahiti as well as West African problems. Although Salisbury would not commit himself on any matters of detail, prospects of a wide ranging agreement again seemed favourable.

On the question of defining Sierra Leone boundaries the Foreign Office had been working on a plan to offer the Los Islands to France.[5] But Colonial Office obstinacy prevented the formula-

---

[1] It was the aim of British representatives in Lagos ultimately to establish authority over the coastline which separated Lagos from Accra. Any increase in existing French establishments there, which they hoped to suppress, was therefore objectionable.

[2] See J. D. Hargreaves, *Prelude to the Partition of West Africa*, p. 226.

[3] For these proposals and French reactions see ibid., pp. 227, 228.

[4] For this meeting see ibid., pp. 229–30.

[5] See J. D. Hargreaves, *Prelude to the Partition of West Africa*, pp. 230, 231.

tion of any definite offer. While these negotiations were suspended news arrived in early November 1879 of Ussher's[1] seizure of Ketenou.[2] Though Salisbury expressed anger at the action of this 'insupportable proconsul',[3] there was no doubt that, at the cost of provoking the French, Britain's position at Lagos had been much improved. Waddington protested in restrained terms and continued to pin his hopes on the Gambia exchange. Here the local position had altered and there was some reason to believe that opposition to the transfer of the colony to France was now, for a variety of reasons, declining.

Although Waddington resigned at the end of the year Salisbury found his successor, Freycinet,[4] equally in favour of comprehensive settlement. Salisbury himself was now definitely anxious to promote the Gambia exchange. Colonial Office objections prevented him from making a positive offer but, in putting forward new proposals concerning the Sierra Leone and Lagos situations, he indicated that he soon hoped to be in a position to do so. Elections were pending in England and Salisbury relied on a new majority to carry through his plans. It was the Liberals, however, who returned to power and Kimberley who became Foreign Secretary. He was known to be against the session of Gambia[5] and so, once again, prospects of a comprehensive settlement receded. The French did make a further effort in July 1880 but the only result was a limited agreement on Sierra Leone boundaries, reached after somewhat acrimonious discussion in May 1881.[6]

In the meanwhile there were signs of a reviving interest on the part of Frenchmen and Englishmen in penetrating inland in West Africa. On the whole, servants of the state were responsible for promoting French expansion while private enterprise dominated British expansion. Neither government showed any marked enthusiasm but during Ferry's[7] ministry (Sep 1880–Nov 1881)

---

[1] Herbert T. Ussher, Governor of the Gold Coast 1879–80.

[2] Ketenou adjoined Porto Nuovo and its seizure followed a gunboat visit to Porto Nuovo to extract compensation claims from its ruler.

[3] See J. D. Hargreaves, *Prelude to the Partition of West Africa*, p. 213.

[4] Charles Louis de Saulces de Freycinet (1828–1923), Premier of France 1879–80, 1882, 1886, 1890–2.

[5] See pp. 24–5.

[6] See J. D. Hargreaves, *Prelude to the Partition of West Africa*, pp. 247–52.

[7] Jules François Camille Ferry (1832–93), President of the Council 1880–1, 1883–5.

and Gambetta's[1] (Nov 1881–Jan 1882) some increasing French Government support for the ambitions of officials on the spot was in evidence. As early as 1879 money had been voted to study projects for a Trans-Sahara and for a Senegal–Niger Railway. In December 1880 approval was given for the construction of a Dakar–St-Louis line.[2] Even this very limited scheme indicated a growing interest. In September 1880 a new military district of Upper Senegal was established.[3] While the French were thus moving forward in Senegambia, British influence was developing on the Lower Niger. By stages, with the formation of the United Africa Company in 1879 and the National Africa Company in 1882, Goldie[4] was building up a powerful trade monopoly. Where French interests existed he was anxious either to buy them out or eliminate them by force; where they might develop he was keen to establish a prior claim.

Thus forces were at work in West Africa in 1882 which presaged increasing Anglo-French friction however much the two governments might remain eager to avoid it.

Such attention as they might have been compelled to devote to this question was, however, rudely diverted by nationalist stirrings in Egypt and the Egyptian crisis which ensued. The movement was diverse in origin. Leaders of an Islamic revival were opposed to the westernising secularism which Khedive Ismail had encouraged. European-educated politicians who had found a platform in the Chamber of Notables, set up by Khedive Ismail in 1866, resented the fact that khedival absolutism had become a cloak for European control. In the Army feeling among Egyptian-born officers against the pretensions of the Turkish-Circassian-Albanian officer caste was growing, creating a new kind of national consciousness in the process. For different reasons all these groups opposed khedival rule as it had developed under Ismail but their discontents were muted by fear while he remained Khedive. His deposition, resulting from a show of independence calculated to win their sympathies, emphasised the extent of Egypt's servitude on the one hand and removed the

---

[1] See p. 23.
[2] See J. D. Hargreaves, *Prelude to the Partition of West Africa*, pp. 254, 255.
[3] Ibid., p. 262.
[4] Sir George Goldie (1846–1925), founder of the Royal Niger Company. For a recent study see J. E. Flint, *Sir George Goldie and the Making of Nigeria*.

main barrier to overt agitation on the other. Khedive Tewfik did
not inspire the same fear as his father, while his subjection to
Anglo-French control was more obviously underlined. It was not
surprising that the forces of discontent rallied and found, in
attacking Dual Control, a measure of common ground.

The initiative came from the Army. In February 1881 a group
of army colonels under the leadership of Ahmed Arabi[1] succeeded
in forcing the resignation of the Minister of War and in securing
his replacement by one of their own nominees. On 9 September
they surrounded the Palace and then compelled the Khedive to
dismiss his Ministry, to convene the Chamber of Notables and to
promise to restore the Army to full strength. Sherif Pasha[2] was
then appointed Prime Minister and Arabi soon joined the new
ministry as Under-Secretary of War.

He soon began to use his authority to effect a series of army
purges against Turkish, Circassian and Albanian officers. At this
stage a rift between the basically conservative Sherif government
and the revolutionary army leadership began to develop.

The situation in Egypt caused immediate alarm in France and
resulted in pressure for a firm line. Gladstone's unhappy Cabinet
was faced with a most unwelcome problem.[3] Co-operation with
France was accepted as a basic concept of policy. On the other
hand the majority of ministers, and Gladstone in particular, at this
time dreaded any further entanglement in Egyptian affairs. And
yet even Gladstone could not contemplate giving the French a
free hand in Egypt. Tunisia, and at a pinch Morocco, might be
allowed to become French Protectorates. This must not be
Egypt's fate. As Granville[4] put it 'we wish to act cordially with
France without allowing her any predominance'.[5] But action to

---

[1] Ahmed Arabi Pasha (1839–1911), leader of the army demonstrations against the
Nubar Government in Feb 1879.

[2] Sherif Pasha (1819–87), Egyptian statesman who had established himself as the
leader of the 'Constitutionalists' in opposition to Dual Control. He had resigned as
Prime Minister shortly after Ismail's abdication. His return to power was now
recommended by the Controllers, perhaps in the hope of dividing the nationalist
ranks.

[3] For a good account of Gladstone's dilemma and the whole ensuing crisis see
R. Robinson and J. Gallagher, *Africa and the Victorians*, pp. 89–121.

[4] Granville Leveson-Gower, 2nd Earl Granville (1815–91), Foreign Secretary
1880–5.

[5] Granville to Dufferin (Ambassador at the Porte), 15 Oct 1881. Lord Edward
Fitzmaurice, *Life of the Second Earl Granville*, vol. ii, p. 252.

Granville meant inaction and the hope that the Egyptian situation, jogged along by Anglo-French diplomatic manœuvres at Constantinople and Cairo, would gradually right itself.

With the advent to power of Gambetta[1] in November 1881, the attitude of France predictably stiffened. In reply to his proposals for joint Anglo-French intervention the British Government turned to the notion of joint diplomatic pressure combined with the possibility of invoking military action by Turkey. Gambetta refused to consider Turkish intervention but produced a draft of a Note which resembled an ultimatum. Gladstone wished to dissociate England but the majority of the Cabinet insisted that solidarity must be maintained in the interests of the French alliance. As far as Egypt was concerned they regarded it as a policy of bluff. The note was presented on 8 January. It inflamed nationalist opinion everywhere and temporarily closed the gap between Arabi and the leading nationalist politicians; on 5 February a new ministry was formed with Arabi as Minister of War.[2]

In the meanwhile further British proposals to invoke Turkish intervention had been dropped in deference to Gambetta's wishes. This conciliatory gesture was facilitated because Gambetta's government was now tottering and by the time Arabi became Minister of War in Egypt, Freycinet[3] had succeeded Gambetta in France. British anxiety to procrastinate over Egypt now met with more sympathetic response in France. Freycinet's government, though not yet prepared to invoke Turkish support, was obviously less eager for Anglo-French military action.

In Egypt the Khedive's authority was rapidly declining and alarmist predictions of imminent anarchy were current in European circles. Gladstone's bewildered Cabinet wrestled with the problem of how to prop up the Khedive by means short of force, yet acceptable to the French. Conscious that Bismarck was exploiting the situation to create Anglo-French tension, even Granville began to feel that some action was required. The notion of a warning from Turkey backed by an Anglo-French naval demonstration, merely to be used as a bluff, won some support in a deeply

[1] See p. 37.
[2] Sherif was replaced as Prime Minister by Mahmoud Pasha Sami, previously Minister of War and an army nominee.
[3] See p. 36.

divided Cabinet. By 12 May Freycinet formally proposed the dispatch of an Anglo-French naval force to Alexandria and agreed reluctantly to the possibility of a Turkish military expedition under Anglo-French control should circumstances make any further steps necessary. On 15 May the Khedive, taking courage from the naval demonstration, dismissed Arabi. Violent nationalist reaction followed and the Khedive promptly recalled Arabi to power. The naval demonstration had obviously failed. Anglo-French demands that Arabi should be exiled were followed by the resignation of the Arabist ministry on 27 May and its reinstatement on 28 May. On 11 and 12 June there were antiforeign riots in Alexandria and some fifty Europeans were killed. The British Consul was assaulted. As has been well said, 'in stirring the Egyptian pot, Britain and France had made it boil over'.[1]

The Alexandria riots created new ferment in Gladstone's Cabinet. Hartington[2] now bitterly attacked Granville and demanded action in Egypt. He was still anxious that it should be Turkish action but he insisted that the only way of getting the Turks to move and the French to agree to such action was for Britain to show willingness to intervene alone. While Hartington argued with Granville hopes of any kind of Turkish intervention gradually faded. At Bismarck's prompting the Turks eventually offered an Egyptian Protectorate to Britain. Gladstone and Granville naturally refused this offer. They were however increasingly impressed by fears, currently expressed in England and loudly echoed by Hartington, for the safety of the Canal.[3] These fears they conveyed to Freycinet, who denied their validity. This confirmed suspicions, already prevalent in some sections of the Cabinet, that the French were now ready to do a deal with Arabi at England's expense.

Since the June riots in Alexandria even Gladstone had come to regard Arabi as a dangerous military adventurer and few liberals remained who could see in him the leader of a nation struggling to be free. Little by little in the Egyptian crisis Anglo-French roles were reversed and it was Gladstone's Cabinet which,

---

[1] R. Robinson and J. Gallagher, *Africa and the Victorians*, p. 103.

[2] Spencer Compton Cavendish, Marquess of Hartington and subsequently 8th Duke of Devonshire (1833–1908), Secretary of State for India 1880–2; Secretary for War 1882–5.

[3] The suggestion was that Arabi might resort to sabotage.

however uneasily, adopted brinkmanship tactics. The Admiral in command of the British naval force appealed for permission to bombard Alexandria if defensive works there were not stopped. Knowledge of this appeal resulted in a withdrawal of the French naval contingent to Port Said. On 8 July, and for differing motives, the Cabinet approved the Admiral's request. In fact he exceeded his orders and demanded not merely that works should be stopped but that the forts should be surrendered. When his ultimatum expired on 11 July he bombarded Alexandria. Egypt rallied to Arabi. The Khedive took refuge in Alexandria and placed himself under the protection of the British fleet.

This latest stage in the Egyptian revolution, triggered off by the bombardment of Alexandria, inevitably confirmed fears for European life and property and also for the safety of the Canal. On 13 July the British invited Freycinet to take joint measures for its protection and this time he agreed. During 18–22 July military intervention was debated in the British Cabinet. Bright[1] resigned and, with Gladstone still protesting, it was decided to send an expeditionary force under Wolseley[2] to Cyprus and Malta in preparation for operations in any part of Egypt. A mandate for intervention was then sought from the Conference which was still in session at Constantinople, but without success. Instead a joint Anglo-French declaration emerged stating that the two powers would protect the Canal with the help of any other powers who chose to assist. On 23 July Freycinet announced that, although France would co-operate in this venture, her troops would not share in any invasion of the interior. While joint occupation of the Canal zone was being planned Freycinet found himself under increasing pressure in the Chambers. In the Commons Gladstone's $1\frac{1}{2}d$ on income tax to raise £2,300,000 was carried by 275 votes to 19 but in the Chamber, Freycinet, appealing for a much lesser sum, was defeated on 29 July. Clemenceau led the opposition, thundering against a wastage of French resources on matters in no way vital to French security. Even Gambetta voted against Freycinet in disgust at what he castigated as a half-measure.

[1] John Bright (1811–89), Cobden's partner in the Free Trade struggle and firm supporter of his views on foreign policy. At this time an elder statesman and Chancellor of the Duchy of Lancaster.

[2] Garnet Joseph, 1st Viscount (1833–1913). Field-Marshal 1894. Commander-in-Chief, British Army 1895–9.

On the day of Freycinet's defeat Wolseley was ordered to land his forces at Port Said, to proceed thence to Ismailia, to assure fresh water supply to the Canal towns and to complete the protection of the Canal by crushing Arabi's forces. Now at last the Turks offered their intervention but the British Government, having finally swung around to action, brushed aside this proposal.

Wolseley landed on 16 August 1882 and crushed Arabi's army at the battle of Tel-el-Kebir on 13 September.

3

The Niger and the Nile

FROM then on the Egypt which had been a bond, though not always a comfortable one, between England and France, was to develop into a festering sore. Although Gladstone's government immediately declared that the withdrawal of all British forces was an irrevocable principle of British policy, this could obviously not be effected until the Khedive's authority, with a loyal army to support him, had been restored. Equally, while British troops remained in Egypt, British influence there would obviously be paramount. Dual Control was dead. This the British were soon obliged to make clear. Under British tutelage, Egyptian independence must now be encouraged to develop on lines which would satisfy bondholders, safeguard the Canal and also appeal to Egyptians. There was some solace in such a programme for each group among the divided Liberals.

In France the Duclerc[1] ministry at first professed itself satisfied with British withdrawal promises. But the demise of Dual Control proved a bitter pill to swallow. After consultation had failed to produce French acquiescence, the British Government simply gave notice of their intention to assume sole responsibility for the regeneration of Egypt. The withdrawal of British troops, which was to begin by withdrawal from Cairo to Alexandria, would continue by phases. It was to be completed as soon as the Khedive's government was effectively re-established. Even Cromer's[2] first

[1] Charles Théodore Eugène Duclerc (1812–88); succeeded Freycinet as President of the Council (Aug 1882–Jan 1885).

[2] After his appointment in Sep 1883 as British Agent and Consul-General. He had been replaced as Controller in Jun 1880 on appointment as Financial Member of the Governor-General's Council in India. He was to remain Consul-General in Egypt until his retirement in 1907.

The valley of the Nile

reports however, though relatively optimistic, suggested that time, perhaps about three years, would be needed for this task. Britain's assumption of authority in Egypt, inevitable after France's failure to join in military intervention, equally inevitably destroyed the much-prized Anglo-French *Entente*. History went against easy acceptance of such a blow to French pride. The fact that the blow was in fact self-inflicted was irrelevant. It was easier to forget the mistake than to suffer its consequences.

On 21 February 1883 Jules Ferry[1] formed his second ministry. He had the backing of former followers of Gambetta, who had died in December 1882. His own views on the advantages of colonial expansion, although he remained aware of difficulties and dangers, had now taken more definite shape. He was prepared to pursue a forward policy in Indo-China, in Tunisia, in West Africa and in the Congo, where de Brazza[2] was building an Empire. He hoped thereby to achieve useful gains for France and, at the same time, to restore French prestige. While ready to do business with England if and when British troops were withdrawn from Egypt, he was eager, in the meanwhile, to score points against England.

These dispositions were encouraged by events in the Sudan which on the one hand embroiled England even further in Egypt and on the other rendered her situation more vulnerable. Egypt's Sudanese Empire was a relatively recent acquisition. Mohammed Ali had inaugurated a policy of military conquest in 1820. In 1842 the Sultan recognised him as Viceroy. After Mohammed Ali's death Egyptian control relaxed. Ismail, however, not only re-established that control but pushed the boundaries of Egypt's Sudanese Empire in the East to the Red Sea, becoming involved in Abyssinian wars in the process; in the west he occupied Darfur and Bahr el Ghazal; in the south he formed the new province of Equatoria, whose boundaries were supposed to extend to the as yet unknown sources of the White Nile. Anxious for practical and prestige reasons to present his expansionist policy in the guise of a civilising mission Ismail claimed, among his objectives, suppression of the slave trade. General

---

[1] See p. 36.
[2] Pierre Savorgnan de Brazza (1852–1905), French explorer and leading agent of French expansion in Central Africa.

Charles Gordon, first as Governor of Equatoria (1874–6) and then as Governor-General of the whole of Sudan (1876–9), did his best to substantiate this claim.[1] In the process he inevitably antagonised the powerful slave-traders of Northern Sudan. Accordingly, when in July 1881 Mohammed Ahmed[2] proclaimed himself the Mahdi, designated by God to lead a revolt against Egyptian rule, they rallied to his support. Egypt, already in the throes of internal crisis, was in no position to meet this distant challenge. Before the end of 1882 the Mahdi, now in control of Kordofan, was encouraged by news of the annihilation of the Egyptian army at Tel-el-Kebir to press forward towards Khartoum.

Under British tutelage the Egyptian Government, virtually without an army and in dire financial straits, eventually appointed Colonel Hicks, commander of the Egyptian forces in the Sudan, to defend Northern Sudan and to protect Egyptian frontiers. But the Khedive, against British advice and mainly for prestige reasons, decided that Hicks, with the poor forces at his disposal, must lead an expedition into Kordofan. On 22 November 1883 news of the annihilation of Hicks's army[3] reached London. It was just at the time when British troops were scheduled to be withdrawn from Cairo and Cromer at once warned that this step must be postponed. In the Cabinet Hartington[4] urged that British forces should assist Egypt to hold Khartoum and the Sudan east of the White Nile. He insisted particularly that the Red Sea ports must be held to defend the route to India.[5] But the Cabinet refused to accept such wide commitments. They were prepared to guarantee Egypt and the Red Sea ports but the Khedive must be ordered to abandon the Sudan. On 16 December 1883 Cromer warned Granville that this would be a terrible blow to the Khedive, that he could not be expected to accept such a command, that he would find no ministers to serve him and Britain would be compelled to accept direct responsibility for the government of Egypt. On 4 January 1884 the Cabinet considered Cromer's

[1] Gordon resigned from Egyptian service in protest against the deposition of Khedive Ismail.

[2] Mohammed Ahmed of Dongola (1840–85), leader of a fanatical Dervish sect who believed in the advent of a guide or Mahdi who would continue the work begun by the Prophet and complete the world's conversion to Islam.

[3] On 5 Nov 1883 at Shaikan.

[4] See p. 40. He was now Secretary for War.

[5] See R. Robinson and J. Gallagher, *Africa and the Victorians*, p. 133.

warning but insisted that the Khedive must be ordered to abandon the Sudan.[1] In the event the Khedive bowed to the ultimatum, and although Sherif Pasha[2] and the other ministers resigned, Nubar Pasha[3] eventually proved willing to constitute a ministry of some kind. Cromer's worst fears had not been realised but the Khedive's position, so vital to British plans, had been seriously undermined. On 18 January the decision was taken in London to send General Gordon to Egypt, with the title of Governor-General of the Sudan, to evacuate the remaining Sudanese forces and to try to secure Egypt's frontiers.

In the meanwhile Cromer was faced with pressing financial problems. The cost of the Khedive's expedition against the Mahdi, the claim of £4,500,000 for damage during the Alexandria riots and a deficit of £1,000,000 on the Egyptian administrative budget, convinced him that only a new loan could avert bankruptcy. After gloomy and acrimonious discussions in Gladstone's unhappy Cabinet it was decided on 2 April 1884 to offer the Powers an unconditional promise to withdraw from Egypt as soon as possible in return for their consent in the raising of a new international loan.[4] For this purpose Granville called a conference in London. Before the conference met private negotiations with Ferry were opened. Granville proposed that Egypt should be neutralised and evacuated at the latest within three and a half years and Ferry guaranteed that France would not occupy Egypt after Britain's withdrawal save by agreement. This bargain was dependent on French acceptance of the British financial proposals.

The conference met on 28 June 1884. The French then rejected all British proposals for balancing the Egyptian budget.[5] They refused to reduce interest on the existing debt or to transfer any portion of the debt revenues to meet administrative and defensive costs. This attitude was partly explained by Ferry's confidence that the British were now 'on the run' and that he would eventually be able to strike a better bargain, and partly out of deference to the interests of the French bondholders. Bismarck, complaining of Granville's obstruction to Germany's colonial claims in South

---

[1] Ibid., p. 135. [2] See p. 38. [3] See p. 30.
[4] See R. Robinson and J. Gallagher, *Africa and the Victorians*, p. 142.
[5] Ibid., p. 143.

and West Africa and in the Western Pacific, backed French objections and laid the foundations of a Franco-German compact on
Egyptian and other colonial issues.

While France and Germany co-operated in blocking British
projects for Egyptian financial reform the plight of Gordon at
Khartoum was becoming desperate and the question of a relief
expedition, pressed in the Cabinet by Selborne,[1] created further
division and made the problem of Egyptian finances even more
pressing. Northbrook[2] visited Egypt to assess the situation on the
spot. In his report, he recommended against any prompt withdrawal from Egypt and in favour of assuming sole responsibility
for Egypt's finances by making a £9,000,000 loan. After a further
spell of violent discussions Gladstone, who had in the meanwhile
consented to a small-scale relief expedition for Gordon, won the
day by obtaining support for retiring from Egypt as soon as
possible and making a further effort, via France, to obtain international support for Egyptian finances.

The French terms were stiff. The international loan must be
internationally guaranteed. The *Caisse de la Dette* must be retained
and strengthened by the addition of German and Russian commissioners. In the administration of the debt, concessions proposed against the interests of bondholders were to be declared
temporary and reduced to a minimum consistent with the avoidance of bankruptcy. These French proposals were accepted and
embodied in the London Convention of March 1885. By this
agreement Egyptian finances remained firmly fettered to international control. British acceptance of such an unsatisfactory
settlement was based on the premise that Britain would soon
cease to be responsible for the government of Egypt. But even if
Britain had withdrawn it is difficult to see how an independent
Egyptian government could have carried on with national
resources effectively in pawn. Cromer indeed was ultimately able
to effect a financial miracle but Cromer's presence and his authority
were tied to British occupation.

Before the conclusion of these crippling arrangements news of

---

[1] Roundell Palmer, Lord (later Earl) Selborne (1812–95), Lord Chancellor 1872–4
and 1880–5.

[2] Thomas George Baring, 1st Earl of Northbrook (1826–1904), First Lord of the
Admiralty 1880–5.

the death of Gordon[1] reached London. Anger and shock gave courage to Gladstone's opponents in the Cabinet. There was a demand for Wolseley's expedition to be instructed to crush the Mahdi and reoccupy the Sudan. Gladstone, under stress, agreed that the Mahdi ought to be crushed but insisted that the Sudan must then be evacuated. This compromise appealed to neither wing within his party and eventually, under cover of the Penjdeh incident,[2] Wolseley's duties were confined to the protection of the Egyptian frontier and to the completion of withdrawal from the Sudan.

While Gladstone's Cabinet was so wretchedly preoccupied with the Egyptian question and its Sudanese ramifications the French were little disposed to avoid friction by self-denial elsewhere in Africa. Their forward policy was opposed by Granville, not out of covetousness for the territories which the French sought, but in order to preserve them from the prohibitive tariffs which were a part of French colonial policy. As a possible check to de Brazza's rapidly expanding empire Granville developed the notion of trying to reserve the future of the rest of the Congo by pressing it on the Portuguese.[3] When this plan was frustrated by French and German intervention Granville, partly to mollify the Germans, almost gratefully accepted King Leopold's own Congo solution. On the Ivory Coast, though an Anglo-French commission met in December 1883, the French rejected any bargain.[4] They also failed to ratify the Sierra Leone agreement.[5] In the Lagos area the French took the initiative by declaring, on 2 April 1883, a renewed Protectorate over Porto Nuovo.[6] This led to local irritation, retaliation and a running quarrel. The British became fearful for the security of their own interests on the Lower Niger and the Oil Rivers; Gambia was once again considered as a means of buying off the French. In the meanwhile, with French approval, the Germans now joined in making West African claims. Partly

[1] He was killed on 26 Jan 1885. Steamboats of the relief expedition arrived two days later.

[2] In Mar 1885 a Russian military expedition clashed with the Afghans at Penjdeh, north of Herat. The Government prepared for the possibility of war against Russia in defence of India.

[3] See G. N. Sanderson, *England, Europe and the Upper Nile*, p. 23.

[4] See J. D. Hargreaves, *Prelude to the Partition of West Africa*, p. 288.

[5] Ibid., pp. 289–94 and see p. 35.

[6] Ibid., pp. 294–301.

because the British resented the Germans less as occupiers than
the French and partly in vain endeavours to secure German co-
operation over Egypt, Britain eventually registered approval of
Germany's acquisitions in Togoland and the Cameroons. But
Franco-German co-operation in West Africa, which might have
proved even more embarrassing to England, was limited because
the French were, quite rightly, suspicious of Bismarck's motives.
They had joined, however, in backing his proposals for a colonial
conference. The Berlin Conference[1] did not, in the event, constitute
a diplomatic revolution. Nor did it redraw the colonial map of
Africa. Generally the *status quo* was ratified and some rules laid
down for future expansion. Granville was able to protect, at least
as far as words went, British interests and claims on the Niger.
It remained to be seen whether British governments would, in
the future, be willing to meet the financial and possibly military
consequences of seeking to defend those interests and of pressing
those claims.

In March 1885 a military set-back in Indo-China precipitated the
fall of Ferry's government. He had increasingly identified himself
with a policy of colonial expansion but, notwithstanding the
growing popularity of Empire and the current irritation against
Great Britain, such a policy was still very vulnerable to parliamentary attack, particularly when accompanied by an apparent
measure of Franco-German co-operation.

With the disappearance of Ferry, Anglo-French friction in West
Africa subsided. There was a pause in French moves towards the
Upper Niger. On the British side, as Gladstone's administration
ground to a halt, there was little disposition to take up the options
reserved at the Berlin Conference.

When Salisbury succeeded Gladstone as head of a caretaker
government in June 1885 he showed no greater inclination for
action on the Niger. Nor, in spite of previous recriminations
about Gordon's fate and government weakness over Egypt, did
he opt for any tougher line there. On the contrary he reaffirmed
intentions to withdraw as soon as possible from Egypt and, as
evidence of his purpose, he sent Drummond Wolff to Constantinople in August 1885 to open negotiations with the Sultan.

[1] Nov 1884–Feb 1885.

Salisbury's attention was almost entirely absorbed by the Bulgarian crisis and here he needed all possible support from Germany and France.

There was no change in priorities when Gladstone returned to office as Prime Minister in February 1886 with Rosebery as Foreign Secretary for the first time. Withdrawal from Egypt remained official policy while Drummond Wolff, together with a Turkish commissioner, were studying the situation in Cairo and preparing a report. In order to avoid expense and yet to preserve British interests on the Niger the policy of handing over responsibility to Goldie[1] was eventually crystallised on 25 June 1886 by the setting up of the Royal Niger Company.

In August 1886 Salisbury, now with a large majority, returned to the Premiership.[2] The Bulgarian question and the supposed Russian threat to Constantinople continued to dominate his attention,[3] and he remained eager for German and French support. Withdrawal from Egypt was not only desirable in itself but a means of placating France. At first he was handicapped in his pursuit of this policy by the attitude of Lord Randolph Churchill[4] who was then in a commanding position in the Cabinet. Churchill was plotting a diplomatic revolution. He advocated a deal with Russia and, to protect the route to India, a permanent occupation of Egypt. Although he was not able to impose his own views he successfully inhibited Salisbury from the pursuit of any positive policy. It was, therefore, with relief that the Prime Minister snapped up Churchill's petulant offer of resignation in December 1886. With Churchill out of the way Salisbury was able to respond to Italian proposals, made in conjunction with Austria, to guarantee Constantinople against the Russians. In September and October 1886 the Italians had offered Great Britain support in Egypt.[5] This implied support against the French and was of little interest to Salisbury who wanted backing against Russia. In January 1887, however, when the Italians changed their tune and

[1] See p. 37.
[2] After Jan 1887, when Lord Iddesleigh died, he combined the offices of Premier and Foreign Secretary.
[3] For a recent study of Salisbury's Mediterranean policy see C. J. Lowe, *Salisbury and the Mediterranean 1886–1896*.
[4] Lord Randolph Churchill (1849–95), then Chancellor of the Exchequer.
[5] See C. J. Lowe, *Salisbury and the Mediterranean*, pp. 11, 12.

spoke in terms of Constantinople, Salisbury was far more prepared to listen.[1] The result was the first Mediterranean agreement of February 1887. This arrangement had the blessing of Bismarck who was only too pleased to devise some means of containing Russia provided England, and not Germany, was committed to the task.

Fortified by his Mediterranean Agreement, obtained on terms which did not oblige him to divulge its contents to the House of Commons, Salisbury had somewhat less need of French support. On the other hand he remained fully determined to go ahead with his policy of withdrawal from Egypt and of using it, if possible, to promote Anglo-French *rapprochement*. By now Drummond Wolff's long preparatory work had been completed[2] and he was instructed to enter into final negotiations with the Sultan. Agreement was eventually reached on 22 May 1887 after Drummond Wolff had accepted a Turkish amendment that Britain should guarantee to evacuate Egypt after three, instead of the five, years originally proposed. Britain's main condition was the right of re-entry, open to both British and Turks, if law and order were threatened or if the Khedive failed to fulfil his international obligations. But the Convention, although in principle concluded, still required the Sultan's ratification. Germany, Austria and Italy, in line with their previous promises, put pressure on him to sign. Russia and France threatened him should he do so. The Egyptian question divided England and France; its solution would facilitate an Anglo-French alignment against Russia. Russian opposition was easy to understand but the French attitude is more difficult to explain. In the autumn of 1886, Freycinet[3] had been pressing for precisely this kind of solution. Although England's right of re-entry was a difficult pill to swallow there now was at least a firm promise of withdrawal. Internal problems probably provide the clue to this change of mind. The Boulangist crisis[4] in May made it dangerous to touch on a sensitive Egyptian nerve. Acceptance of any British proposal would no doubt have been unpopular. This, combined with Russian pressure and the value, against

[1] See C. J. Lowe, *Salisbury and the Mediterranean*, pp. 13–16.
[2] See p. 50.
[3] See p. 39. He was again President of the Council.
[4] General Georges Boulanger (1837–91), Minister of War, Jan 1886–May 1887. After the fall of Freycinet's ministry and Boulanger's dismissal his popularity, in the midst of chauvinist agitation, was dangerously high.

Germany, of even a hint of Russian collaboration, probably proved decisive.

On 15 July 1887 Salisbury, weary of the Sultan's continued prevarications, ordered Drummond Wolff to break off the negotiations.[1] He did not, however, abandon his hopes of mollifying the French. Discussions about a Suez Canal agreement, already in progress in response to French pressure, were continued and were brought to a successful conclusion by the signature of a convention at Constantinople on 29 October 1888. This convention, which stipulated freedom of passage to all vessels in time of peace or war was, however, not to become operative until after the end of the British occupation of Egypt.[2] The temporary nature of that occupation was thus again implicitly stressed.

Although the Suez Convention was intended as an emollient to France and although Waddington[3] tried to impose a 'realistic' attitude towards Egypt on his own government, various influences were combining to pull Britain and France further apart. An ambitious French naval programme had in 1887 aroused Italian alarm. By 1888 the alarm had communicated itself to England and the awkward prospect of facing Franco-Russian fleets in the Mediterranean was providing naval strategists with a theme which was to haunt British foreign policy.[4] If Franco-Russian influence was paramount at Constantinople and if the French and Russian fleets worked in unison how could Constantinople be defended against a Russian *coup*? In search of some kind of answer to Britain's problem the Italians suggested that the Turks might be invited to join the Mediterranean Agreement.[5] Salisbury could not accept this, partly because the secrecy of the agreement would obviously be jeopardised and partly because, in his view, the Turks might need to be defended at Constantinople even when they themselves refused to take cognisance of their danger. But he reacted more favourably to an alternative Italian suggestion that the existing Mediterranean Agreement should be tightened. In consequence new arrangements were made in December 1887 which virtually committed Britain to war in defence of the

[1] See R. Robinson and J. Gallagher, *Africa and the Victorians,* p. 266.
[2] See J. Marlowe, *Anglo-Egyptian relations,* pp. 79, 80.
[3] See p. 30. He was now, since 1885, Ambassador in London.
[4] See A. J. Marder, *British Naval Policy 1880–1905,* pp. 126–32.
[5] See C. J. Lowe, *Salisbury and the Mediterranean 1886–1896,* p. 20.

Straits. Although Salisbury was still able to avoid making any awkward disclosures to Parliament he had, in deference to Austrian and Italian pressure and with Bismarck's benign backing, drawn closer in an alignment which, while directed against Russia, was obviously hostile to France.

In France, agitated by Boulangism, anti-British attitudes offered an outlet for demonstrations of patriotism. It was less dangerous to grumble about Egypt than to call for the return of Alsace-Lorraine. Honour could be vicariously satisfied more easily by an anti-British than by an anti-German press.

In spite of this cloudy atmosphere a Gambia exchange project was again aired in 1888 and in 1889 a comprehensive Sierra Leone frontier settlement was eventually achieved.[1] In June 1889 Spuller, the French Foreign Minister, reopened the Egyptian question. France, he now declared, was ready to accept the Drummond Wolff convention. But Salisbury, though still desirous of accommodation with the French, had somewhat altered his views. Cromer's work of rehabilitation in Egypt was beginning to show impressive results. His influence had grown accordingly. He now argued that viable Egyptian independence was conditional on a longer period of British superintendence. This argument seemed convincing. Furthermore Salisbury had now begun to take an interest in the problem of the whole valley of the Nile. Even if the evacuation of Egypt was still regarded as eventually desirable, Egypt's independence could not prudently be restored while there was a danger that any other major European power might establish control over the Nile waters. Salisbury's attention, therefore, was directed to eastern and southern Sudan where Italian and German pretensions might contain the seed of awkward problems.[2] Until these problems had been settled, and indeed until the whole situation in the Sudan had been cleared, it would not be safe or sensible to hand Egypt back to the Egyptians.

Salisbury looked first to an accommodation with Germany which would keep the Germans from reaching the Nile. He was

[1] See J. D. Hargreaves, *Prelude to the Partition of West Africa*, pp. 342–3.

[2] An Egyptian victory at Tushki in Aug 1889 suggested that the Khalifa's military power was beginning to crumble. See G. N. Sanderson, *Egypt, Europe and the Upper Nile*, p. 43.

prepared to offer Heligoland as bait. Bismarck, at one stage, seemed ready to go much further and proposed an Anglo-German alliance. The projected alliance, however, was clearly directed against France and would have removed any chance of good Anglo-French relations. Salisbury, therefore, rejected the suggestion but continued his efforts to reach an African agreement with Germany. Here Bismarck was not in any hurry and Salisbury's real opportunity came after Bismarck's fall. The Kaiser was prepared to pay quite heavily for a token of British friendship with the promise of closer relations and more tangible benefits to come. Furthermore he set greater store than Bismarck had done on acquiring Heligoland. Salisbury was thus able to buy up German claims in Kenya and Uganda at a bargain price.[1] By the agreement of 1 July 1890 Britain gained a free hand in the whole of those vast territories as well as recognition of her Protectorate over Zanzibar. In return, apart from Heligoland, Germany obtained territories previously under British control in the region of Lake Nyasa[2] and formal recognition of her East African colonies.

This Anglo-German agreement provoked complaints from back-benchers in the French Chamber and which Delcassé voiced with particular effect,[3] that the Government had been caught napping and had lost the chance of gaining compensation for Britain's Zanzibar Protectorate. In fact negotiations with Salisbury were already in progress. Their object was to secure Britain's approval for the annexation of Tunisia. But Salisbury, who wished to avoid irritating the Italians and by implication the Triple Alliance, was not prepared to make Tunisia the basis of bargaining. He therefore turned to West Africa as a means of satisfying the French. There he was willing to make widespread concessions. By the agreement of 5 August 1890 France recognised Britain's Protectorate over Zanzibar and Pemba in return for a free hand in Madagascar and the right to occupy vast territories of

---

[1] See R. Robinson and J. Gallagher, *Africa and the Victorians*, pp. 292–4.

[2] Sacrifice of these territories meant abandonment of the Cape to Cairo dream. But that, compared to the Upper Nile question, seemed to Salisbury of much less importance.

[3] It was Delcassé's first major speech since his election as deputy (see p. 78) and it seems to have made a considerable impact. For an analysis and an extravagantly eulogistic description of the event see A. Néton, *Delcassé*, pp. 100–5.

central and western Sudan. In effect French claims from the hinterland of Algeria to the northern boundary of the Royal Niger Company's possessions were recognised. The whole of the Upper Niger by implication became French,[1] and French possessions on the West African coast were now linked by internal desert communication. In defending the agreement Salisbury argued that 'the land is what agriculturalists call "very light land"; that is to say it is the desert of the Sahara'.[2] There was much truth in this description but, as far as local British West African interests were concerned, the conclusions were painful and direct.

The agreement roused immediate protest from the Italians who complained that the reversion of Tripoli, which remained their objective, had been prejudiced. Crispi[3] tried to use this complaint to draw Salisbury into a yet closer Italian alliance. He offered support in Egypt and suggested an Anglo-Italian condominium in the Sudan.[4] This was no part of British Nile policy. In March 1890 Cromer had written: 'I have no hesitation in saying that I should prefer to see the Dervishes in possession of Kassala and Khartoum than that those places should be held by the Italians.'[5] Salisbury fully endorsed this view and refused to be drawn into any negotiations which would allow the Italians a place on the Nile Valley. Crispi's insistence on Italy's rights to Kassala resulted in the suspension of discussions at Salisbury's instruction on 10 October 1890. As he explained to Cromer on 21 November 1890:

> the Dervishes are rendering us a service in keeping Italy out. . . . If the Dervishes have occupied the valley of the Nile, they do not pledge the future in any way. Whenever you have money enough to go to Khartoum, the resources of civilization will be adequate to the subjugation of the country. If you leave them for the present where they are they can destroy nothing, for there is nothing to destroy: they cannot erect any domination which shall make the conquest of them a more formidable task, for they have, practically speaking, neither cannon nor machine

---

[1] The Niger boundary then established was known as the Say–Burrauwa line.

[2] Salisbury to Baring 31 Aug 1890, quoted in R. Robinson and J. Gallagher, *Africa and the Victorians*, p. 303.

[3] Francesco Crispi (1819–1901), Italian Prime Minister 1887–91, 1893–6; ambitious for colonial expansion, largely responsible for anti-French bias in Italian policy.

[4] See C. J. Lowe, *Salisbury and the Mediterranean*, p. 62.

[5] Quoted ibid.

guns, nor even the ammunition for ordinary rifles. Surely, if
you are NOT ready to go to Khartoum, this people were created
for the purpose of keeping the bed warm until you can
occupy it.[1]

Salisbury was of course preaching to the converted. Although,
as Cromer complained, 'I can hardly move a step without a jar of
conflicting international interests',[2] he had effected a financial
miracle in Egypt. The resources so painfully husbanded were
desperately needed for public works on which further prosperity
depended. Nothing filled him with greater apprehension than the
thought of diverting Egyptian money to reconquering the Sudan.
Signs of the weakening of the Khalifa's authority were therefore,
at this point, ominous rather than welcome. No countenance
could be given to Crispi's designs.

In February 1891 Crispi fell from power. His successor Rudini
was more disposed to negotiate on British terms. In March and
April agreements were reached which encouraged Italian pretensions in Abyssinia in return for surrender of any claims to
Nile Valley territory.[3] Reassurances of British support for Italy
over Tripoli and against France if attacked were also vaguely but
comfortingly given.

The new bogy of a Franco-Italian war and the old fear of a
Russian *coup* at the Straits compelled Salisbury, in the light of
growing Franco-Russian solidarity,[4] to look closely at the naval
situation in the Mediterranean. The views of the directorate of
the Admiralty were most pessimistic.[5] They rated the Russian
Black Sea fleet and the French Mediterranean fleet as a dangerously
powerful combination. The Straits, they pointed out, were now
defended against entry from the Mediterranean only; Turkey was
thus equipped to resist Britain and not Russia. The Germans
echoed the pessimism of the British naval authorities and pressed
Salisbury to strengthen his naval forces in the Mediterranean. On
the basis of expert advice Britain was no longer in a position to

---

[1] Quoted ibid., p. 63.

[2] Cromer to Salisbury 2 January 1891, quoted Lord Zetland, *Lord Cromer*, p. 183.

[3] See C. J. Lowe, *Salisbury and the Mediterranean*, p. 80.

[4] The visit of a French squadron to Kronstadt in July 1891 provided spectacular
evidence.

[5] See A. J. Marder, *British Naval Policy*, pp. 152–60.

guard Constantinople against Russian attack without exposing
herself to naval humiliation at the hands of the French and perhaps
even jeopardising national security. On this assumption Salisbury's
whole foreign policy was now based on bluff. Although he dis-
trusted expert advice and was loth to accept this verdict he was
sufficiently impressed to recognise that the situation called for a
foreign policy reappraisal. On the other hand a General Election
was pending and he was despondent about his chances of victory.
The moment for major decisions seemed inopportune. So he
merely concentrated on the avoidance of quarrels with France
and on the maintenance of existing links with the Triple Alliance.

In August 1892 Gladstone formed his fourth ministry with
Rosebery again at the Foreign Office. In opposition Rosebery
had watched Salisbury's foreign policy with admiration and
approval. He returned to the Foreign Office determined to continue that policy whatever the views of the rest of the Cabinet.[1]
Indeed, as leader of the Liberal Imperialists he considered that one
of his main duties was to combat the influence of anti-imperialist
colleagues. In this frame of mind he at once accepted Cromer's
premise, which Salisbury had endorsed, that there could be no
prompt withdrawal from Egypt. Indeed he assumed that occupation would be permanent. He also accepted the opinion, which
appealed less to Cromer but which Salisbury had come to hold,
that Uganda was essential for the security of the Nile. Salisbury's
attempt to find funds for a Uganda Railway had been blocked and
he had only managed to secure £20,000 for a survey.[2] In the
meanwhile Mackinnon's chartered company, partly owing to its
own incompetence and partly to the loss of confidence which
postponement of the railway project had generated, was facing
bankruptcy and threatening to abandon Uganda. In the teeth of
bitter cabinet opposition Rosebery conducted a carefully laid
Uganda campaign. Company finances were propped up by charitable subscription. Government aid on a limited scale and for a
limited period was made available. Finally, a Uganda Protectorate
was declared.[3]

[1] See R. R. James, *Rosebery*, p. 255.
[2] See R. Robinson and J. Gallagher, *Africa and the Victorians*, p. 369.
[3] For details of Rosebery's road to the Protectorate, achieved in Mar 1894,
shortly after he succeeded to the Premiership, see ibid., pp. 311–30.

It was not only in Uganda that Rosebery seemed prepared to move further than Salisbury in his concern about the Nile Valley. He began anxiously to consider the future of the two south-westerly provinces of the former Egyptian Sudan, Equatoria and Bahr el Ghazal, where Egyptian garrisons had continued to maintain a precarious existence. Cromer insisted that they should be permanently abandoned. Very unwillingly he had in 1886 contributed £10,000 to finance an expedition led by Stanley[1] for the relief of Emin Pasha,[2] who had remained there as Governor-General.[3] Stanley arrived with orders from the Khedive for Emin Pasha to withdraw and with proposals from Leopold of the Belgians and the East African Chartered Company for conflicting policies of territorial aggrandisement. Emin's troops mutinied and although he was rescued by Stanley all other plans collapsed. Germany had at one time seemed likely to take some interest in Equatoria but all plans were abandoned after the 1890 agreement with England.[4] These vast and inaccessible territories now lay at the mercy of any adventurous claimant. Rosebery was determined that they must be denied to any major power other than Britain. He therefore opened negotiations with King Leopold to whom he offered the territories on lease.[5] As part of the agreement King Leopold contracted to lease to Britain a strip of territory in the Congo which would have reopened the possibility of a Cape to Cairo railway. News of the treaty, which was published on 14 May 1894, led to violent protest in Rosebery's cabinet. It also led to violent objections on the part of the Germans and of the French. Combined pressures against Leopold and against Rosebery made Leopold back out of the agreement and forced Rosebery into welcoming this conclusion. He now could do no more than reserve, in Egypt's name, Egyptian rights over all her former possessions. But the ultimate fate of these territories remained an awkward open question.

[1] Sir Henry M. Stanley (1841–1904), American journalist and explorer.
[2] Mehmed Emin Pasha (1840–92), born Eduard Schnitzer, a German who entered the Khedive's service and succeeded Gordon as Governor of Equatoria (see p. 46).
[3] For details of this expedition and its consequences see G. N. Sanderson, *England, Europe and the Upper Nile*, pp. 26–46.
[4] See p. 55.
[5] For details of the Anglo-Congolese agreement and its failure see G. N. Sanderson, *England, Europe and the Upper Nile*, pp. 163–87.

Rosebery's suspicions of French designs in Equatoria were heightened by signs of French activity and revived Anglo-French rivalry in West Africa. The agreement of 1890 had reserved to the Niger Company the whole of the Lower Niger and the Kingdom of Sokoto thus, at least in theory, blocking France's road to Lake Tchad. The French had accepted these dispositions in the belief that Goldie's claims to have established some kind of territorial control were well founded. Gradually the French explorers, backed by the *Comité de l'Afrique française*,[1] learned more of the truth. From Senegal and from Dahomey[2] the French began to press forward. Goldie was alarmed. There were settled boundaries with Germany[3] but he still needed to reckon with the French. The race between Decœur[4] and Lugard[5] to Borgou was symptomatic of the struggle; although Lugard reached his goal he was not able to leave any effective force behind him to deal with even the mildest French military challenge. Responsibility for coping with this awkward situation was left entirely to Goldie. In Rosebery's view West African interests were expendable and, as Salisbury had postulated, only significant as bargaining counters in relation to the far more important question of Egypt and the Upper Nile.

In January 1893 Khedive Abbas[6] with French encouragement carried out what amounted to a *coup d'état* in Egypt.[7] Cromer protested to Rosebery and asked for troop reinforcements. These were provided and Abbas was forced to toe the British line. This French provocation, culminating in further French humiliation, took place when conversations between Gladstone and Waddington, based on familiar formulas of eventual British withdrawal

---

[1] This powerful pressure group was formed in Nov 1890. By its periodical the *Bulletin du Comité de l'Afrique française* and by its lobby in the Chamber of Deputies it rapidly became a national institution. Delcassé was a founder member.

[2] Military operations, after long hesitation, had resulted in the formal establishment of a colony.

[3] The German Cameroons colony had been recognised. See p. 50.

[4] A captain in charge of the French expeditionary force. It consisted of 145 soldiers.

[5] Frederick Lugard, later Lord Lugard (1858–1945), at this time a captain in the employment of the Niger Company – he had 40 soldiers under his command.

[6] Abbas Hilmi II (1874–1944) succeeded his father as Khedive in 1892. Was deposed in 1914 when Egypt became a British Protectorate and spent the rest of his life in exile.

[7] The Khedive dismissed his ministers and appointed new ones without consulting Cromer.

from Egypt, had been in progress. Ribot[1] showed signs that he
would have been prepared to be reasonably 'realistic' over Egypt
in return for a freer hand in Morocco and in Madagascar. But
Rosebery effectively dampened this initiative.[2]

To the French colonialists and particularly to Delcassé,[3] the
Colonial Under-Secretary, it seemed, in the light of this rebuff in
London and of recent humiliation in Cairo, that Britain would
only understand arguments from strength. Pressure must be
brought to bear at a vulnerable point if Britain's withdrawal from
Egypt or any major compensatory concession elsewhere was to be
obtained. Accordingly Delcassé, without confiding in his immediate superiors, prepared for action.[4] Monteil[5] was to be his
instrument.[6] Starting from Brazzaville and proceeding via the
Ubanghi, Monteil was to lead an expedition to Bahr el Ghazal
and from there to occupy Fashoda. Once France had established
a position on the Upper Nile, the British would be forced to
negotiate in a much humbler spirit. But Delcassé also had a
further and unavowed objective. In his calculations the Monteil
mission was designed not only to bring pressure on England, but
to counter the ambitions of King Leopold. The *Comité de l' Afrique
française*, whose secretary[7] was in Leopold's pay,[8] was unaware of
Delcassé's ulterior motive and, no doubt under its secretary's
influence, opposed any action until agreement with the King had
been reached.

Guided by the *Comité* Monteil contrived to delay his departure
and arranged to be sent in the meanwhile to negotiate with the
Germans.[9] By the time he returned Delcassé had resigned. Eventually, however, after a welter of complicated intrigues, Monteil

---

[1] Alexandre Ribot (1842–1923); Foreign Minister from 1890, he became President
of the Council from Jan to Mar 1893. He was again President of the Council from
Jan to Oct 1895.

[2] See R. Robinson and J. Gallagher, *Africa and the Victorians*, pp. 324–5.

[3] See p. 79.

[4] For details of Delcassé's manœuvres see G. N. Sanderson, *England, Europe and the
Upper Nile*, pp. 140–61.

[5] Parfait Louis Monteil (1855–1925), French officer and explorer who had been
the recent hero of an expedition from Senegal to Lake Tchad and back via Tripoli.

[6] Monteil apparently accepted the mission only after a direct appeal from the
President of the Republic.

[7] Hippolyte Percher, better known by his pen-name Harry Alis.

[8] See G. N. Sanderson, *England, Europe and the Upper Nile*, p. 137.

[9] Ibid., p. 146.

set sail, only to find, after Delcassé's return to office, new orders that his expedition was to be diverted to dealing with troubles on the Ivory Coast. The Monteil mission was important because it aroused British suspicions and because it provided a blueprint for the eventual Marchand[1] mission. In support of his original plan Delcassé had initiated approaches to Emperor Menelik of Abyssinia which, however unrealistic, were also to be pursued as part of the Marchand plan strategy. During the autumn of 1894 a further move towards the settlement of outstanding Anglo-French differences was attempted. This time Rosebery was in favour but the negotiations eventually foundered on the question of the Upper Nile.[2] Hanotaux[3] lacked the courage to accept a self-denying ordinance and so left the road open for pursuit of Delcassé's original Fashoda plan.

On 28 March 1895 Grey[4] warned, in the House of Commons, that a French advance into Bahr el Ghazal would be regarded as an unfriendly act. This move was not a calculated one because it came in reply to a parliamentary question for which Grey had not been prepared.[5] Rosebery, however, completely supported his attitude even though Kimberley,[6] in answer to French protests, tried somewhat to soften the threat. In fact, in anticipating this kind of confrontation, the British assumed that French preparations were far more advanced than was the case. The French on the other hand became convinced that a British move to reconquer the Sudan was imminent. They were quite mistaken.

Rosebery had not been able to make any plans for action. As Prime Minister he found that his control over foreign policy was much weakened. Furthermore, in spite of his concern about the African question, he was being harassed by wider foreign policy considerations. The naval scare which had been building up when

---

[1] See p. 65.

[2] British concessions in West Africa and elsewhere depended on French renunciation of any Upper Nile ambitions.

[3] Gabriel Hanotaux (1853–1944), appointed Foreign Minister in May 1894, he had already served in that Ministry for many years as a Civil Servant.

[4] Edward Grey, subsequently Viscount Grey of Fallodon (1862–1933), at this time Under-Secretary for Foreign Affairs. He had been selected by Rosebery and was in close sympathy with his views.

[5] See G. N. Sanderson, *England, Europe and the Upper Nile*, pp. 212–17.

[6] See p. 24. Kimberley had become Foreign Secretary when Rosebery succeeded Gladstone as Prime Minister in Feb 1894.

Salisbury left office gained ground with the tightening of Franco-Russian relations.[1] Gladstone's final resignation and Rosebery's accession to the Premiership were, in fact, consequences of Gladstone's refusal to support naval estimates. But even with an increased naval programme, the Admiralty still deprecated the possibility of intervention at Constantinople while France remained Russia's ally. Armenian massacres made the question one of more than academic interest. There seemed little prospect of bringing pressure on Turkey by concert of powers. It was difficult for England to do nothing and yet unilateral action, according to naval advice, represented an unthinkable risk. Inaction, on the other hand, allowed the possibility of a sudden Russian *coup*. To Rosebery, at any rate, the situation seemed critical. Links with the Triple Alliance, however valuable in theory, could in practice bring little support to the British Navy. In any crisis, the Navy was faced with a task apparently beyond its powers. On 10 May 1895, in an effort somehow to improve relations with France, Kimberley suggested to the French that if they would recognise an Egyptian sphere of influence on the Nile as far south as Fashoda, he would agree to a standstill agreement in the rest of the valley.[2] There was not enough in this to tempt Hanotaux and, when Rosebery's government fell in June, Britain was still faced with an unsolved Egyptian question which now embraced the whole valley of the Nile, and a Mediterranean dilemma which the Franco-Russian Alliance posed and the Triple Alliance could not resolve. The weakness of Britain's position was emphasised in April 1895 when Germany, Russia and France co-operated to protect China against the consequences of her defeat by Japan. It seemed as if England, hitherto the champion of China and enjoying a lion's share of Chinese trade, had been outmanœuvred. Henceforth the difficulty of preserving British interests in the Far East was added to the agenda of immediate problems. Small wonder that available resources seemed to be sorely stretched and that new experiments in the conduct of foreign policy appeared indicated.

[1] The Franco-Russian Alliance became a definite reality after an exchange of Franco-Russian notes concluded on 4 Jan 1894 which confirmed the draft agreement prepared fifteen months previously.

[2] See R. Robinson and J. Gallagher, *Africa and the Victorians*, p. 338. See also G. N. Sanderson, *England, Europe and the Upper Nile*, pp. 222-4.

Salisbury, returning to office on 25 June 1895 with an overwhelming majority, was faced with a challenge of new dimensions.[1]
Never a believer in British isolation, he assumed that British
interests could best be served by combining with other Powers
for particular purposes. What he tried to avoid was the crystallising of alignments. Situations obviously were constantly changing
and so, in Salisbury's view, must alignments. He had no wish to
involve England in permanent enmity with any power. In the past
it had often seemed necessary to seek combinations against Russia
but, while doing so, he had never wished to close the door to
possible co-operation and he was certainly most unwilling to be
involved in any permanent attitude of hostility to France in the
process. It was for this reason that he had rejected Bismarck's
1889 alliance proposal. The long-term price was too high for the
immediate advantage. In Salisbury's view the conduct of foreign
policy was a dynamic and not a static exercise. Britain needed
friends in Europe to serve her interests. But partners must change
according to circumstances.

It was this readiness to experiment which explains Salisbury's
manœuvres on his return to office. Old formulas did not seem
adequate to meet the dangers which lay ahead and which obviously
he was anxious to anticipate. Constantinople was still the most
burning question. The Russian threat, highlighted by Armenian
massacres, had achieved new urgency with the solidifying of the
Franco-Russian Alliance and the consequent conclusions of British
naval experts; the failing power of the Khalifa meant that the
question of the Upper Nile would have to be faced sooner rather
than later; French susceptibilities over the continued occupation
of Egypt, quickened by a colonial Press and Russian inspiration,
called for caution; German interest in Delagoa Bay contained a
hint that Germany might seek to exploit British difficulties in
South Africa; and finally there was a problem which Salisbury was
beginning to consider more seriously than all the others. In terms
of British trade China was infinitely more valuable than Africa.
But, in the Far East, the alignment of Russia, France and Germany
left Britain isolated and vulnerable. Although Armenian massacres
might be deplored, the logic of practical politics made it seem

[1] For a recent study of the last phase of Salisbury's foreign policy see J. A. S.
Grenville, *Lord Salisbury and Foreign Policy*.

more important to protect China than Constantinople from the
Russians.

In the light of this appraisal Salisbury tentatively explored the
possibility of bargaining with Russia. He hinted both to the
Germans and to the French that, in the event of the complete
collapse of Turkey, he would be prepared to make important concessions to Russia. This was the germ of the plan which he later
elaborated into a scheme for dividing the Near and the Far East
into spheres of preponderating influence. At this time neither
France nor Germany was prepared to play the role of 'honest
broker' in arranging an Anglo-Russian deal. The Germans suspected a trap while the French viewed the prospect of Russian
advance at Turkey's expense with positive distaste. Salisbury then
attempted a more frontal approach to Russia and proposed joint
action to the Russians over the Armenian question. His overture
was rejected. Finding it difficult to establish any line to Russia,
Salisbury made a determined effort at *rapprochement* with France.
On 13 August 1895 he began serious discussions on Siam[1] and by
October a bargain had been concluded. The resulting agreement
was signed on 15 January 1896. At the same time Salisbury
began to press for a resumption of Anglo-French negotiations on
West Africa.[2] In November, however, Berthelot[3] authorised the
appointment of Captain Marchand[4] as Governor-General of the
Upper Ubanghi. The Monteil scheme had thus been revived and
the Marchand mission was born. But there were no immediate
signs of any intention to mount a major operation. Berthelot had
made a gesture for the benefit of those who argued that the road

[1] French encroachments from Indo-China and British advances from Burma had
created an explosive situation. In reply to the British occupation of Muong Sing to
the east of the Mekong on 5 May 1895 the Governor-Geenral of Indo-China proposed to send warships to Bangkok and to declare Siam a French Protectorate.
Instead Hanotaux authorised the occupation of neighbouring villages as a sign of
practical protest. Salisbury was now prepared to withdraw from Muong Sing and to
accept the Upper Mekong as the frontier between Burma and Indo-China in return
for French guarantees of Siamese security. For details see J. D. Hargreaves, 'Entente
Manquée', *Cambridge Historical Journal*, XI, 1 (1953) 69–72.

[2] For details of the negotations which eventually followed and for the background
of this whole diplomatic manœuvre see J. D. Hargreaves, 'Entente Manquée',
Cambridge Historical Journal, XI, 1 (1953) 65–92.

[3] Pierre Eugène Marcelin Berthelot (1827–1907), a distinguished chemist, Foreign
Minister in succession to Hanotaux from 1 Nov 1895 to Mar 1896.

[4] Jean-Baptiste Marchand (1863–1934), an officer and explorer who was already a
legendary colonialist hero.

to good bargains with Great Britain lay through Fashoda. He himself preferred to seek for bargains without seriously trying to implement threats.

As Anglo-French relations seemed to be improving Berlin took alarm. The Jameson Raid was seized as an opportunity to enfold Britain closer to the Triple Alliance. But the Kruger Telegram, a clumsy device, badly misfired. Far from reminding Salisbury of the importance of German support, the telegram, apart from resulting in a wave of hostility against Germany, confirmed his growing doubts about the reliability of the Kaiser and strengthened his desire for better relations with France.

With England in this mood de Courcel[1] opened the Egyptian question with Salisbury. He recognised that it would suit neither England nor France to restore Egypt to anarchy and he suggested that employment of French officials in Egyptian service might form the basis of a new compromise. Salisbury, and even Cromer, were prepared, with some misgivings, to explore these possibilities. The preliminary talks on West Africa were, however, not proceeding satisfactorily. On 15 January 1896 it had been agreed to appoint commissioners to settle frontiers on the Lower Niger. They soon reached deadlock. Initially Chamberlain[2] had objected to the concessions which Salisbury would have liked to offer. But the extent of French pretensions, when they became known, violently angered Salisbury. He concluded that, although Berthelot and de Courcel were eager for accommodation, their influence was undermined at every turn by the now powerful West African lobby. Short of total surrender, which Salisbury neither wished to attempt nor would have been able to carry against Chamberlain, there was no easy route to appeasement in West Africa.

Though difficulties obviously still lay in the way of an Anglo-French understanding, it continued to be increasingly attractive

---

[1] Baron Alphonse Chaudron de Courcel (1835–1919) Ambassador at Berlin (1881–6) and at London (1894–8). He was known to favour Anglo-French *rapprochement*.

[2] Joseph Chamberlain (1836–1914), Colonial Secretary 1895–1903. Since his split with Gladstone over Home Rule in 1886 Chamberlain's political vision had become increasingly dominated by current Imperialist economic theory. Even the most unrewarding colonial possessions now seemed to be potentially valuable. But, quite apart from theory and in the light of his own temperament, Chamberlain would no doubt have been unwilling to submit without question to the alienation of any territories under his department's control.

to both sides. Apart from the general European advantages of good relations with England the French resented their growing dependence on Russia and the fact that Russia seemed intent on pointing the alliance against England and not against Germany. As far as Salisbury was concerned relations with his partners in a Mediterranean enterprise were proving awkward. The Austrians, acting under German influence, pressed him for an answer as to whether the Mediterranean Agreements were still in force.[1] Salisbury felt bound to give a somewhat guarded reply. He admitted that British naval action at Constantinople had been rendered almost impossible in the light of the Franco-Russian Alliance. He also doubted whether British public opinion would now be prepared to back any war in defence of Turkey. The Austrians insisted that this meant the end of the Mediterranean Agreement alignment. Salisbury had no wish to draw any such drastic conclusion but Austria's attitude made it much harder to preserve the vestiges which he still valued. It was his attempts to do so which were soon to interrupt the process of *rapprochement* with France.

The Italians, under pressure in Abyssinia, were clamouring for a British gesture of support. Because the links with Vienna and Rome were so frayed Salisbury felt bound to attempt some response. Early in March 1896 he decided that an Egyptian advance against the Khalifa as far as Dongola would serve the purpose.[2] From his correspondence with Cromer it is quite clear that this move was diplomatic and not the prelude to any re-conquest of the Sudan.[3] At that time Salisbury still believed in waiting until railway preparations in Uganda would permit an advance into the Southern Sudan. Though Dongola was stated to be the objective, Salisbury was more concerned with the gesture than with the objective. To Cromer, however, the situation appeared in a different light. Although he was not ready to promote a reconquest of the Sudan, he realised that no Egyptian government could be expected to back an expedition unless that

---

[1] For this diplomatic manœuvre and its consequences see C. J. Lowe, *Salisbury and the Mediterranean 1886–1896*, pp. 108–97. See also J. A. S. Grenville, 'Goluchowski, Salisbury and the Mediterranean Agreements 1895–97', *The Slavonic and East European Review*, xxxvi (Jun 1958) 340–69.

[2] See C. J. Lowe, *Salisbury and the Mediterranean 1886–1896*, p. 113.

[3] See G. N. Sanderson, *England, Europe and the Upper Nile 1882–1899*, pp. 244–9.

objective were in sight. Otherwise Egypt would merely be being used as a tool of British diplomacy. Cromer therefore became desperately anxious that the venture should be pursued with sufficient vigour to show at least some concrete results.[1]

The announcement of the projected Dongola expedition on 12 March 1896 inevitably affected Anglo-French relations. Although de Courcel clearly divined Salisbury's real motives and although Berthelot listened to his arguments Léon Bourgeois, the Prime Minister, was more inclined to share in the general feelings of anger and betrayal.[2] Nevertheless, notwithstanding a stiffening in France's attitude, negotiations were for a while continued. Salisbury was prepared to make promises that this new move in no way altered Britain's determination eventually to withdraw from Egypt. In the meanwhile Egyptian funds were required to finance the expedition; France was unwilling to agree to such expenditure without more concrete concessions. The Germans insisted that a decision at the *Caisse de la Dette* must be reached at once. The *Caisse* met on 26 March. The French and Russian Commissioners walked out of the meeting. Two days later Berthelot was forced out of office and the negotiations were dead.[3]

The Egyptian question had been revived in a manner which made discussion difficult and Salisbury concluded that such discussion was now better avoided. He continued, however, in far less favourable circumstances, to work for good relations with France. In June he reverted to the theme of spoils in the decaying Ottoman Empire and suggested that the French might eventually be interested in acquiring Syria; in August he offered Crete; and early in 1897 he dropped heavy hints about Morocco.

The French were disinclined to rise to such dangerous bait. They were beginning to take firmer steps to bring pressure on Britain more seriously. Léon Bourgeois, who succeeded Berthelot as Foreign Minister, reactivated the Marchand Mission.[4] When Hanotaux returned to the Foreign Office on 29 April 1896 preparations were already well under way. He accepted the *fait accompli*.[5]

[1] See G. N. Sanderson, *England, Europe and the Upper Nile 1882–1899*, pp. 246–7.
[2] See J. D. Hargreaves, 'Entente Manquée', *Cambridge Historical Journal*, XI, 1 (1953) 87.
[3] Ibid., p. 91.
[4] See G. N. Sanderson, *England, Europe and the Upper Nile 1882–1899*, p. 280.
[5] Ibid., pp. 280, 281.

He was more inclined to do so because Russia now seemed to be prepared to co-operate over the Egyptian question. There were plans for joint Franco-Russian manœuvres in Abyssinia. Hanotaux hoped somehow that Marchand's mission might prove a trump card.

Marchand himself landed in the French Congo on 24 July 1896. There he found a situation of almost total disorder and he was forced to cope with local problems before he could begin to make his own preparations.[1] These, too, proved slow and difficult. Such interest as had been aroused in England by news of the mission soon subsided. Salisbury, however, was quite aware that Marchand might succeed in hoisting a French flag somewhere on the Upper Nile. But he was convinced that what mattered was not the staking of claims but the actual means of maintaining them. On this score he felt confident about British long-term superiority. Less sanguine about a southern approach since the failure of the ill-fated Macdonald Mission,[2] he now began to think seriously in terms of an advance from the north. Two factors influenced his conversion to this more positive policy.

In the first place he had gradually capitulated to the naval expert's point of view that Constantinople was not defensible. One of the consequences of this conclusion was the need for Alexandria as a British Mediterranean naval base.[3] This suggested continued occupation of Egypt and an abandonment of the use of promises to withdraw as a diplomatic bargaining counter. In those circumstances there was no longer any sense in unduly delaying a settlement of the awkward Upper Nile question. The second consideration was purely local. After some early successes against the Dervishes, Kitchener,[4] in an optimistic mood, calculated that with a modest increase in military expenditure he

[1] Ibid., pp. 285, 286.

[2] Major Macdonald, British military commander in Uganda, was instructed to proceed, in Jun 1897, with a force of five hundred to Fashoda. But a mutiny of the Sudanese garrison in Uganda and other local troubles made it impossible for Macdonald to make any move until the prospect of his reaching Fashoda before Marchand had totally disappeared. See R. Robinson and J. Gallagher, *Africa and the Victorians*, pp. 362–3.

[3] See A. J. Marder, *British Naval Policy 1880–1905*, p. 270.

[4] Horatio Herbert Kitchener (1850–1916), created Baron 1898, Viscount 1902, Earl 1914. Served in the Sudan 1884–5. Appointed Sirdar (Commander-in-chief) of the Egyptian army in 1890. He occupied Dongola on 23 Sep 1896.

could achieve complete and relatively rapid victory over the Khalifa.[1] He met with a sympathetic response from Cromer. Since a British loan would now almost certainly be required to meet the cost[2] Cromer, influenced by the need to satisfy Egyptian opinion, was prepared to recommend that the amount be increased in order to permit the more extensive and conclusive operations which Kitchener proposed. With Cromer's blessing Kitchener visited London to press the argument in person. Their joint efforts convinced Salisbury. But, in the event, Kitchener was proved to have underestimated Dervish resistance. Soon he was obliged to plead for direct British military reinforcements. Thus was the original Dongola expedition transformed by stages into a major military operation to reconquer the Sudan.

Now it was Salisbury's turn to be in a hurry. He foresaw awkward moments ahead and even the chance of a headlong collision with France should Marchand have established himself at any point on the Upper Nile. This did not imply any race for Fashoda but simply that once the decision to destroy the Khalifa's power had been taken, the whole Upper Nile question must be settled on Britain's terms even at cost of direct confrontation with France. In order to avoid the tangle of problems which might result from claiming the recovery of former Egyptian territories, Salisbury hit on the notion of treating the Khalifa's empire as an independent state.[3] If the Khalifa was defeated all his possessions would fall to the victors, Egypt and Britain, by right of conquest. An Anglo-Egyptian condominium could then be declared, and the Sudan would be protected from all the awkward international restrictions which tied Cromer's hand in Egypt. This ingenious device was bound to provoke French resentment. But Salisbury was ready to take that risk, confident that on such an issue France would be, for practical purposes, isolated. In single combat with France, British naval superiority must prove decisive.

[1] For Kitchener's assessment of the situation and Cromer's conversion to his point of view, see G. N. Sanderson, *England, Europe and the Upper Nile 1882–1899*, pp. 252–253.

[2] Because the advance made by the *Caisse de la Dette* as a result of a decision taken in the absence of the French and Russian representatives (see p. 68) was likely to be declared illegal by the Mixed Courts, to whom the matter had been referred.

[3] For the various alternative possibilities and Salisbury's eventual solution see G. N. Sanderson, *England, Europe and the Upper Nile 1882–1899*, pp. 266–9.

In the meanwhile, anticipating an awkward moment ahead in Anglo-French relations, Salisbury decided to make another effort to solve the Niger question. It was obviously worth trying to avoid simultaneous crises on the Niger and on the Nile, particularly since French pressure in West Africa was now revealing the inadequacies of Goldie's resources. When the Commissioners resumed their discussions in Paris in October 1897[1] Great Britain was in a poor bargaining position. And yet Chamberlain was loth to make major sacrifices. In February 1898 the frontier force which he had created was under instruction to press as far forward in the Lagos hinterland as its commanders dared without headlong collision with the French. However, in spite of this provocation, once Hanotaux appreciated that the Niger negotiations would not in any way be linked with the Nile he was prepared to consider a West African solution on its own merits and the Commissioners were gradually able to reach a settlement. By the beginning of June 1898 haggling was reduced to the fate of Bona and of Ilo. Chamberlain would have wished to insist on retaining both but in deference to Salisbury's pressure he gave way on Bona. On 14 June the Niger Convention was signed. By its terms the French obtained access to the navigable Niger and they retained the disputed regions of Mossi and Nikki. Borgou was divided between the contestants. British claims had receded considerably since Salisbury hopefully drew the Say–Burruwa line in 1890.[2] However, in the light of the situation on the spot, Salisbury still contrived to make a useful bargain. Hanotaux's willingness to settle was influenced mainly by the fact that, while French opinion was very sensitive over the Egyptian question, there was much less emotionalism over West Africa.

While Salisbury had thus cleared the board in Africa for a possible confrontation with France over the Upper Nile, he continued to look for solutions to his other main foreign policy problems. The summer of 1896 had convinced him that the Powers were not willing to give England any support in taking

---

[1] Their deliberations had been suspended after the announcement of Kitchener's mission to capture Dongola on 12 Mar 1896. They had been resumed in Apr 1896 but French pretensions had, inevitably as a result of the Dongola news, increased rather than diminished and negotiations again lapsed in May 1896. See J. D. Hargreaves, 'Entente Manquée', *Cambridge Historical Journal*, XI, 1 (1953) 92.

[2] See p. 56.

Armenian massacres seriously and that Constantinople was, in fact, at Russia's mercy. He began to make a more determined bid towards striking a bargain with Russia. It culminated in an offer of partition of preponderance in the Near and Far East. In effect he was offering a freer hand to Russia in the Near East in return for a self-denying ordinance in China. But the Russians were by now more interested in China than in the Near East. This they showed by making an agreement with Austria in May 1897 to put the Near East on ice. In China the Russians coveted the whole inheritance, though not in any hurry. Germany's seizure of Kiaochow[1] was therefore, from Russia's point of view, an annoying episode. It was only after hesitation that the Russians decided to make the best of a bad job and establish their own claims at Port Arthur.[2] Salisbury, after making new advances to the Russians and trying somehow to put the clock back, finally snatched at Weihaiwei, just 'as a matter of pure sentiment'.[3]

Salisbury's tentative moves in Russia's direction had proved a failure. Chamberlain, who had favoured a far more decisive approach, was critical of the results. He now concluded that the containment of Russia in the Far East was essential and that a German alliance was the only effective means of achieving this result. In order to obtain such an alliance he characteristically assumed that it was simply necessary to set the wheels of negotiation in motion. Impatient of the kind of delays and reservations which he associated with Salisbury as Foreign Secretary and with diplomacy in general he seized the opportunity provided by Salisbury's absence on a convalescent holiday[4] abroad for direct talks with Hatzfeldt.[5] When, on his return to England, Salisbury received

---

[1] A bay in the Gulf of Pechili in Northern China occupied by German naval units in Nov 1897, ostensibly as a reprisal for the murder of two German missionaries.

[2] They obtained from China a twenty-five-year lease of the Liaotung Peninsula, including the harbours of Port Arthur and Talienwan, in Mar 1898.

[3] Salisbury had used the phrase in a letter of 30 Dec 1897 to Chamberlain, after complaining that 'the public will require some territorial or cartographic consolation in China'. He was then thinking in terms of Chusan. See J. L. Garvin, *Life of Chamberlain*, vol. II, p. 249.

[4] Salisbury had been seriously ill earlier and left England as soon as he was fit to travel on 28 Mar 1898, returning on 1 May. During his illness and absence his nephew Balfour deputised informally as Foreign Secretary.

[5] Count Paul Wildenburg von Hatzfeldt (1831–1901), German Ambassador in London 1885–1901. Hatzfeldt had been trying to pave the way with Balfour, during Salisbury's illness, for a discussion of colonial questions. Balfour had suggested a

a full report from Chamberlain of these talks, he doubted whether they contained any ground for optimism that Germany would be prepared to back England against Russia in China. On the contrary it seemed to him that Germany was only interested in extracting such concrete tokens of British goodwill as could be obtained without Far Eastern commitment. But, partly for the sake of restoring cabinet solidarity, he did not allow his doubts to prevent some discreet endeavours to pursue Chamberlain's initiative. German reactions, however, seemed fully to justify his scepticism. Chamberlain, in spite of sporadic and embarrassing personal solicitations to Germany,[1] gradually came to recognise this during the spring and early summer of 1898. In August, however, the darkening situation in South Africa made Chamberlain anxious to renew his approaches to Germany even without reference to the Far East. This time he successfully negotiated an agreement whereby Britain and Germany appointed themselves residuary legatees of Portugal's African Empire.[2] His subsequent efforts to achieve a closer alignment were, however, rejected by Germany. The Portuguese bargain, although not entirely to Salisbury's taste,[3] was nevertheless opportune. Quite apart from the South African question, it suited Salisbury that some compact with Germany should have been achieved when Anglo-French confrontation on the Nile was imminent. With Kitchener on his way to Khartoum and rumours of Marchand's presence at Fashoda already current, a crisis seemed inevitable.

After the Anglo-German agreement France, even if she had wished to find it, could not expect support from Germany. The Anglo-German *rapprochement*, however tenuous in reality, was also an apt reminder to France of the weakness of her own European

---

private talk with Chamberlain and this led to their meeting on 29 Mar. Hatzfeldt was quite unprepared for Chamberlain's sudden alliance proposals. They had further talks on 1 Apr and on 25 Apr. Chamberlain also had talks on 22 Apr and 26 Apr with Baron von Eckardstein. For Chamberlain's memoranda of these conversations see J. L. Garvin, *Life of Joseph Chamberlain*, vol. 3, pp. 259–77. For a recent study of the negotiations and of Salisbury's attitude and subsequent reactions see J. A. S. Grenville, *Lord Salisbury and Foreign Policy*, pp. 148–76.

[1] Particularly his 'Long Spoon' speech at Birmingham on 13 May 1898.

[2] The Anglo-German agreement of 30 Aug 1898.

[3] While the treaty was being negotiated Balfour was in control of foreign affairs because further ill-health had again obliged Salisbury to take another prolonged holiday in France. He backed Balfour's endorsement of Chamberlain's policy but did not hide his misgivings. See J. A. S. Grenville, *Lord Salisbury and Foreign Policy*, p. 97.

position. Russia, with her sights set on China, was not likely to offer any substantial aid. Furthermore Salisbury's naval experts were now beginning to play down the strength of the Russian and French navies. Quite rightly he calculated that, from Britain's point of view, the moment was propitious to settle Nile scores with France. If Britain was isolated then so was France. Isolation, in those circumstances and on that issue, was not dangerous.

4

The Advent of Delcassé

THE year 1898 was one of crisis, not only in Anglo-French
relations, but for the Third Republic. Jules Méline, head of a
ministry of 'moderates' since April 1896, opened the year by
declaring with Canute's kind of confidence: 'there is no Dreyfus
affair'.[1] The rising tide of doubt could, however, no longer be
stemmed. Esterházy's[2] acquittal was followed by Zola's *J'accuse!*;[3]
the novelist's subsequent trial loosed the floods of publicity. The
Third Republic was more bitterly and noisily divided than ever in
its angry history. Elections, held in May 1898, returned a Chamber
which duly reflected divisions and where majorities were more
ready to oppose than to back any kind of ministerial combination.
Méline's relatively long-lived administration proved an early
casualty. After three fruitless attempts to form a broad-based
ministry of conciliation Brisson, on 30 June 1898, finally assembled
a shaky team of radicals and radical sympathisers with no 'moderate'
representation. It was in this ministry, doomed to be short-lived
and surviving for four months mainly because the summer recess
intervened, that Delcassé[4] accepted the portfolio of Foreign Affairs;
he was to hold it for seven years through four successive ministries
of very varying complexion until his own resignation in July 1905.

Théophile Delcassé,[5] the mainspring of the *Entente Cordiale*, was

[1] Captain Alfred Dreyfus (1859–1936) had been court martialled for treason in
Oct 1894 and sentenced to imprisonment on Devil's Island.

[2] Count Maria-Charles-Ferdinand Walsin Esterházy (1847–1923). Since 1894 a
formidable volume of evidence had been amassed pointing to the innocence of
Dreyfus and the guilt of Esterházy.

[3] Clemenceau published an open letter to the President of the Republic written by
Zola in his newspaper *L'Aurore* under this inspired title.

[4] See p. 62.

[5] There is, as yet, no adequate biography of Delcassé. *Delcassé* (Paris, 1952) by
Alberic Néton, a friend and former junior colleague, is full of gaps and almost

born at Pamiers, then a small country town in the foothills of the
Pyrenees, in 1852. His father combined the functions of bailiff,
tipstaff and process-server and, as a minor law officer, ranked
among the lower middle class of a predominantly farming com-
munity. Delcassé grew up in an atmosphere where the soil was
sacred and local pride an article of faith; there was no element of
cant in the passionate attachment which he retained throughout
his life for the region of his birth and schooling. At eighteen, after
diligent and promising studies at Pamiers, he was admitted to the
University of Toulouse where, after two previously unsuccessful
attempts, he graduated as a Master of Arts in November 1874.
No doubt encouraged by his father he considered the law as a
profession but soon decided to seek his fortune in Paris as a
writer.

Inspired by Racine and the classic literature of France, he
lavished his energies on a five-act tragedy which he submitted to
the Théâtre-Français[1] where it languished in a forgotten file.[1] While
dedicated to creative art he made a living by teaching and occasional tutoring. He also became increasingly interested in politics.
His upbringing and his literary proclivities resulted in a romantic
patriotism[2] which embraced the glories of the past and was symbolised by Joan of Arc and Louis XIV.[3] Among living Frenchmen Gambetta[4] had been his hero since university days and it was
towards Gambetta that he now looked for the regeneration of

---

entirely uncritical. The nearest approach to any comprehensive biographical study
is still Charles W. Porter, *The Career of Théophile Delcassé* (Philadelphia, 1936). On
Delcassé's foreign policy, however, a major study, C. M. Andrew, *Théophile Delcassé
and the Making of the Entente Cordiale* (1968), is now available; it also contains valuable
biographical material.

[1] Passing by the theatre many years later he jokingly remarked that he felt inclined
to go in and collect his manuscript. See A. Néton, *Delcassé*, p. 35.

[2] 'For France, everything, always' was his own choice of epitaph: ibid., p. 28.

[3] 'They are my national deities: without them there would be no France' he confessed to Paléologue. See M. Paléologue, *Un Grand Tournant de la Politique Mondiale*
(Paris, 1934) p. 191. Maurice Georges Paléologue (1859–1944), who claimed descent
from Byzantine Emperors, was France's Ambassador to Russia in 1914; a prolific
writer and member of the French Academy, he was an Assistant Under-Secretary at
the Ministry of Foreign Affairs during Delcassé's tenure of that office. His diary,
covering the years 1904–6 and published in 1934, no doubt contains literary and other
embellishments. Delcassé is obviously cast in the role of the hero. But even if
Paléologue romanticises Delcassé, his appreciation of the man and of his policies was
based on very close contact and, allowing for some licence, conveys what is probably
the most authentic note.

[4] See p. 23.

France. Drawn into the orbit of Gambetta's disciples he was presented to the master in 1879 and pressed into journalistic service. Gambetta used the newspapers under his control, *La République française* and *La Petite République*, to provide a political apprenticeship for his most promising supporters. When in 1880 Barrère, Gambetta's foreign affairs expert, was launched on a diplomatic career Delcassé was groomed to succeed him. The assignment became a mission. Delcassé allowed himself few distractions. He took some pleasure in the serious theatre and he could appreciate music but mostly he was absorbed in his work and oblivious of his surroundings. Apart from his delight in sport, chiefly fencing and riding, and his eagerness to snatch holidays in the Pyrenees, he looked for no respite from labour. Although he had a Frenchman's appetite he drank little wine and despised all manner of frivolous amusement. In company he was generally silent. Only among his closest friends did he ever unbend and then it was suddenly to recite Racine.[1] Small in stature, dark, wiry, shortsighted and with a bushy moustache he proved an eager, erudite and bustling reporter; his political ambitions and his talents were equally evident. In 1881 Gambetta encouraged him to stand for municipal elections in Paris. 'Throw yourself into the water, my boy,' he said 'it is the only way to learn how to swim.'[2] The advice was not original but the experience, even though he failed to win his seat, was valuable. This failure was a small blow compared to the defeat of Gambetta's government on 26 January 1882. Delcassé relieved his feelings by publishing a pamphlet entitled *Alerte! Où allons-nous?*, which established him as a personality in the world of political journalism. The new Government came to fear his pen and, after Gambetta's death in 1882, he continued in his master's name, though with more reference to a Gambetta legend than to Gambetta's latter policies, to harass ministries for weakness and indecision in foreign and colonial policy. He backed Jules Ferry[3] as Gambetta's heir and, in 1885, he presented himself for election to the Chamber of Deputies at Foix on a Ferry ticket. Prejudice against *Le Tonquinois*[4] was running high and Delcassé met with vigorous heckling from the right and from the left.

---

[1] See A. Néton, *Delcassé*, pp. 24, 25.   [2] Ibid., p. 45.   [3] See p. 36.
[4] Ferry's endeavours to pursue a forward policy in Indo-China earned him the nickname.

After the first ballot a Republican bargain was struck at Delcassé's expense and he withdrew, not without some credit, from the contest. During the election campaign one of Foix's traditional Republican representatives, M. Massip, died. Delcassé had previously acted as private secretary for this wealthy deputy. In 1887 he married his widow thus inheriting both the Massip fortune and his political connections. From henceforth Delcassé was sheltered from all financial problems. His wife, who shared his interest in music, was self-effacing and devoted to quiet domesticity. They had three children and seem to have enjoyed a close and contented family life. The reserved and withdrawn side of Delcassé's personality was emphasised rather than diminished by his marriage. His comfortable home was a refuge which made his dedication to work easier and no doubt more congenial. Visitors – and they were usually confined to the closest of old friends – might now occasionally find Delcassé in an expansive conversational vein; even then his wife worked silently at her embroideries.[1]

In 1889 Delcassé was elected, on a broad Republican ticket, as a Deputy for Foix and he continued to represent his home constituency for the next thirty years. By the time of his election, in addition to his regular work on *La République française* Delcassé had become foreign editor of *Le Paris*.[2] He was by now recognised as one of the leading French journalists and above all as an expert in foreign affairs. He continued to claim that his opinions had been entirely formed by Gambetta. There were, however, already many varying interpretations of Gambetta's political legacy. The version adopted by Delcassé was a simple one. To him Gambetta had stood for restoring the greatness of France which had been in jeopardy since 1870. This could only be achieved, given the unfavourable balance of population and economic resources between the German Empire and France, if France were able to attract the support of other powers and if she were able to build up a colonial empire which would be a source of strength rather than of weakness. These objectives could sometimes seem to be in opposition. It was necessary to pursue them simultaneously. This could only be done from a position of strength. Strength implied the maintenance of powerful armed forces, both military and naval,

---

[1] See A. Néton, *Delcassé*, p. 24.
[2] Edited by one of Gambetta's former supporters.

and an active, confident diplomacy. It was chiefly here that Delcassé was critical of government policies currently pursued. In terms of power politics he was in favour of alliance with Russia, of bringing an end to the feud with Italy and, perhaps above all, of bargaining from strength with England. Where colonies were concerned, he was dubious about the value of Indo-China but he believed that North Africa could be a major source of strength.[1] In this sense he was a colonialist and he was prepared, on the African continent, to pursue a generally forward policy. In the first speech which he made on 6 November 1890 in the Chamber, after characteristically claiming that he was 'a government supporter by inclination and on general principle',[2] he launched into a detailed and critical survey of recent foreign and colonial policy. Affirming that friendship with England was a desirable major objective, he denied that the appeasing policies which he discerned would ever lead to this goal. Quoting Gambetta, he insisted: 'You may be certain that the English, like the good politicians they are, will only value allies who know how to make themselves respected and how to take their own interests into account.'[3] Softness over Egypt and elsewhere in Africa was no doubt well-intentioned but surely mistaken.

In the two years that followed Delcassé established a reputation as a leading advocate of naval armament and colonial expansion. Work on a budget committee, where he was given special responsibility for colonial affairs, brought him into close contact with the Under-Secretary, Étienne, a colleague on *La République française*; he was also a disciple of Gambetta and recognised as leader of the 'colonial' group. When the Government fell in the wake of the Panama scandal[4] Delcassé was offered, in the new Ribot ministry formed in January 1893, the Colonial Under-Secretaryship. This office reverted significantly to dependence on the Ministry of Commerce rather than on the Admiralty.[5]

---

[1] See M. Paléologue, *Un Grand Tournant de la Politique mondiale*, p. 202.

[2] Quoted A. Néton, *Delcassé*, p. 550, from the *Journal Officiel* of 7 Nov 1890.

[3] Ibid., p. 553, from the *Journal Officiel* of 7 Nov 1890.

[4] The Panama Canal Company, with de Lesseps as President, became bankrupt in 1889. Subsequent investigations led to a major political scandal which, for many years, compromised Clemenceau's career. Delcassé had been a member of the commission of enquiry which led to the Government's fall.

[5] The separate identity of the office was more easily discernible under the Ministry of Commerce than under the Admiralty.

Delcassé had made his acceptance of the appointment conditional on carrying this point. He had previously been active in pressing for the elevation of the Colonial Office to the status of a ministry. Although this step had not yet been taken Delcassé was able to move his department from the Admiralty to the *Pavillon de Flore*. His establishment in these splendid premises was a decisive step towards departmental independence. On 30 March, when Ribot was succeeded by Dupuy, Delcassé remained in office. On 15 May he won a vote in the Chamber for converting the Colonial Under-Secretaryship into a ministry.

When the Dupuy government fell in November 1873 Casimir-Périer[1] invited Delcassé to stay on, but, contrary to his usual habit, this time he chose to resign with Dupuy. New elections were pending and he had little faith in the vigour of the Casimir-Périer régime. At Foix, Delcassé was re-elected with an overwhelming majority and when, on 30 May, Dupuy again formed a government he returned to the Colonies which had now been elevated, as decided in May 1893, to the status of a ministry. It was as Minister for the Colonies that Delcassé helped to lay the preliminary plans for a challenge to Great Britain on the Upper Nile.[2] These plans chimed with his general principle of negotiations from strength.

The Dupuy ministry fell on 14 January 1895. In the new Ribot[3] cabinet of 28 January 1895 no place was found for Delcassé. He continued to speak on colonial matters and he also began to make a serious study of naval policy. His journalistic training proved invaluable in ferreting out information by private investigation; the knowledge he gained made him a master of awkward questions in the Chamber. Though again offered no office, he began by generally supporting the Méline[4] government of 'moderates' formed in April 1896. But as the shadow of the Dreyfus affair loomed larger, he came to believe that it was Méline's duty to try to create a Republican-rally government and he considered that Méline was failing in this task. He complained in the Chamber that government spies had tampered with his

---

[1] Jean Paul Pierre Casimir-Périer (1847–1907), grandson of one of the leading political figures in the making of the July Monarchy. In addition to the Premiership he also took over the Foreign Affairs portfolio. He later became President of the Republic (1894–5).

[2] See p. 61.   [3] See p. 61.   [4] See p. 75.

correspondence.[1] Clemenceau, who bore Delcassé a grudge for the part he played in the Panama commission of enquiry and who cordially disliked his rather smug and introverted personality, for once wrote of him in favourable terms. Unlike Delcassé, Clemenceau found anti-government attitudes congenial.

In the May 1898 elections Delcassé found himself opposed by a ministerial candidate at Foix. As a Dreyfusard and as an opponent of the 'government of moderates' he campaigned on a 'Radical' ticket. Apart from this occasion Delcassé seldom took any interest in domestic controversies other than to deplore them. He was satisfied to be a Republican but he had no time for debate about the character of that Republic. Now however he was entitled to a 'Radical' label. Consequently when, after Méline's fall and the failure of attempts to substitute a broad-based Republican ministry,[2] Brisson formed a cabinet of Radicals and Radical sympathisers, he felt able to offer Delcassé the Foreign Office portfolio. As soon as the offer had been made Brisson was petitioned by powerful 'moderate' opinion outside the Government to transfer Delcassé to the Navy. Delcassé, it was argued, was too well known, on account of his colonial policies, as an anglophobe to be a 'safe' Foreign Minister. Brisson, however, refused to be deflected from his original decision.

When he took over the Foreign Office, Delcassé's views on foreign policy were clearly and definitely formed. Talking to Paléologue[4] on 29 December 1898 he said, 'for Russia, as for France, England is a rival, a competitor whose proceedings are often very disagreeable; but she is not an enemy and certainly not THE ENEMY! ... Ah my dear Paléologue if only Russia, England and France could be allied against Germany!'[3] He confessed to being 'haunted' by the notion of an Anglo-French alliance. Its achievement was his mission. But he was fully aware of the difficulties which lay in his path and he was determined to follow the road without sacrificing colonial aspirations which, by now, centred mainly on Morocco. Behind hopes of a triple Anglo-French-Russian alignment there was a double purpose; it would provide the means of successful resistance against any

[1] See A. Néton, *Delcassé*, pp. 168, 169.
[2] See p. 75.
[3] M. Paléologue, *Un Grand Tournant de la Politique Mondiale*, p. 13.

possible German aggression and a platform from which gains, in certain circumstances, could be obtained without use of force. The loss of Alsace-Lorraine had, in Delcassé's opinion, created an abyss between France and Germany. While those provinces remained German there could be no question of 'any close colla-boration between France and Germany';[1] there might be limited co-operation but never close co-operation. Delcassé rejected the desirability of directly planning a war of *revanche* against Germany; but he did envisage the possibility of a German attack. Victory in such a war, depending on the support of England and Russia, would be one way of recovering the lost provinces. The other way however, and the one which Delcassé favoured, was by peaceful means. He believed that the death of Franz Joseph was likely to result in a crisis in the Hapsburg Empire which would lead to its disruption. With the support of England and Russia, France should be able to secure the reversion of Alsace-Lorraine in return for approving the incorporation of German Austrian territories into the German Empire.[2] Although this may have been wishful thinking, and Delcassé very seldom mentioned Alsace-Lorraine at all, the lost provinces were uppermost in his mind when seeking diplomatic combinations which would enable France to face war against Germany or to snatch opportunities which peace could provide.

What qualities did Delcassé bring to his self-appointed task? He possessed a detailed knowledge of recent diplomatic history and of current colonial questions. He was, however, determined not to be circumscribed by the past in formulating policies for the future. In this sense he affected to despise history[3] and, as Paléologue remarked, quoting an expression of Talleyrand's, he

[1] See M. Paléologue, *Un Grand Tournant de la Politique Mondiale*, p. 163. During the Boer War Delcassé did try to explore the possibilities of securing German support in an anti-British alignment. See C. M. Andrew, *Théophile Delcassé and the Making of the Entente Cordiale*, for new evidence of the lengths he was prepared to travel in this direction. But there is no suggestion that he was ever willing to consider a bargain which would have reaffirmed recognition of the loss of Alsace-Lorraine. He did, how-ever, toy with the notion of offering the French Indo-Chinese Empire to Germany in return for the restoration of Alsace-Lorraine to France.

[2] M. Paléologue, *Un Grand Tournant de la Politique Mondiale*, p. 196.

[3] 'Do you think', he once remarked to Paléologue, 'that in any difficult serious situation I would go and consult a history book? No certainly not! In such a situa-tion what counts above all is flair, coolness, courage, resolution, dexterity.... My dear Paléologue, beware of history.' Ibid., p. 83.

had 'beaucoup d'avenir dans l'esprit'.[1] Although the fastidious Cambon[2] regarded him as somewhat hasty and even prone to jump at a poor bargain, he was a patient and flexible negotiator. He revelled in the exercise of diplomatic art. He was supremely self-confident. As he often repeated to Paléologue, 'It is the duty of a chief to be optimistic.'[3] He was persistent. He never lost sight of the end in view because he never ceased to contemplate it. This concentration was, at times, a weakness. Withdrawn by temperament, he liked to work on his own; he made a virtue of secrecy; he showed his hand to trusted members of his diplomatic staff but seldom to his cabinet colleagues. He became notorious for his silence.[4] Like Holstein,[5] there was something of the spider about Delcassé; but the web which Delcassé spun was of tougher and more lasting fibre. Even though he was disavowed and forced to resign in 1905, the lines of policy which he had drawn were so firmly established that they could not be overthrown. In seven years at the Foreign Office he achieved almost all his objectives.

Reporting on 1 July 1898 on the new French Cabinet, Monson[6] predicted that Delcassé would prove 'a very combative Minister'.[7] 'M. Denis Guibert,' he added, 'the Anglophobe writer in the *Figaro*, welcomes this morning his advent at the *Quai d'Orsay* in the confident hope that he will signalise it by vigour in dealing with the Egyptian Question.'

On 10 July Captain Marchand,[8] with other French officers and 120 Senegalese troops, reached Fashoda. There was, of course, at that time no precise knowledge of his whereabouts either in London or in Paris. But Salisbury was fully alert to the contingency. Although, after the occupation of Khartoum,[9] there were to be 'no further military operations on a large scale or involving

---

[1] Ibid., p. 190.   [2] See p. 222.
[3] Ibid., p. 8.
[4] It was commented upon at various times by most of his colleagues. See for instance Raymond Poincaré, *Au Service de la France*, vol. 2, p. 83, where he describes his conduct as Navy Minister in the Cabinet in 1912.
[5] Baron Friedrich August von Holstein (1837–1909), leading policy-maker in the German Foreign Ministry.
[6] Sir Edmund Monson (1834–1909), Ambassador at Paris 1896–1905.
[7] Monson to Salisbury, 1 Jul 1898, *BD* 1, no. 183, p. 158.
[8] See p. 65.
[9] It followed the battle of Omdurman on 2 Sep 1898.

any considerable expense'.[1] Kitchener was authorised to send 'two flotillas, one up the White and the other up the Blue Nile'. He was to command the White Nile flotilla and he was to be warned that 'a French force might be found in occupation of the Nile Valley'. In that event Kitchener was not to be furnished with any detailed instructions but he was 'to endeavour to convince the Commander of any French force with which he may come in contact that the presence of the latter in the Nile Valley is an infringement of the rights both of Great Britain and of the Khedive'.

Salisbury now had no doubts about adopting a firm line. Kitchener, once he had completed the Mahdi's defeat, would be in an impregnable military situation in the Sudan. Locally the French and their Abyssinian ally would be quite powerless. War between England and France could only mean a naval war, and here, even if Russia stood by her ally, Salisbury reckoned that, as he now no longer felt committed to holding the Straits, there was nothing to fear. Recent naval intelligence appreciations in any case suggested that the Russian Navy had been over-estimated and that British naval power had re-established a supremacy which only recently had seemed seriously threatened. From this position of strength Salisbury was quite prepared to meet a Fashoda crisis with uncompromising resolution. Too much had been spent and too many sacrifices made to safeguard the Egyptian road to India for there to be any hesitations at this final stage in the operation. While Salisbury discounted the dangers of provoking French susceptibilities Monson reported from Paris expressing his fears that, in the circumstances, there might be difficulty in obtaining ratification of the West African Convention.[2] Étienne[3] was already whipping up hostile agitation, and Monson speculated uneasily on the influence which he might be able to exert once Khartoum was conquered and French public opinion thus sharply reminded of its 'sentimental' Egyptian grievance. Although Delcassé seemed determined to defend the Convention his task would not be an easy one in such an atmosphere.

---

[1] Salisbury to Cromer 2 Aug 1898, *BD* I, no. 185, p. 160. These instructions were conveyed by Cromer to Kitchener under sealed orders which he opened, according to instruction, after the Omdurman victory.

[2] See Monson to Salisbury, 4 Aug 1898, *BD* I, no. 186, p. 161.   [3] See p. 79.

Delcassé did indeed find himself in a position of considerable difficulty. His long-term objectives were clearly at odds with the developing situation. Anxious to defend the West African Convention for the sake of good understanding with England he found himself in conflict with the colonial groups whom he had championed when out of office. Critical in the past of ministries who had been 'soft' on Egypt, he now had to face the prospect of final evidence of England's paramount and unassailable position. Furthermore there was the problem of Captain Marchand. Even though Delcassé had originally been in favour of the project he was out of office when the expedition was finally authorised and the circumstances in 1898 were vastly different from those obtaining in 1895. Not only had all the linked projects met with failure, but Kitchener's army was now an all-powerful reality. In his own mind Delcassé seems to have utterly rejected the possibility of meeting this challenge by war. If he could have cut his losses by wishing Marchand out of existence no doubt he would have done so. But it seemed inevitable that Marchand would be encountered at any rate in the vicinity of his destination and that France must be exposed to added humiliation on this most sensitive of Egyptian issues. Delcassé, champion of the strong line, would be forced to take a soft one. It was a highly disagreeable prospect and Delcassé could only hope to mitigate the disaster by diplomatic art. Although Marchand's presence at Fashoda could not now be regarded as a bargaining counter Delcassé must contrive to create an illusion that there were bargains to be made. A diplomatic success of some kind must be salvaged from the wreckage. And in the meanwhile every effort must be made to lull British suspicions and cultivate British goodwill.

On 7 September Delcassé received Monson and congratulated him on Kitchener's Khartoum victory.[1] He went on to say that he presumed the British flotilla would now be pushing up the Nile and that there was a possibility of an encounter with Captain Marchand. 'He had', Delcassé explained, 'been distinctly told that he is nothing but "an emissary of civilization" and that he has no authority to assume the decision of questions of right which appertain exclusively to the competence of the British and French

[1] See Monson to Salisbury, 8 Sep 1898, *BD* I, no. 188, p. 163.

governments.'[1] All differences between England and France, Delcassé insisted, could 'be amicably arranged by the exercise of patience and conciliation'. When Monson asked for definite information of the whereabouts of Captain Marchand Delcassé claimed ignorance. On receipt of this news Salisbury at once instructed Monson to declare categorically that 'all the territories which were subject to the Khalifa' had 'passed to the British and Egyptian governments by right of conquest'.[2] This right was not open to discussion. In reply Delcassé merely remarked that 'territories subject to the Khalifa was rather vague'.[3]

On 18 September Delcassé stressed to Monson his desire to maintain 'the most harmonious relations with Great Britain'.[4] With that end in view he had recommended the appointment of Paul Cambon[5] to succeed Baron de Courcel,[6] who was due to retire, as Ambassador in London, and he hoped that this would be regarded as proof of his intention. When Monson raised the question of Captain Marchand, Delcassé refused to accept that, if indeed he were at Fashoda, he had no right to be there. 'However,' he added 'it would be useless to discuss these details now. If the British approached the matter "in a friendly spirit", there could be no reason why a satisfactory arrangement should not be quickly arrived at.' Thus Delcassé tried to establish that a round of bargaining might at some stage be opened.

On 25 September a telegram from Kitchener reached London via Cairo giving full details of his Fashoda confrontation with Captain Marchand and thus providing the first official news of the fate of the expedition.[7] After exchanges of civilities Kitchener informed Marchand that 'the presence of a French force at Fashoda and in the Valley of the Nile was regarded as a direct infringement of the rights of the Egyptian Government and of Great Britain'. Marchand insisted 'that he had precise orders to occupy the country and to hoist the French flag over the government buildings at Fashoda and that it was impossible for him to retire without receiving orders from his government to that

---

[1] Monson to Salisbury 8 Sep 1898, *BD* I, no. 188, p. 163.
[2] Salisbury to Monson, 9 Sep 1898, *BD* I, no. 189, p. 164.
[3] Monson to Salisbury, 10 Sep 1898, *BD* I, no. 190, p. 165.
[4] Ibid., 18 Sep 1898, *BD* I, no. 191, p. 165.
[5] See pp. 92–5.   [6] See p. 66.
[7] See Rodd to Salisbury, 25 Sep 1898, *BD* I, no. 193, pp. 167, 168.

effect...'. Kitchener then caused the Egyptian flag[1] 'to be hoisted on a ruined bastion of the old Egyptian fortification 500 yards south of the French flag'. Before leaving Fashoda, Kitchener handed Marchand a formal protest and appointed a Commandant, with a garrison force, to take charge of the Fashoda district. 'In his present position,' Kitchener summed up, 'he [Captain Marchand] is powerless, but I hope that Her Majesty's Government will take the necessary steps for his removal as soon as possible, as the presence of a French force and flag on the Nile is manifestly extremely undesirable.'[2]

On 27 September Delcassé received Monson.[3] His immediate purpose was to play for time. He said that he was awaiting reports which Marchand had addressed to him in duplicate, one via Abyssinia and one via the Congo, and that it would be awkward for the French Government to reach any decisions until this report was available. He suggested that a telegram from Cairo instructing Marchand to forward a copy via Cairo might be helpful. When Monson pressed for an answer as to whether instructions to recall Marchand must await receipt of the report, Delcassé said that he would be prepared to enter discussions but must not be asked to concede more.

British insistence on the immediate recall of Marchand continued to meet with evasion. 'Do not ask me for the impossible, do not drive me into a corner',[4] Delcassé appealed. While public opinion in England and in France was beginning to run dangerously high, Delcassé pinned his hopes on being able eventually to announce that 'talks had begun' and so avoiding the impression of unconditional surrender.

On 1 October Salisbury required Kitchener to be informed that 'it has become clear that the French Government will not instruct

---

[1] This was not strictly in accordance with his instructions but had he also displayed the Union Jack, Marchand might have felt compelled to make a token show of resistance. See G. N. Sanderson, *England, Europe and the Upper Nile*, pp. 333-5.

[2] In his report Kitchener exaggerated the hopelessness of Marchand's position. As Marchand had no means of making any speedy independent report, Kitchener's version of the plight of the expedition provided useful ammunition for the British Government to press the French to give a withdrawal order. For a critical study of Kitchener's reporting see ibid., pp. 337-9.

[3] For Monson's account of their meeting see Monson to Salisbury, 27 Sep 1898, *BD* I, no. 196, pp. 169, 170.

[4] Monson to Salisbury, 28 Sep, *BD* I, no. 198, p. 171.

M. Marchand to leave Fashoda. They expect that her Majesty's
Government will purchase his departure by large concessions of
territory. This Her Majesty's Government will not do.'[1] For the
present Kitchener was to make 'M. Marchand's position as unten-
able as possible. If he is in want of food supplies, it will be very
necessary to use circumspection in helping him to obtain them.
Until he expresses his intention of going down the river, no such
supplies should be furnished to him except in case of extreme
necessity.'

On 5 October, via de Courcel, Delcassé again pressed for the
opening of negotiations and gave some indication of French territorial pretensions.[2] Although Monson held out no hopes to
Delcassé of this kind of solution, he had been impressed by the
implied threat in several of their conversations that France would
fight rather than accept total humiliation.[3] The angry temper of
French opinion gave colour to Delcassé's warning. But, in his
game of bluff, the vehemence of French public opinion was probably more of an embarrassment than an asset.

As Delcassé's hopes of achieving a successful salvaging operation at this stage became more remote, he began to take what steps
he could to lower the temperature of public opinion.

On 10 October Monson wrote enclosing a copy of a leading
article published in *Le Matin* on the subject of Fashoda, 'which,
in view of the tone previously adopted by that organ with
regard to the questions, almost verges on the ludicrous, so sudden
and complete is the change of front taken up'.[4] The pith of the
article, Monson explained, was that the abandonment of Fashoda
was perfectly compatible with the preservation of national
honour.

At a meeting with Monson on 11 October Delcassé 'contrasted

---

[1] Salisbury to Rodd, 1 Oct 1898, *BD* 1, no. 201, p. 172.
[2] See Salisbury to Monson, 6 Oct 1898, *BD* 1, no. 203, pp. 173–5.
[3] See Monson's dispatches to Salisbury of 30 Sep and 7 Oct 1898, *BD* 1, no. 200,
p. 172, and no. 204, pp. 175, 176. Delcassé's vehemence seems to have stemmed from
a mistaken belief, encouraged by a secret intelligence report, that Monson had an
ultimatum ready for immediate delivery in his pocket. Delcassé remained convinced
that his attitude had averted its presentation. See C. M. Andrew, *Théophile Delcassé
and the Making of the Entente Cordiale*, pp. 99, 100. Although Delcassé was wrong about
the ultimatum, the impression which he made on Monson was not entirely without
salutary influence on British policy.
[4] Monson to Salisbury, 10 Oct 1898, *BD* 1, no. 208, p. 178.

the moderation of the Paris press with the excited language of the London dailies'.[1] He again pressed for negotiations and he warned that 'the knowledge of his friendly disposition towards us is injuring his position here'. 'If he has to retire,' commented Monson, 'his successor, whoever he may be, will certainly not err in the same direction.' It was now, in fact, on Delcassé's part very much of a rearguard action and Monson concluded: 'For the rest, his arguments, like those of M. de Courcel, went over the old ground of the French having as much right to be on the Nile as the English, Germans and Belgians, but I repeat that I think he is prepared to retreat eventually, and after negotiation, from his position if we can build him a golden bridge for that retrograde movement.'

Salisbury was not in any desperate hurry to provide the golden bridge. From Cromer he received, on 17 October, a report from Kitchener dated 8 October and proposing 'a frontier line, granting large concessions to France, that might from a military point of view . . . be given them without injuring our position in this part of Africa'.[2] With de Courcel, Salisbury was ready to speak informally of territories which might be made available for French colonial expansion. But he remained adamant that negotiations could not begin until Marchand had been withdrawn. In reply to characteristic enquiries from the Italian Government, transmitted via Sir Philip Currie,[3] about the possibility of war between England and France and their own need to take naval precautions Salisbury answered: 'Such information as we have of the preparations at Toulon does not point to intentions of immediate attack, but it is of course necessary to take precautions in time. As far as we are concerned, we shall endeavour to avoid any step which may seem aggressive or provocative, but we are unable to discuss questions of frontier between Egypt and the French Congo as long as the French flag remains at Fashoda. In the present state of affairs at Paris it is difficult to foretell how long the tension may last or to what solution it may tend.'[4]

A Cabinet crisis in France inspired Delcassé to make a further

[1] Monson to Salisbury, 11 Oct 1898, *BD* 1, no. 209, p. 179.
[2] Cromer to Salisbury, 8 Oct 1898, *BD* 1, no. 207, p. 177.
[3] Sir Philip Currie (1834–1903), cr. Baron Currie 1899, Ambassador at Rome 1898–1903.
[4] Salisbury to Currie, 27 Oct 1898, *BD* 1, no. 219, p. 183.

attempt to press for negotiations. He could not remain in office, he urged, in a new Ministry unless French territorial claims were first considered.[1]

Meanwhile Captain Marchand, without instructions, left Fashoda and reached Khartoum on 28 October. Delcassé professed to be rather 'irate' at this 'escapade'.[2] He now said that Marchand must return to Fashoda to arrange evacuation. But evacuation could only be agreed if there was an undertaking that England would 'negotiate on the principle of a grant to France of an outlet to her commerce on the Nile. If this is not acceded to,' Delcassé added, 'a humiliation will be inflicted on the French which he personally cannot accept; and as a war with England, which is the only alternative, would be alike contrary to his avowed policy, and repulsive to his principles he would be obliged to retire from his post as Minister of Foreign Affairs.'[3]

Before receiving news of Delcassé's latest pleas Salisbury had again and unequivocally insisted to de Courcel that the evacuation of Fashoda must be unconditional.[4] Afterwards the British Government would be willing to examine questions of frontier delimitation; but such examination was bound to take time and no definite promises regarding results could be made at this stage.

On 30 October Monson concluded that Delcassé's 'pertinacity' was 'invincible' and that it might be best if he retired from office.[5] But Delcassé remained and on 3 November Monson was able to report to Salisbury that a cabinet council had wired instructions to de Courcel to announce that 'Fashoda would be evacuated with the least possible delay'.[6] Delcassé told Monson that 'it had cost him much to continue in office with the prospect of having to adopt the step which he had just communicated . . .'.[7]

There was no doubt that Kitchener's victorious campaigns and the triumph of Salisbury's militant diplomacy had dangerously turned the knife in the Egyptian wound. It is sometimes a mistake to make the most of a favourable situation and Anglo-French

[1] See Monson to Salisbury, 28 Oct 1898, *BD* I, no. 221, pp. 184, 185.
[2] See Monson to Salisbury, 29 Oct 1898, *BD* I, no. 222, p. 186.
[3] Monson to Salisbury, 29 Oct 1898, ibid.
[4] See Salisbury to Monson, 30 Oct 1898, *BD* I, no. 223, p. 187.
[5] See Monson to Salisbury, 30 Oct 1898, *BD* I, no. 225, p. 188.
[6] Monson to Salisbury, 4 Nov 1898, *BD* I, no. 227, p. 188.
[7] Monson to Salisbury, 4 Nov 1898, *BD* I, no. 228, p. 189.

relations might have been better served if Salisbury had allowed Delcassé to retreat, as he so desperately sought, on known rather than on hypothetical conditions. In the event even Delcassé's unconditional surrender did not bring an immediate end to the crisis. Partly as a guarantee of French good faith and partly because of reports that the French were still arming, British naval preparations continued in evidence;[1] persisting tension inevitably prolonged the humiliation of France. For Delcassé, who had looked forward to *rapprochement* with England negotiated from a position of strength, the first few months of his tenure as Foreign Minister could hardly have proved more miserable and frustrating.

[1] See A. J. Marder, *British Naval Policy 1880–1905*, pp. 332–5.

5

Cambon at the Court of St James

IT was still under the shadow of Fashoda that Paul Cambon[1] arrived in London on 8 December 1898 to succeed de Courcel as ambassador; he was to remain until he resigned on 20 December 1920. Though his name will always remain linked with his historic London Embassy his career before 1898 was already a distinguished one. Born in Paris 1843 he was brought up by his widowed mother in affluent circumstances and in an atmosphere of *salon* politics. Her home was a rallying point for leading antibonapartists. When he started, none too enthusiastically, on a legal career, he was already a member of the young *élite* of the opposition and on terms of close friendship with Thiers[2] and the Ferry brothers.[3] When after Sedan and the collapse of the Empire Jules Ferry became Prefect of Paris, he appointed Cambon as his secretary. In this capacity Cambon played an adventurous role during the provisional government's confused withdrawal to Versailles and he was even obliged, no doubt for the first and only time in his life, to use his fists in a scuffle. From Versailles he was sent as secretary to the Prefect first at Nice and then at Marseilles. On 2 February 1872 he was promoted to Prefect of the Aube Department. His civil service career was interrupted by the fall of Thiers in May 1873 but he eventually secured a job in Paris as inspector of child welfare. In 1876 he returned to the higher ranks of government service as Prefect of Doubs, but resigned after the

---

[1] K. Eubank, *Paul Cambon*, is the most recent and valuable biography.
[2] See p. 23.
[3] Jules François Camille Ferry (1832–93), see p. 36 and Charles Émile Léon Ferry (1834–1909).

16 May crisis which had removed his moderate Republican friends from office. With the turn of the political tide he was appointed in December 1877 Prefect of the important Nord department with his headquarters at Lille. There he remained until his appointment as Minister Resident in Tunisia in February 1882. From Tunisia he was transferred in 1886 as Ambassador to Madrid and thence in 1891 to Constantinople. He remained in Constantinople until his London appointment.

An anti-bonapartist and a liberal by upbringing, Cambon was a conservative by instinct and temperament. Order and moderation were his watchwords; he believed that sound administration was the supreme goal. He could not understand why a strong government of 'moderate' Republicans dedicated to this purpose should in fact have proved a Utopian dream. The constant clash of opinions and personalities seemed, in his critical appraisal, to represent no more than exhibitions of human weakness, folly and intrigue. Unlike Delcassé he had no hero among the politicians. Jules Ferry approximated most closely his conception of a 'sound' leader but even his admiration for Ferry was qualified. In 1880 he considered entering the political arena himself but he was too disillusioned with politics and politicians to make any serious attempt. His public service, he thereafter decided, must be rendered outside the political arena; only thus could he hope to carve out a congenial career and at the same time contribute, despite politicians, to national welfare. The role of Prefect was too narrow and too closely related to politics to be satisfying and in 1881 he wrote: 'we have discussed with Jules[1] whether it would not be suitable, if necessary to go into the diplomatic service . . . the lack of talent is terrifying'.[2]

In this mood he welcomed the offer of a mission to Tunisia. He believed that firm and efficient government by indirect rule was the requisite formula. He demanded a completely free hand and above all the subordination of the military commander to his authority. He received the necessary promises but was constantly frustrated by lack of support from Paris. When General Boulanger was given military command in Tunisia a major clash could hardly be avoided. It says much for Cambon's persuasive tenacity

---

[1] His brother, Jules Martin Cambon (1845–1935).
[2] 29 Dec 1881, *CC* I, p. 142.

that, in the course of their inevitable quarrel, he eventually won his case and secured the General's recall. But Boulanger, relieved of his Tunisian command, re-emerged as Minister of War. Like many proconsuls Cambon had more difficulty in dealing with his own government than in contending with problems on the spot. Although he had achieved victory in principle the fight had been so bitter that, with Boulanger at the Ministry of War, he concluded that good relations between the civil and military authorities in Tunisia could best be promoted by his own withdrawal. The Rome and Constantinople Embassies were offered to him but his Tunisian policy had made him unpopular with both governments concerned and so he found himself relegated to the relative backwater of Madrid. During the leisurely years as Ambassador in Spain, Cambon's views on foreign policy began to crystallise; these he developed in a voluminous private correspondence with leading personalities of the Third Republic. Soon he became accepted, together with Barrère[1] and his own brother Jules, as the core of an exclusive syndicate of professional diplomats upon whom transient foreign ministers could rely for inspiration and guidance. On 11 March 1889, replying to Spuller's[2] invitation for his views on foreign affairs in general, he wrote: 'I consider that the reconciliation of France and Italy and later the *Entente* of these two powers with England is the goal which must be recommended for French policy.'[3] French blunders had provided England's opportunity in Egypt. There was no sense in continuing to repine over the past. On the contrary, efforts should be made to rescue any remnant of capital from this mistake and to concentrate on building up good relations for the future.

As he had outlined the policy so was Cambon invited to join in its execution by being offered the London Embassy in 1891. Personal considerations, however, compelled him most reluctantly to decline the post. In January 1875 he had married Anna Guépratte.[4] Two years later, as a result of an accident, Mme Cambon became a semi-invalid; henceforth her health became a

---

[1] See p. 77.
[2] See p. 54. He was a disciple of Gambetta and at that time Foreign Minister.
[3] *CC* I, p. 332.
[4] Her mother was English and her father was a French general. Their only son, Henri, born in 1876, followed his father into the diplomatic service. He also wrote a biography of his father and edited his correspondence.

matter of prime consideration for her husband. He was advised that the English climate might prove fatal and it was this advice which compelled him to reject the London Embassy. Instead he accepted a transfer to Constantinople. There he constantly reverted to the theme of Anglo-French *rapprochement*. Never a blind partisan of the Franco-Russian alliance, he argued that Anglo-French co-operation at Constantinople was essential both for France's Mediterranean interests and for her general security. He was, during these years, frequently very critical of official policy. 'In Paris', he wrote characteristically on 23 November 1895, 'no idea, no direction. It is as if we had confided our Foreign Office portfolio to Baron de Monroheim.'[1] Within the limits imposed by official policy Cambon did strive to establish a measure of Anglo-French co-operation at Constantinople; but he was more often frustrated than satisfied.

When his wife died in the early summer of 1898 there were no longer any personal reasons for remaining at Constantinople; he was, therefore, at last able to respond to Delcassé's invitation to accept the London Embassy. He was then fifty-five years old, a small white-bearded man with a slight limp, the result of two riding accidents, and an immense confidence in his own judgement. He had an army of disciples, including Bompard[2] and his own son Henri, in the French diplomatic service. Critical and fastidious, but capable of inspiring strong loyalty and affection, he was respected among professionals as an oracle of wisdom. His appointment was regarded, in itself, as a declaration of policy on Delcassé's part. Anglo-French *rapprochement* was seen, in French diplomatic circles, to be the objective.

And yet, as Cambon prepared to present his credentials, the outlook seemed bleak. On 8 December Delcassé had a somewhat stormy interview with Monson.[3] While reiterating France's desire for good understanding, he objected to continued British naval preparations and he threatened that, if war resulted, France would have Germany as well as Russia on her side. But, as Monson explained to Salisbury, Delcassé had a sore throat and his angry

---

[1] *CC* I, p. 397. Baron de Monroheim was the Russian Ambassador to Paris.
[2] Louis Maurice Bompard (1854–1935), French Ambassador to St Petersburg, 1902–8.
[3] See Monson to Salisbury, 8 Dec 1898, *BD* I, no. 238, pp. 196, 197.

agitation, typical of 'a native of the south of France', should not perhaps be taken too seriously. On 9 December, when Monson was writing this somewhat discouraging report, Cambon was received at Windsor by the Queen. He gave a detailed description of the occasion to his mother-in-law,[1] whom he always addressed as 'my dear mother', almost the only English words he seems to have used even in correspondence. He found the food at Windsor detestable, but he approved the simplicity of the arrangements. Earlier in the day he had been received by Salisbury and they found some further opportunity for conversation at Windsor. 'My impressions', Cambon reported to Delcassé, 'after my first contact with Lord Salisbury have not been too bad. It is obvious that personally he is well disposed and that he is trying to contend with public opinion. It is equally certain that of all questions Madagascar is causing him most concern.'[2] Cambon himself had been critical, as an advocate of indirect colonial government, of the annexation of Madagascar and he now pointed out to Delcassé the adverse effects on Anglo-French relations of the protectionist policy which had accompanied that annexation. To Salisbury he had hinted at the possibility of eventual tariff revision and this line he recommended to Delcassé as a palliative. On the subject of Bahr el Ghazal Cambon reported that he had made a reference to 'a commercial outlet on the Nile for France' and judged that this might be obtainable. 'It will serve', he commented, 'no other purpose than to save our face but after Fashoda that is not a result to be despised.'[3] Salisbury summed up his first two conversations with Cambon in lighter vein: 'At Windsor he gave me a very interesting lecture on French philosophy during the past two centuries and in London a full explanation of the difference between the principles of French and English colonial administration.'[4]

In fact it was not until 11 January 1899 that Salisbury and Cambon had their first serious conversation.[5] Cambon opened the proceedings by a formal declaration that Fashoda had now been

[1] See Cambon to Mme Guépratte, 9 Dec 1898, *CC* II, pp. 9–12.

[2] Cambon to Delcassé, 13 Dec 1898, *CC* II, p. 13.

[3] Cambon to Delcassé, 13 Dec 1898, *CC* II, p. 14.

[4] Salisbury to Monson, 19 Dec 1898, F.O. 27/3399, quoted J. A. S. Grenville, *Lord Salisbury and Foreign Policy*, p. 232.

[5] See Salisbury to Monson, 11 Jan 1899, *BD* I, no. 240, pp. 197, 198.

evacuated. He then reminded Salisbury of his own previous statement to de Courcel that, once this operation was completed, he would be prepared to study boundary delimitation in the Bahr el Ghazal area. Salisbury recognised the fact but insisted that Great Britain could not accept the presence of the French flag anywhere in the Nile Valley. Cambon confirmed that France did not wish to press for territorial claims but was anxious to secure a commercial outlet to the Nile. Salisbury agreed that there was a basis for negotiation. Cambon proposed a demarcation line 'starting from the south-eastern end of Tunis, passing to the east of Lake Tchad, leaving Darfur to Egypt, and then separating the Bahr el Ghazal from the Ubanghi'.[1] Salisbury replied that the questions were 'geographical' and that he could not deal with them 'without maps'; he 'readily admitted', however, that Cambon's observations contained the elements of a satisfactory settlement. Thus encouraged Cambon invited Salisbury to raise any other question of Anglo-French difference. In the ensuing discussion about Madagascar, Cambon tried to calm Salisbury's complaints by reverting, in greater detail, to the possibility of gradual revision of French tariff policy. Salisbury 'assented to the opinion that much of the strained feeling between France and England was due to the extravagant protectionist policy that France had pursued'.[2] According to Cambon, as the interview seemed to be drawing to a close, Salisbury remarked: 'I do not speak to you of Newfoundland. For sixty years it has been an object of discussion between us. Now the Newfoundlanders have joined in. It becomes a triangular duel. That may last a long time.'[3] Cambon interpreted this remark as an indication that Salisbury did not wish to become involved in any discussion of the Newfoundland problem. He did not yet know his Salisbury. On the contrary Salisbury was deliberately trying to draw Newfoundland into the bargaining and he reluctantly concluded that 'M. Cambon did not show any inclination to enter upon any discussion of that question'.[4] Although they failed to pursue the Newfoundland question Salisbury and Cambon both emerged with increased confidence in the prospect of improvement in Anglo-French relations. 'From this long

[1] Salisbury to Monson, 11 Jan 1899, *BD* I, no. 240, p. 198.   [2] Ibid.
[3] Cambon to Delcassé, 12 Jan 1899, *DDF* i, xv, no. 14, p. 27.
[4] Salisbury to Monson, 11 Jan 1899, *BD* I, no. 240, p. 198.

discussion', Cambon significantly commented, 'I have gained the impression that Lord Salisbury has a sincere desire to look for an *entente* basis and that, of all the questions which we have touched upon, he regards Madagascar as the most serious.'[1]

On 18 January Salisbury and Cambon had a further discussion;[2] Salisbury raised the question of possible Italian interest in the Tripoli hinterland and Cambon, while taking note of the matter, argued that a boundary could be defined which would not offend Italian pretensions. On 21 January friendly discussion of the territorial settlement was resumed. Salisbury took this opportunity to refer again to Madagascar and to Newfoundland. Now Cambon gained the impression that Salisbury was trying to establish a correlation between the two questions. He deprecated the notion of a Newfoundland–Madagascar bargain but he was no longer unaware of Salisbury's interest in including Newfoundland on the bargaining agenda.[3] During this meeting with Salisbury, Cambon alluded to a speech of Chamberlain's at Wolverhampton on 18 January and he regretted an offensive reference to the Nile Valley question. 'All our affairs', Salisbury soothingly interrupted, 'would settle themselves much better if Mr Chamberlain spoke less but,' he added with a sigh, 'how can Mr Chamberlain be stopped from speaking?'[4] Convinced of Salisbury's goodwill Cambon remained worried by the state of British opinion and the nagging Madagascar question. 'I think', he confided to Delcassé, 'that we will have difficulties with the English so long as we do not adopt a policy of commercial freedom in our colonies. In Tunis and on the Niger we have done so. Why not in Madagascar? public opinion should be prepared for an abandonment of our narrow protectionist system ... I say and I repeat: the important question is neither Newfoundland nor the Bahr el Ghazal, it is Madagascar. What would we do if the English, excited by Chamberlain and Rosebery, declared that they would not recognise our annexation? War! Really it would be sad for a question of tariffs.'[5] On 25 January Salisbury and Cambon met again. Cambon submitted a draft boundary delimitation which Salisbury

[1] Cambon to Delcassé, 13 Jan 1899, *DDF* i, xv, no. 15, p. 31.
[2] See Cambon to Delcassé, 18 Jan 1899, *DDF* i, xv, no. 25, pp. 39–43.
[3] See Cambon to Delcassé, 21 Jan 1899, *DDF* i, xv, no. 39, p. 63.
[4] Ibid., p. 64.
[5] Cambon to Delcassé, 21 Jan 1899, *CC* ii, p. 20.

seemed broadly to approve, but which, he declared, would need further study.[1] To Cambon's relief he did not refer to Madagascar or to Newfoundland. On 2 February Salisbury showed Cambon a draft prepared by Cromer, whose advice had in the meanwhile been sought, proposing delimitation with the whole of Darfur included in the British zone.[2] Delcassé, writing to Cambon on 7 February, indicated that he would, if necessary, be prepared to accept the British demand for Darfur but wished to make this conditional on an extension of French territory in the Bahr el Ghazal region.[3] On this point Cambon found Salisbury quite uncompromising and, with Delcassé's approval, he abandoned the attempt.[4] After a good deal of further but amicable discussion agreement was finally reached on 21 March.[5] At Delcassé's suggestion it took the form of a declaration to be appended to the Niger Convention of 14 June 1898. Details of boundary delimitation, which, for lack of precise knowledge on either side, had proved intractable, were to be settled by a mixed boundary commission.

By this agreement the French vastly increased the size of their desert empire and the British set the seals on their claim to exclusive control over the Nile Valley. In spite of the friction which the Fashoda dispute had engendered on both sides of the Channel the spirit in which the agreement had been made was a friendly one and the road to further *rapprochement*, in the light of these first contacts between Salisbury and Cambon, seemed open. But passions, once roused, proved difficult to calm and public opinion, as reflected both among politicians and the Press in England and France, remained avid to seize upon any occasion for boasting or recrimination. Though Delcassé and Cambon on the one hand and Salisbury on the other were anxious to rise above this tide of ill will they could not always avoid being carried by it. Not only the Kaiser continued to talk of the inevitability of war between

[1] See Cambon to Delcassé, 25 Jan 1899, *DDF* i, xv, no. 46, pp. 71, 72.
[2] See Cambon to Delcassé, 2 Feb 1899, *DDF* i, xv, no. 57, p. 97.
[3] See Delcassé to Cambon, 7 Feb 1899, *DDF* i, xv, no. 68, pp. 112, 113.
[4] See Cambon to Delcassé, 8 Feb 1899, *DDF* i, xv, no. 70, p. 115; Delcassé to Cambon, 10 Feb 1899, *DDF* i, xv, no. 76, pp. 120, 121; and Cambon to Delcassé, 10 Feb 1899, *DDF* i, xv, no. 77, pp. 123, 124.
[5] See Cambon to Delcassé, 21 Mar 1899, *DDF* i, xv, no. 122, pp. 188–91, enclosing a copy of the agreement signed.

England and France; the theme remained widespread. Even though Monson was convinced of the pacific intentions of the French Government he warned, on 3 February 1899, that 'the fact that France is arming – indeed has armed – to the teeth is notorious',[1] and he added: 'the language of the press in regard to relations between France and England is becoming offensive in proportion as that of the English press becomes more conciliatory'.[2]

Not surprisingly English restraint was not in evidence for long. While Cambon and Salisbury were putting the finishing touches to their African boundary agreement a minor quarrel flared up which illustrated quickness of temper on both sides. The French opened negotiations with the Sultan of Muscat in order to obtain a lease of territory for a coaling station. The Sultan, threatened by British naval bombardment if he complied, suspended negotiations. Cambon complained to Salisbury on 22 February 1899 that he had seen the incident described on hoardings in London as 'a new check for France'.[3] On 15 March Cambon referred Salisbury to the Muscat question 'not so much for the purpose of making any new arrangement but rather for that of drawing general conclusions as to the present attitude of the two countries towards each other'.

> He represented with great earnestness and at considerable length that it was a position not at all free from danger. He said that he had ascertained by his residence in this country that no one had the slightest desire for war; and returning to France he was convinced, as he had been ever since the commencement of the Fashoda incident, that a similar abhorrence of any war between the two countries existed in almost every part of the French community. He reiterated several times such a war would be absurd. But he said he thought that there was a tone prevalent in England which might have the effect of driving the pacific sentiments of France to despair, and leading Frenchmen to think that there was no hope of tranquil relations with this country. In several incidents which had recently occurred between the two countries, notably in the case of the Fashoda affair and in regard to the proposed extension of the French settlement at Shanghai, and then later in the matter of Muscat, France was

---

[1] Monson to Salisbury, 3 Feb 1899, *BD* I, no. 243, p. 200.
[2] Monson to Salisbury, 3 Feb 1899, ibid., p. 201.
[3] See Salisbury to Monson, 22 Feb 1899, *BD* I, no. 255, p. 209.

treated, in all expressions that were given of the sentiments of the British government or officers, in an exceptionally unfavourable and humiliating manner.[1]

Salisbury avoided giving the conversation a more 'irritating turn' by forbearing 'to point out in detail how the menacing action of French officers in various parts of the world had forced upon us considerations of self-protection'.

The Muscat quarrel simmered during the spring and summer of 1899 and was gradually forgotten amid more serious disputes and misunderstandings. In England Salisbury and Chamberlain, though they differed on the means of meeting the situation, were equally preoccupied with the problem of preserving British trading pre-eminence in China. The main threat, it was agreed, came from Russia. Chamberlain still favoured the notion of combating this danger by a German alliance. Salisbury, doubting Germany's willingness to join sincerely in such a combination on any terms, favoured compromise with Russia. In fact he was prepared to jettison the 'Open Door' policy and to carve up China into spheres of influence reserving the Yangtze basin for Great Britain. In pursuit of this aim a preliminary agreement on railway concessions was reached with Russia on 29 April 1899.[2] French suspicions of Salisbury's China policy, though no doubt exaggerated, had already become acute. On 20 April 1899[3] Cambon advised Delcassé that the wisest policy for France would be to attempt a revival of the Far Eastern Triplice. On 2 May he expressed grave fears of the consequences of the Anglo-Russian agreement and reiterated his advice to attempt active co-operation with Russia and Germany against Great Britain. 'Our inertia in Egypt', he commented, 'has cost us too dear for us to allow ourselves to be dragged along by events in China also.'[4] At the *Quai d'Orsay*, after seriously considering the possibility of trying to strike a direct bargain with England, the line suggested by Cambon was eventually adopted. Thanks partly to the attitude of France the Far Eastern Triplice was in fact restored. Neither Salisbury's hopes of compromising with Russia nor Chamberlain's

[1] Salisbury to Monson, 15 Mar 1899, *BD* i, no. 257, p. 211.
[2] See Salisbury to Bax-Ironside, 30 Apr 1899, *BD* i, no. 61, pp. 40, 41.
[3] See Cambon to Delcassé, 20 Apr 1899, *DDF* i, xv, no. 150, pp. 233–5.
[4] Cambon to Delcassé, 2 May 1899, *DDF* i, xv, no. 164, p. 264.

dream of finding a powerful partner against Russia seemed to be meeting with any success.

This failure was particularly awkward when it became increasingly apparent, in September 1899, that a South African War would not be avoided. The French Press, not surprisingly, had already taken sides. If England, over South Africa, provided an easy target France, over the Dreyfus retrial verdict, was equally vulnerable. A spate of anti-French articles envenomed the atmosphere. The Queen, on her own initiative, sent a telegraphic message *en clair* to the Paris Embassy expressing her horror at the news of this 'monstrous verdict'. Thanks to the good sense of the French Ministry of the Interior and discreet government intervention in England there was no leakage of information.[1] If, as seemed almost certain, the telegram had been published in the Press a major crisis in Anglo-French relations could hardly have been avoided. Even without the Queen's intervention the situation was bad enough.

With the commencement of hostilities in South Africa French reporters and cartoonists pursued their campaign with added and self-righteous virulence. The possibility of Anglo-French conflict was openly canvassed on both sides of the Channel. Muraviev's[2] visit to Paris in October lent colour to the notion of a continental league against England.[3] Although Delcassé later tried to cover his tracks he does seem to have been tempted by the possibility of playing a leading part, under threat of force, in imposing mediation.[4] The Kaiser, although never as enthusiastic as Delcassé subsequently alleged, on the one hand does seem to have given some countenance to the notion, and on the other certainly tried to claim credit in England for having defeated it. Whatever thoughts of intervention Delcassé may have entertained the combination of British jingoism and French Press polemics was in any case highly combustible. Both governments concluded, plausibly if

[1] For this incident see J. A. S. Grenville, *Lord Salisbury and Foreign Policy*, pp. 430, 431.

[2] Count Muraviev, Russian Foreign Minister 1896–1900.

[3] For Muraviev's proposal and for French and German reactions see J. A. S. Grenville, *Lord Salisbury and Foreign Policy*, pp. 270–4.

[4] For this first attempt by Delcassé to approach Germany via Muraviev and for its failure see C. M. Andrew, *Théophile Delcassé and the Making of the Entente Cordiale*, pp. 162–5.

erroneously, that the other was contemplating military action. Monson's alarmist dispatches from Paris were matched by Cambon's from London. Writing on 11 November 1899 he argued that once England had successfully liquidated her difficulties in the Transvaal she would be free to pick a quarrel with France; in the present mood of violent anti-French feeling aggression would be so popular that it must be feared; protraction of the war in South Africa was, from a French point of view, the best safety-valve; in the meanwhile Cambon could only counsel the speeding up of French naval preparations.[1] Later he claimed that he had deliberately sought 'to put the wind up the Quai d'Orsay' in order to stimulate French rearmament;[2] in his opinion it was still the best guarantee of peace and eventual *Entente*.

Even if Cambon's faith in *Entente Cordiale* as an ultimate objective remained unshaken this, in the light of aggressive French attitudes, was hardly apparent to Salisbury. The question in his mind was how far it might be worth trying to turn the other cheek and to meet insult by conciliation. In present circumstances there seemed little to be gained. France, however hostile, did not represent a threat to British communications with South Africa. Nor could French friendship, even if purchasable, contribute appreciably to any improvement in Britain's Far Eastern situation. As far as South Africa was concerned, Portugal was of more importance than France. And in October it was with Portugal that Great Britain signed a secret treaty, arousing German suspicions about the validity of the previous Anglo-German agreement.[3] Portuguese co-operation was thus secured at the cost of irritating Germany. To repair this damage now became a major British objective; Germany's attitude was of direct importance in South Africa and might even be turned to valuable account in China. At last therefore Salisbury resigned himself to giving Kaiser William some satisfaction over Samoa.[4] The way was thus paved for the Kaiser's projected visit to Windsor. Although care was exercised in Germany to stress the family character of the visit, it was welcomed

---

[1] See Cambon to Delcassé, 11 Nov 1899, *DDF* i, xv, no. 297, pp. 514-17.

[2] See Cambon to Jules Cambon, 19 Mar 1900, *CC* ii, pp. 36-7.

[3] The Anglo-Portuguese agreement was signed on 14 Oct 1898. On the question of conflict with the previous Anglo-German agreement over Portuguese Colonies of Aug 1898, see J. A. S. Grenville, *Lord Salisbury and Foreign Policy*, pp. 260-3.

[4] The Anglo-German Samoan Convention was signed on 14 Nov 1899.

in England and feared in France as a sign of improved Anglo-German relations. The fact that the whole Press of Europe was so hostile to Great Britain's South African war gave the visit a special significance. The Kaiser, on this occasion, was on his best behaviour.[1] While the death of Lady Salisbury temporarily removed the Prime Minister from the scene, the Kaiser had interviews with Balfour and for the first time directly with Chamberlain.[2] His amiability and Bülow's[3] warm platitudes encouraged Chamberlain to believe that the prospects for alliance were fair. He hinted broadly at the possibility of concluding special arrangements to ensure Anglo-German co-operation in Asia Minor and Morocco. Though German reactions to Chamberlain's advances were non-committal he interpreted them favourably. Even if sceptical of more positive results and suspicious of Chamberlain's attempts to secure them, Salisbury could not but be gratified at the improvement in Anglo-German relations which the Kaiser's visit symbolised.

On 30 November, the day after the Kaiser's departure from England, Chamberlain, in a speech at Leicester, complained bitterly of the attitude of the French Press and, in contrast, painted a glowing picture of the future of Anglo-German relations which he described, in spirit if not in fact, as an alliance. French protests followed at once.[4] Sanderson, on behalf of the Foreign Office, disclaimed responsibility for the sentiments expressed. To Delcassé Monson explained that Chamberlain was not Foreign Minister and that he would resign should Chamberlain ever occupy that office.[5] Somewhat mollified by these disclaimers Delcassé was further reassured by German reactions. Official response, deferring to a violent outburst on the part of public opinion, was so frigid that Anglo-German relations, far from improving on the lines assumed by Chamberlain, suffered a sharp set-back. However, although the French Foreign Minister might be reassured, French opinion was even further exacerbated.

[1] For details of the visit see J. A. S. Grenville, *Lord Salisbury and Foreign Policy*, pp. 277–81.

[2] On 21 and 24 Nov 1899.

[3] Prince Bernhard von Bülow (1849–1929), German Foreign Minister 1897–1900; Chancellor 1900–9.

[4] See Cambon to Delcassé, 1 Dec 1899, *DDF* i, xvi, no. 16, pp. 26–9 where he reports the official protest which he made to Sir Thomas Sanderson, the Permanent Under-Secretary at the Foreign Office.

[5] See Delcassé to Cambon, 7 Dec 1899, *DDF* i, xvi, no. 22, pp. 37–9.

One of the ways in which anti-British feeling in France could be vicariously gratified was by demonstration of sympathy for the Egyptian nationalist movement. Not surprisingly Mustapha Kamil,[1] the Egyptian nationalist leader, had become a hero in the French Press. But Cogordon,[2] reporting from Egypt, on 20 December 1899, on the growing strength of this nationalist movement in Egypt, warned Delcassé of the dangers of trying to use this weapon against British influence in Egypt.[3] Mustapha Kamil, he pointed out, represented a brand of Islamic nationalism which was hostile to all European influence; France herself possessed too many Moslem subjects to give active encouragement to such a movement. This caution was readily understood by Delcassé, and Cogordon's attitude in Cairo mitigated the effects of a pro-Kamilist campaign which constituted yet another source of Anglo-French tension.

In the meanwhile from London Cambon's reports were becoming slightly more hopeful. British reverses in South Africa seemed to preclude the possibility of rapid victory. Writing on 21 December 1899, he concluded that the possibilities of an early conflict with France were less threatening. 'We must not however', he warned, 'be lulled into sleep by exaggerated optimism. At risk of wearying Your Excellency, I will not stop repeating that the best way of living with our ambitious neighbours is to neglect no military precautions destined to enable us to withstand attack one day or another.[4]

Delcassé, somewhat reassured regarding immediate British intentions but still nervous about the state of feeling in both countries, made a number of efforts both public and private to lower the temperature. He was, therefore, particularly aggrieved in the early months of 1900 when the Léandre[5] affair brought feelings, once more, to boiling point. Of all the caricaturists who had lampooned Queen Victoria Léandre had caused most offence

---

[1] Mustapha Kamil (1874–1908) had been a law student in Paris and had maintained close links with numerous French politicians and writers, particularly Mme Juliette Adam of the radical *Nouvelle Revue*.

[2] François Georges Cogordon (1849–1904), French Consul-General at Cairo 1894–1902, Political Director at the French Foreign Office 1902–4.

[3] Cogordon to Delcassé, 20 Dec 1899, *DDF* i, xvi, no. 34, pp. 53–6.

[4] Cambon to Delcassé, 21 Dec. 1899, *DDF* i, xvi, no. 37, p. 63.

[5] Charles Lucien Léandre (1862–1934), French artist and cartoonist.

by a cartoon of Chamberlain hiding behind the Queen's skirts. When Léandre was decorated with the Legion of Honour by the Minister of Fine Arts this was interpreted by Queen Victoria as a deliberate and personal insult. The matter was canvassed in the Press. The Queen privately urged that Monson should be recalled from Paris; in fact he moved less ostentatiously to Cannes. She decided to abandon her usual spring holiday in France and marked the point by a visit to Italy instead. There was talk of a British boycott of the Great International Exhibition. The Prince of Wales, who should have presided at the opening, decided, in spite of appeals from Salisbury, against attending the Exhibition at all. Writing on 22 March 1900 after seeing Salisbury, when they discussed the attitudes of the Press and the general situation, Cambon felt that he could at last detect signs of a *détente* even though the harm done by the incident was 'not yet effaced'.[1]

In the meanwhile, as a result of Russian prompting, Delcassé once again considered the possibility of an 'amicable' intervention to restore peace in South Africa.[2] He was prepared to co-operate provided that the lead in approaching Great Britain was taken by Germany; only in these circumstances was he willing to take the risk that Britain might respond to any such demand by a declaration of war. Before his views had been made known to the Russians, Muraviev had already made an approach to Germany and received a somewhat dusty answer. The Kaiser indicated that the Russians should first enquire whether any mediating intervention would be acceptable to the British and at the same time he warned the British Government of Muraviev's proposal rendering it, in his version, rather more sinister. As far as the French were concerned any obligations to treat the Russian proposal seriously disappeared when the Russians reported that the Kaiser was not willing to be associated with any mediation offers unless the nations concerned were prepared to give one another mutual guarantees of territorial possession. Recognition of the loss of Alsace-Lorraine was too heavy a price for Delcassé to pay in order to gain German compliance in a venture which, though tempting,

[1] See Cambon to Jules Cambon, 22 Mar 1900, *CC* II, pp. 41, 42.

[2] For Muraviev's second intervention proposal and its consequences see J. A. S. Grenville, *Lord Salisbury and Foreign Policy*, pp. 285–90. See also C. M. Andrew, *Théophile Delcassé and the Making of the Entente Cordiale*, pp. 169–74.

also filled him with misgivings. The results of this incident, as far as Salisbury was concerned, were heightened suspicion of Russia, qualified gratitude to the Kaiser and renewed reflection on the dangers of the Franco-Russian alliance. These reactions, in Chamberlain's case, were heightened into concluding that Russia was seeking an opportunity to strike at the British Empire, that France was bound to support Russia and that a German alliance was even more urgently to be sought.

The views of the Indian Government and the reports of the service chiefs in England swayed the Cabinet towards Chamberlain's more alarmist assessment of the situation.[1] Russian activity in Persia and Afghanistan confirmed suspicions. The defence of India became a major preoccupation and the prospects seemed bleak. Though Curzon[2] remained confident that Russia could be successfully resisted military experts in London were gloomy and plans for the defence of India, which included the probability of being obliged to fight against Russia and France simultaneously, were undertaken in a spirit of profound pessimism, unrelieved by the fact that the Chancellor adamantly rejected schemes involving major additional expenditure. In the meanwhile Russian advances in Persia, to Curzon's disgust, were allowed to proceed unchecked.

Although British governments were not able to appreciate the point, Russian pressure on the borders of India was not the prelude to any grandiose plan for aggression against India. Russian sights were firmly set on China. But, from a British point of view, the fact that Russian objectives were Chinese rather than Indian was almost equally disturbing. Russia's predominant interest in China was confirmed during the aftermath of the Boxer rising.[3] Under impetus of the initial shock European powers rallied against Chinese nationalism. But mutual suspicions flourished in the process. Russia's determination to establish her grip over Manchuria was patently obvious. In order to keep German goodwill Great Britain reluctantly consented to the Kaiser's plan for

---

[1] See J. A. S. Grenville, *Salisbury and Foreign Policy*, pp. 290–303, for a useful analysis of the Indian defence problem.

[2] George Nathaniel Curzon (1859–1925), cr. Viscount 1898, Earl 1911, Marquis Curzon of Kedleston 1921; Viceroy of India 1898–1905 and Foreign Secretary 1919–24

[3] The Legation in Peking were besieged from early June until their relief by an international force on 14 Aug 1900.

confiding command of an expeditionary force to Field-Marshal von Waldersee. The Field-Marshal arrived after the emergency was over but in time to increase the disruption of China by exacting revenge and reparation. Russia was, paradoxically able to pose as China's friend and protector. Salisbury, struggling to keep China open to British trade, was forced further towards a policy of fixing spheres of influence while yet seeking to preserve the fiction of China's political integrity. Co-operation with Germany and with Japan seemed to be the only means available of checking Russia. Sceptically and reluctantly Salisbury negotiated the Anglo-German China Agreement to which Japan also subscribed.[1] Chamberlain envisaged it as an important first step in his cherished diplomatic revolution. To Salisbury it was a temporary device unlikely to stand the strain of any serious testing.

Its conclusion, however, suggested that the Boxer rebellion had resulted in increased Anglo-Russian tension and in Anglo-German *rapprochement*. In these circumstances, although Anglo-French relations did not deteriorate, there was little prospect of any positive improvement.

During the negotiations for the Anglo-German agreement England had been in the throes of a General Election. The hero of the Government's successful campaign in the Khaki Election had been, not the ageing Prime Minister, but Chamberlain at the height of his brash, domineering, 'new image' oratory. In the Cabinet not only his critics, but also his friends and relations, considered that the time had come for Salisbury to lighten the load of his duties.[2] Younger men at the Foreign Office agreed with Chamberlain that masterly inactivity was now no more than a cloak for a dead hand in control. Those who still had faith in Salisbury's omniscience and who feared Chamberlain's impetuosity believed that their chief's health was too precarious, and too important, for him to continue to be burdened with the detailed administration of foreign affairs. Fully aware of these pressures, Salisbury hesitated before reaching any decision; new appointments at the Admiralty and at the War Office were not

---

[1] The agreement was signed on 16 Oct 1900. For details of the negotiations, and particularly for the divergence in approach between Salisbury and Chamberlain, see J. A. S. Grenville, *Lord Salisbury and Foreign Policy*, pp. 310–18.

[2] Ibid., p. 324.

accompanied by any announcement concerning the Foreign Office. Eventually, however, on 23 October Salisbury advised the Queen that he wished to propose Lord Lansdowne as his successor. She agreed 'on the strict understanding' that he would closely supervise the work of the new Foreign Secretary.[1] The appointment of his eldest son, Lord Cranborne,[2] as Parliamentary Under-Secretary for Foreign Affairs seemed further designed to avoid any abrupt transition. Nevertheless, to those impatiently pressing for change at least some prospect of new development in the direction of foreign affairs appeared to have been won.

[1] See Queen Victoria, memorandum, 23 Oct 1900, *Queen Victoria Letters* III, pp. 611–12, quoted J. A. S. Grenville, *Lord Salisbury and Foreign Policy*, p. 325.

[2] James Edward Hubert Gascoyne-Cecil, Viscount Cranborne (1861–1947). He succeeded his father as 4th Marquis of Salisbury in 1903.

6

Lansdowne at the Foreign Office

'WHEN I pass by your splendid house in London', Dr Jowett[1] wrote in 1867, 'I feel a sort of wonder that the owner should be reading quietly in Oxford. But you could not do a wiser or a better thing. Wealth and rank are means and not ends, and may be the greatest good or evil as they are used.'[2] The Marquis of Lansdowne,[3] to whom these words were addressed, was then an undergraduate at Balliol and had just succeeded to the title on the death of his father. Destined by birth to rapid promotion in public service, his early accession to the House of Lords, where Whig Peers were already in short supply, was inevitably calculated to hasten the process.

Henry Charles Keith Petty-Fitzmaurice, fifth Marquis of Lansdowne and twenty-eighth Lord of Kerry in direct male succession, was born on 14 January 1845. The Fitzmaurices had adventured to Ireland in the twelfth century and there carved out an empire in the County of Kerry. Though that empire proved ephemeral, the Fitzmaurices rejoined the ranks of great Irish landowners when the twenty-first Lord of Kerry married Anne, only daughter and heiress of Sir William Petty (1623–87). Her grandson, the second Earl of Shelburne and first Marquis of Lansdowne (1737–1805), possessed talents which matched his wealth. With political vision ranging beyond the Whig oligarchy, he bridged the gap between the Pitts whom he served respectively as disciple and as patron.

---

[1] The Rev. Benjamin Jowett (1817–93), then Master of Balliol.
[2] Jowett to Lansdowne, Apr 1867, quoted Lord Newton, *Lord Lansdowne*, p. 7.
[3] The only biography of Lansdowne is Lord Newton's published in 1929.

Prime Minister at last in 1782 he was soon a victim of the system, now represented by the Fox–North coalition, which he loftily despised. Although, compared to its promise, his own political career ended in disappointment, he had occupied the forefront of the stage and henceforth politics, as befitted great landowners, became a family tradition. His second son, later the third Marquis of Lansdowne (1780–1863) became Chancellor of the Exchequer in Grenville's Ministry of All the Talents in 1806. Unlike his father, he made a virtue of the Whig allegiance which was at that stage in his career cemented, and he remained out of office during the long Tory ascendancy until in 1827 he led the Whigs into coalition with Canning. He then served under Goderich and was subsequently included in every Liberal cabinet between 1830 and 1858.

While he thus maintained the family's political tradition his son, eventually the fourth Marquis[1] and Lansdowne's father, vastly increased the family wealth by marrying the daughter of a Scottish heiress and of Count de Flahault. The Count, one of Napoleon's generals and his favourite aide-de-camp, was a natural son of Talleyrand,[2] who thus was Lansdowne's great-grandfather. Through his mother and her connections Lansdowne acquired an early knowledge of the French language and of France. He paid frequent visits to French relatives and in 1868 was the guest of Napoleon III. Apart from the impact of French influence, Lansdowne's youth and education conformed entirely to English aristocratic pattern. From Eton, where Balfour[3] was his fag, he went on, after a spell with a crammer, to Balliol. Fond of sport and enjoying the distractions of undergraduate life, which wealth made so easily inviting, he nevertheless studied with purpose and application. The earnestness and sense of duty which were to characterise his life and career were already firmly in evidence. To his mother, who remained one of his chief correspondents until she died in 1895, he continually confided his fears that, amid all the pleasures of life at Oxford, he was failing to work as hard as he should. When, after his father's death and his own accession to the title, he took his final examinations in 1867 and obtained a

---

[1] He died in 1866.   [2] See p. 16.
[3] Arthur James Balfour (1848–1930), subsequently 1st Earl of Balfour, Salisbury's nephew and his successor as Prime Minister.

Second instead of the First Class Honours on which his heart had been set, he was bitterly disappointed. Dr Jowett pontifically commiserated:

> I am sorry about the Class List, both for your sake and Lady Lansdowne's and also for the sake of Oxford and Balliol. You failed not from want of ability, but from a certain want of interest and from the cares of this world coming upon you too soon; and I failed in making you understand the amount of interest and of hard work which was required.
>
> But I should be much more sorry if I thought that you were going to settle down 'second class' for life. Don't allow yourself to think this for a moment. You have certainly far greater ability than many First Classmen, and by good management, with your opportunities, you may make every year a progress on the one before.
>
> I want you to have objects and dreams of ambition and energy and industry enough to carry it out. A new era of politics is beginning, and unless a man would be a cipher or a paradox he should fit himself for it. Time will show him how to shape his course; though always willing to act with a party, he should still keep his mind above party feelings and motives. It does not do for a young man to begin where an old man leaves off. Knowledge of the world and of political subjects, reticence and self-control, freedom from personal feeling, are the qualities to be aimed at. I don't object to a touch of idealism or speculation also, if kept in its proper place. But how few statesmen have these qualities in any degree?[1]

In his future career Lansdowne seems to have taken much of this advice quite literally. The 'touch of idealism' was still clearly in evidence when, as an old man during the First World War, he wrote his peace letter which *The Times* rejected and the *Daily Telegraph* published.[2] Reticence and self-control were his constant watchwords. It could be suggested that throughout his career he strove anxiously, perhaps too anxiously, to conform to Jowett's image of statesmanlike excellence.

Lansdowne's active political career began very shortly after he first took his seat in the House of Lords. When Gladstone formed his first ministry in December 1868 he offered Lansdowne a

---

[1] Quoted Lord Newton, *Lord Lansdowne*, pp. 9, 10.
[2] On 29 Nov 1917. For the background to the letter and its impact see H. Kurtz, 'The Lansdowne Letter', *History Today*, xviii (Feb 1968) pp. 84–92.

Junior Lordship of the Treasury. Liberal Peers of intellectual ability were in short supply and Gladstone had no hesitation in trying to harness Lansdowne to duty at the earliest opportunity. He responded by diligent application to numerous dull tasks and seemed well suited to meet Gladstone's expectations. In 1869 he married Lady Maud Hamilton, youngest daughter of the Duke of Abercorn, and settled down to domestic felicity amid the pomp and luxury of Bowood. In 1872 he was promoted to the post of Under-Secretary for War. When the Liberals returned to office in 1880 he was offered and accepted the Indian Under-Secretaryship. But doubts over Gladstone's Irish policy made him uneasy in office and in the same year he resigned, although Gladstone tried to make him change his mind by arguing that an Under-Secretary was not responsible for government policy and that he would be quite free to express personal opinions on the Irish Question. Lansdowne's speech explaining the motives for his resignation made a considerable impression and was highly praised by Disraeli in a letter to the Queen. Though the Irish Question divided Lansdowne from the Government, there was as yet no formal breech. He played an active part in parliamentary business and, among other duties, became Chairman of the joint Committee of the two Houses on the Channel Tunnel project which he strongly supported. In 1883, much to his surprise, Gladstone offered him the Governor-Generalship of Canada. He accepted, mainly for financial reasons. In spite of his great wealth the estate had been encumbered since the death of his father and he was averse to reducing his establishments. While in Canada he remained preoccupied by Irish affairs and his own political allegiance shifted, in tune with that of Hartington,[1] from the Liberals to the Conservatives. Salisbury took cognisance of the change by inviting him in 1887 to become the next Viceroy of India. An unassuming proconsul, he ruled India discreetly, in relatively quiet times, from 1888 to 1894. In the spring of 1895 his mother died; after inheriting her Scottish estates and thanks to the profitable sale of land in Ireland, his resources were at last equal to the maintenance of all the remainder of his vast properties. He needed no longer to be an exile. In June 1895 he became War Minister in Salisbury's Unionist Cabinet. He settled to his new

[1] See p. 40.

duties with a tact and modesty rare in ex-Viceroys. Though aware of the deficiencies in army organisation, he characteristically tried to do his best within existing terms of reference. Their inadequacy became apparent during early failures in the South African War. Inevitably, but with doubtful justice, he became a main target for criticism. This he bore with stoicism, but in August 1900, when proposing a measure of reconstruction, he took the opportunity to offer his own resignation, sensibly pointing out to Salisbury that there would be more confidence in changes planned if a new man were appointed to execute them. Salisbury appealed to him to continue in office until after the General Election which would, he confided, not long be delayed. Lansdowne dutifully withdrew his resignation. He was fully conscious that his tenure of the War Office was not regarded as a successful one and he made no claims, for the future, on the Prime Minister. His selection by Salisbury as his successor at the Foreign Office came as a surprise. He certainly had not sought the responsibility but, having accepted it, he was anxious to prove himself and to quench the odour of failure which clung to him as War Minister. Though diffident about his own talents and in no way ambitious, he was nevertheless determined, as a matter of personal pride and of patriotic duty, to respond successfully to this new challenge.

His experience as Viceroy of India made him acutely conscious of the problem of Indian defence. His experience at the War Office convinced him that British resources were not adequate for her imperial commitments and particularly for the defence of India. These preoccupations inclined him towards the opinions of those who were critical of Salisbury's conduct of foreign policy. Though eager to find a way out of difficulties by accommodation with Russia, he nevertheless believed that promises of support against Russia, in the form of concrete agreements, should be more actively sought than Salisbury's attitude seemed to allow. And yet, by temperament and on general principles, Lansdowne was far more in sympathy with Salisbury's measured and professional methods and approach to diplomacy than with Chamberlain's brand of brash dynamism. His reason was on the side of a new deal; his instinct deplored its necessity.

In his first official confrontation with the Russian question, he reacted negatively and cautiously. While the powers wrangled over details of Chinese punishment for the Boxer rebellion, it emerged that Russia was engaged in secret negotiations with China about Manchuria. Revelations about a supposed bargain were received by Lansdowne, and by Salisbury, in a spirit of almost bland resignation.[1] For Britain's part the Agreement recently reached with Germany had been intended to include Manchuria but neither Lansdowne nor Salisbury seem to have been prepared to make a crisis of the issue. The Japanese government, however, reminded Lansdowne that Japan was a party to the Anglo-German Agreement and that Japan interpreted it as safeguarding the integrity of Manchuria. During December 1900 and January 1901 he was under heavy pressure from Japan to adopt a tough line towards Russia and to co-operate in bringing Germany into line.

While Lansdowne was under this pressure an event occurred which led him, indirectly, towards a more responsive attitude. Queen Victoria died on 22 January 1901. The Kaiser had hastened affectionately and dutifully to her death-bed on 20 January. He remained in England until 5 February. On arrival he was hailed in the Press as 'a friend in need'; on departure he was loudly cheered. His interviews with Chamberlain, with Lansdowne and even with Salisbury were cordial. In the background Eckardstein[2] was claiming to the Kaiser that the British ministers were now ready to pay almost any price for noncommital German friendship.[3] In even louder vein, Eckardstein was repeating hints to Chamberlain that Germany was eager for a firm alliance. Although not so sanguine as Chamberlain, Lansdowne was far less suspicious than Salisbury. From the Kaiser's visit he emerged with the impression that a British diplomatic initiative in Germany's direction would not be unwelcome.

During the month of February secret Russian negotiations with the Chinese continued. Japanese remonstrances at St Petersburg were accompanied by threats at Peking. The Chinese unhappily wondered whether, by placating the Russians, they would

---

[1] See J. A. S. Grenville, *Lord Salisbury and Foreign Policy*, p. 330.

[2] Baron Hermann von Eckardstein, First Secretary at the German Embassy in London 1899–1902.

[3] For the most plausible interpretation of Eckardstein's role and for the consequent Anglo-German misunderstanding see J. A. S. Grenville, *Lord Salisbury and Foreign Policy*, pp. 333–5.

not have to face even more dangerous Japanese wrath. Germany and Great Britain were both lukewarm in support of Japan and yet advised China against the consequences of surrender to Russia; Russian designs, however obvious, were constantly denied by the Russian Foreign Minister. In the midst of this imbroglio the Chinese Foreign Minister in London appealed on 1 March 1901 for British mediation.[1] Lansdowne seems to have concluded that the Russians were tightening the screw and that, contrary to his own previous assumptions, diplomatic means of preserving the territorial integrity of Manchuria, as the Japanese desired, were worth attempting. To gain German support he was prepared to pay a high price and he put before the Cabinet a project for a secret treaty of alliance which would, in certain circumstances, have committed England and Germany to war on Japan's side against Russia. Lansdowne circulated a draft declaration to this effect to the Cabinet on 12 March.[2] It seems to have been decided to test German reactions informally before making any official proposals. Lascelles's[3] tentative enquiries alarmed Bülow and on 15 March 1901 he made a declaration in the Reichstag denying that the Anglo-German China agreement was in any way concerned with Manchuria. While Bülow's interpretation of the agreement was open to question there was no doubt whatever about the policy which Germany intended to adopt. Lansdowne's first attempt to tighten Anglo-German bonds had proved abortive. The Manchurian crisis, which had caused the attempt, dissolved with Russia's abandonment of her negotiations with China. This represented Witte's[4] victory over his more adventurous colleagues in Russia rather than any kind of success for British diplomacy.

In spite of disappointment at Bülow's Reichstag speech Lansdowne continued to look towards Germany to redress the Far Eastern balance of power in Great Britain's favour. Determined to take advantage of this mood Eckardstein spoke to Lansdowne in terms of a defensive alliance against France and Russia[5] and

[1] See J. A. S. Grenville, *Lord Salisbury and Foreign Policy*, pp. 38, 39.
[2] See Lansdowne Cabinet Memorandum, 12 Mar 1901, F.O. 46/547, quoted ibid., p. 340.
[3] Sir Frank Lascelles (1841–1920), Ambassador at Berlin 1895–1908.
[4] Sergei Witte (1849–1915), then Russian Minister of Finance.
[5] See Lansdowne to Lascelles, 18 Mar 1901, *BD* II, no. 77, pp. 60, 61.

then, on 19 March 1901, reported to Berlin that such a proposal had been made by Lansdowne.[1] Bülow and Holstein[2] were concerned, not with the Far East where they were determined to avoid quarrelling with Russia on Great Britain's behalf, but with Europe where the Triple Alliance, as a result of obvious Franco-Italian *rapprochement*, seemed to be breaking apart. They therefore decided, on the basis of Eckardstein's report, to respond to Lansdowne's supposed proposal by instructing Hatzfeldt[3] to advise Lansdowne to open negotiations for joining the Triple Alliance with the Austrians.[4] Neither Bülow nor Holstein were over-sanguine of success but at least this approach would relieve them of the embarrassment of seeming to reject British advances out of hand. On receiving his instructions Hatzfeldt, who was in poor health, left matters in Eckardstein's hands. Eckardstein, the victim of his own well-intentioned duplicity, was loth to act as instructed. Instead he first tried to persuade the Austrian Ambassador in London to take the initiative and then, after the failure of this move, resumed conversations with Lansdowne on the general theme of Anglo-German alliance.[5] Not surprisingly he was unable to respond when Lansdowne pressed for concrete proposals. Towards the end of May, however, he decided to take one more chance and he promised a detailed memorandum.[6] At this juncture Hatzfeldt, whose health had improved, renewed contact with Lansdowne. Acting on official instructions, he suggested that England should seek membership of the Triple Alliance. Lansdowne answered evasively and wrote to Eckardstein asking for the promised memorandum. Hatzfeldt opened the letter and at last realised the extent to which Eckardstein had departed from instructions. He replied to Lansdowne that he had not been aware of any promised memorandum and that Eckardstein was now

---

[1] See Eckardstein to Holstein, 19 Mar 1901; Eckardstein, *Ten Years at the Court of St. James*, pp. 207–8. Eckardstein himself confessed: 'the fact was that when dining with Lord Lansdowne on March 16, I had given him a strong hint to approach us with an offer of alliance.... But if I had put this into my telegram to Holstein he would have fallen on me for going too far. Holstein's motto always was: "make me an omelette but break me no eggs".'

[2] See p. 83.

[3] See p. 73 note 5.

[4] See J. A. S. Grenville, *Lord Salisbury and Foreign Policy*, pp. 347, 348.

[5] Ibid., pp. 348–50.

[6] For this move of Eckardstein's and its consequences, see ibid., pp. 350–2.

away in the country. In answer to a further discreet probe from Lansdowne, Hatzfeldt politely made it obvious that there would be no memorandum, however informal. While the Eckardstein bubble was thus being burst, Sanderson[1] had prepared a draft of a possible Anglo-German convention based on Britain joining the Triple Alliance.[2] Sanderson himself was obviously fully alive to the difficulties and the draft seems to have been intended as a starting point for study rather than a matured project. Salisbury responded with a famous deprecatory memorandum.[3] Lansdowne, now aware of Eckardstein's excess of zeal, was prepared 'to mark time' and await any authorised and more promising overtures from Germany. On the other hand, as he showed later, he did not acknowledge the full force of Salisbury's criticisms. Perhaps the present price for German friendship was too high. But, at a lower rate, it was worth pursuing and in his view more possible than Salisbury seemed ready to acknowledge.

Once again a royal funeral[4] seemed to provide an opportunity to communicate informally, and perhaps more fruitfully, with the Kaiser. But the hopes which Lansdowne had entertained of the meeting between Edward VII and his nephew were not fulfilled.[5] On the contrary by conveying the impression that he still regarded the King's ministers as 'unmitigated noodles'[6] the Kaiser hardly seemed anxious to suggest that he wished to do any serious business with them.

Nevertheless, and in spite of further deterioration in Anglo-German relations during the autumn and winter of 1901, Lansdowne continued, with lessening hopes, to strive for a limited agreement on moderate terms. Handicapped by Chamberlain's Edinburgh speech,[7] by the Kaiser's furious reactions to it and by

[1] See p. 104.

[2] See memorandum by Sanderson, 27 May 1901, *BD* II, no. 85, pp. 66–8.

[3] See memorandum by Salisbury, 29 May 1901, *BD* II, no. 86, pp. 68, 69.

[4] The funeral of Empress Frederick, favourite sister of Edward VII and mother of the Kaiser.

[5] See Lascelles to Lansdowne, 25 Aug 1901, *BD* I, no. 323, pp. 259–61 and *BD* II, no. 90, p. 73. See also p. 159.

[6] The Kaiser had used this expression in conversation with Lascelles and in a letter to Edward VII in Apr 1901. See Eckardstein, *Ten Years at the Court of St James*, pp. 216–18.

[7] On 25 Oct 1901 when he defended Britain's conduct of the war in South Africa by favourable contrast with 'barbarity' and 'cruelty' in other wars including, for example, the conduct of the victors in the Franco-German War of 1870.

Hatzfeldt's retirement,[1] Lansdowne kept the question under review at the Foreign Office. On 9 November 1901 Bertie[2] produced a lengthy and strongly argued memorandum.[3] Influenced no doubt by Selborne,[4] who was beginning to take alarm at German naval plans, Bertie had become extremely suspicious of Germany and he now came down firmly against any formal alliance. On 11 November Lansdowne summed up his own views.[5] He refused to be prejudiced by Bertie but he did admit that there were serious obstacles in the way of any comprehensive alliance with Germany. On the other hand he continued to argue in favour of a limited agreement if indeed it could be obtained. This argument was based on the general principle, which he now stressed, that Britain was in need of friends. 'I fully admit', he conceded,

> the force of the Prime Minister's observation that this country has until now fared well in spite of its international isolation. I think, however, that we may push too far the argument that because we have in the past survived in spite of isolation, we need have no misgivings as to the effect of that isolation in the future.
>
> In approaching the Japanese we have, indeed, virtually admitted that we do not wish to stand alone.[6]

In a further memorandum dated 12 December 1901 Lansdowne indicated in some detail and in answer to a query from Salisbury the kind of limited agreement with Germany which he still had in mind. 'My own impression', he concluded, 'is that the German government (or the German Emperor) desire something much more precise and far-reaching than this, and that they would refuse an overture on these lines. Should they do so no great harm will have been done and we shall have put it out of their power to accuse us of having "dropped" them.'[7] This prediction proved

[1] He was replaced by Count Paul Metternich, who remained German Ambassador until 1912.

[2] Sir Francis Bertie (1844–1919), 1st Viscount Bertie of Thame, Assistant Under-Secretary of State for Foreign Affairs 1894–1903; Ambassador at Rome 1903–5; Ambassador at Paris 1905–15.

[3] *BD* II, no. 91, pp. 73–6.

[4] William Palmer, 2nd Earl of Selborne (1859–1942), First Lord of the Admiralty in Nov 1900.

[5] See memorandum by Lansdowne, Nov 1901, *BD* II, no. 92, pp. 76–9. It was in fact in answer to Salisbury's memorandum of 29 May 1901. See p. 118 note 3.

[6] Memorandum by Lansdowne, 11 Nov 1901, *BD* II, no. 92, p. 77.

[7] Memorandum by Lansdowne, 12 Nov 1901, *BD* II, no. 93, p. 79.

correct. Lansdowne did make his proposals for an *entente* to Metternich and Metternich, judging that they would be little appreciated in Berlin, omitted even to report them.[1] But it would be wrong to assume that, because Lansdowne could foresee the possibility of this result, he was not disappointed. On the contrary, even at this stage he would warmly have welcomed a working agreement with Germany.

In the meanwhile his desire to pursue positive policies was bearing fruit in negotiations with the United States and with Japan. The settlement eventually reached with the United States was based on a virtual admission that Great Britain would in no circumstances in the future be prepared to contemplate the possibility of naval action against America.[2] Though 'war games' continued for some time to be played on the contrary assumption, a momentous decision had in fact been reached. The Anglo-Japanese Alliance,[3] although a more spectacular achievement, was in the long run less conclusive. When resuming previous discussions with Hayashi[4] on 16 October 1901, Lansdowne set the pace by making it clear that Great Britain would now negotiate irrespective of German co-operation.[5] Lansdowne was motivated mainly by strategic considerations and by anxiety to forestall a possible Russo-Japanese bargain. On the other hand he did not wish to close the door to Anglo-Russian agreement. The alliance was intended to prod the Russians in this direction just as much as to build a front against them. When pressing the alliance project on the Cabinet, Lansdowne was careful to present proposals for agreement with Russia at the same time. This was not merely a matter of cabinet tactics and the proposals remained a basis for

[1] See J. A. S. Grenville, *Lord Salisbury and Foreign Policy*, p. 362.

[2] The question at issue was the future Panama Canal. By the Clayton–Bulwer Treaty Britain had established a right to equal control of any such canal. That right was abandoned in the Hay–Pauncefote Treaty signed in Washington on 18 Nov 1901. Although the treaty contained provision to safeguard international use of the Canal Lansdowne clearly recognised that it would effectively be entirely under American control. The strategic implications confirmed the conclusion, already prompted by financial reasoning, that in striving to meet naval challenges Britain must be resigned to leaving out the United States as a possible opponent.

[3] For the most recent study see I. S. Nish, *The Anglo-Japanese Alliance of 1902*.

[4] Baron, later Viscount, Tadasu Hayashi (1850–1913), Japanese Ambassador at London 1900–6.

[5] See Lansdowne to Whitehead, 16 Oct 1901, *BD* II, no. 105, pp. 96–8.

possible negotiation even after the conclusion of the Japanese Alliance. Lansdowne certainly was not trying to push Japan into war with Russia. On the contrary he was hoping that the alliance would enable him to negotiate, from a position of greater strength, with Russia. In the event he miscalculated but the ultimate objective, Anglo-Russian compromise, was eventually, though in different circumstances, achieved.

It was a sign of Lansdowne's quiet and persuasive power that the Anglo-Japanese Alliance should have been concluded in spite of persistent criticism and doubts on Salisbury's part.[1] The result was patronisingly welcomed in Berlin,[2] where it was confidently assumed that the alliance would worsen Anglo-Russian and Anglo-French relations and thus in the long run emphasise British dependence on Germany.

Although the Kaiser and his chief ministers were congratulating themselves on having evaded a British trap and finding satisfaction in Britain's commitment to Japan, the mood in England was hardening against Germany. While Bertie at the Foreign Office typified the mistrust of a new generation of diplomats, it was Chamberlain, as usual, who voiced the emotional feelings of less well-informed opinion. Unrepentant after his outburst in October 1901[3] he made it clear on 6 January 1902 at Birmingham that he had abandoned his quest for German alliance by proclaiming, somewhat illogically so shortly before the conclusion of the Anglo-Japanese Alliance, a new faith in isolation. 'We have', he declared, 'the feeling, unfortunately, that we have to count on ourselves alone, and I say, therefore, it is the duty of British statesmen and it is the duty of the British people to count upon themselves alone, as their ancestors did. I say alone, yes in a splendid isolation, surrounded by our kinsfolk.'[4] During a debate which followed the reassembly of the Reichstag on 8 January Bülow made a personal attack on Chamberlain to which he angrily

[1] See J. A. S. Grenville, *Lord Salisbury and Foreign Policy*, p. 413. The treaty was signed on 30 Jan 1902.

[2] 'The noodles seem to have had a lucid interval', was the Kaiser's characteristic comment. See Lascelles to Lansdowne, 8 Feb 1902, quoted Newton, *Lord Lansdowne*, p. 247. It was translated into 'diplomatic language' at the Kaiser's suggestion in Lascelles's official report to Lansdowne on 7 Feb 1903. See *BD* ii, no. 128, pp. 122–3.

[3] See p. 118.

[4] See *The Times*, 7 Jan 1902.

replied in a speech at Birmingham on 11 January.[1] In the midst of
this highly publicised flurry Edward VII, who had received a
letter of complaint about Chamberlain from the Kaiser, wrote
back threatening to cancel the proposed visit of the Prince of
Wales to Germany as it would be better for him not to go where
he is liable to be insulted. . . .'[2]

The policy of seeking closer understanding with Germany,
which Chamberlain had noisily promoted and which Lansdowne
had more discreetly followed, seemed to have ended, not only in
failure, but in a positive development of mutual antipathy. For
this Chamberlain on the one hand and the Kaiser and Bülow on
the other were largely responsible. None of the three could resist
adopting the language of a popular line. But underneath the
recriminations lay wishful thinking on the part of those in Britain,
including Lansdowne, who had seen Germany as a counterweight
to Russia in the Far East and miscalculation on the part of those in
Germany who, with Holstein as their guide, assumed that Britain
would be reduced by force of circumstances to beg for even the
slightest of favours. Eckardstein's good intentions had contributed
materially to this decisive misunderstanding.

The failure of Anglo-German negotiations was a source of
relief and satisfaction to Delcassé, who had been reduced during
their progress to the role of an interested but impotent spectator.
Far less happy, from his point of view, was the conclusion of the
Anglo-Japanese Alliance. Although the terms did not commit
England to come to Japan's aid in a war against Russia unless
Russia were supported by France, tension between Russia and
England seemed bound to be heightened. However earnestly
Lansdowne tried to reassure Cambon that no more was intended
than a warning to Russia, that he had tried to reach agreement with
Russia and that he would continue to work towards that end,[3]
little comfort could be drawn from these reassurances. England
and Russia seemed set on a game of brinkmanship which at worst
threatened to involve France in war against England, and at best

[1] See J. Amery, *Life of Joseph Chamberlain*, vol. 4, pp. 172–3.

[2] See Edward VII to the Kaiser, 15 Jan 1902, quoted Sir Sidney Lee, *King Edward
VII*, vol. 2, p. 138. The Prince of Wales's visit was to attend the Kaiser's birthday
celebrations. After a last-minute appeal from the Kaiser, Edward VII, to Lansdowne's
relief, withdrew his objections and the Prince reached Berlin on 26 Jan.

[3] See Cambon to Delcassé, 12 Feb 1902, *DDF*, I, no. 81, pp. 88–91.

would put new difficulties in the way of Delcassé's Anglo-French *rapprochement* goal. On the other hand the existence of the alliance made that goal even more desirable. During the course of the Anglo-Japanese and Anglo-German negotiations, points at issue between England and France had been, at various times, under tentative discussion. The situation in Siam provided an opening. But it was above all Morocco which, by postulating a major issue between the two countries, eventually prepared the way for serious bargaining.

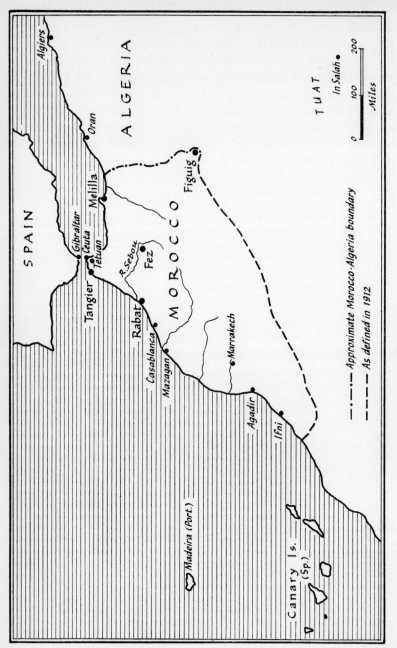

Morocco

7

Morocco

In 1873 Moulay Hassan (El Hassan), who was to reign until his death in 1894, became Sultan of Morocco. At his accession the Shereefian Empire was little more than a geographic expression.[1] By force of arms he succeeded in imposing his authority over substantial parts of the Empire. Others remained effectively beyond his control. While dealing with endemic domestic troubles Moulay Hassan was at first unhampered by foreign interference. Unlike Egypt, Morocco had long been isolated from European impact. In the *Larousse Atlas*, published at the turn of the nineteenth century, it was described, though no longer quite accurately, as 'a closed country, still full of mystery'. In fact at the time of Moulay Hassan's accession there were only three European nations possessing significant interests in Morocco and maintaining any serious contacts. Spain, clinging 'by her eyelids' to scattered remnants of her own Moorish Empire, still cherished the illusion of holding an option on the whole; of more practical importance was a modest coastal trade. Since the conquest of Algeria France had been involved in disputes, some of them military, concerning the southern boundary between Morocco and Algeria; apart from this point of occasionally acrimonious contact trading links with Marseilles were established on a small but solid scale. The bulk of Moroccan trade was carried in British ships and Britain's Morocco merchants were able to muster some kind of a lobby in Parliament. Otherwise Great Britain's sole concern was strategic. Control of the Strait of Gibraltar could be threatened if any other naval power were to be

[1] For a comprehensive study of the internal situation in Morocco and of her relations with the great Powers see J. L. Miège, *Le Maroc et l'Europe (1830–1894)*, vol. 4. The promised fifth volume of this massive work has not yet been published.

allowed to establish a base on the opposite Moorish coast. The
port of Tangier seemed naturally suitable for such a purpose.

While British fears on this score lay dormant, while Spanish
dreams of reconquest were obviously no more than dreams and
while France failed to press the border question, commercial
interests dominated relations between Morocco and the three
interested European powers.[1] In order to bolster his military
forces and in order to reform and modernise his empire Moulay
Hassan was eager for European aid. On the other hand he was
jealous of his independence and anxious to secure aid without
strings. He was, therefore, cautious about awarding concessions
and anxious to preserve the 'impenetrability' of his empire. On
the whole Europeans were confined to the ports and they were
virtually prohibited from owning property or setting up in business inland.

Although not without their own jealousies the European Powers
eventually combined to present a united front in obtaining
privileges for the protection and expansion of their trade. By the
Treaty of Madrid in 1880 Morocco's independence was guaranteed on the one hand, but special rights for foreign nationals were
secured on the other. These rights, including exemption from
taxation, could be extended to Moroccans under foreign 'protection'. This system inevitably led to abuse and proved, within a
relatively short period, one of the main barriers to effective fiscal
and administrative reforms.

The first serious threat to Moulay Hassan's independence came
with the appointment, in December 1881, of Ladislas Ordega[2] as
French Minister Plenipotentiary. The establishment of a French
Protectorate in Tunisia had inevitably served to arouse a greater
degree of interest in Morocco. Already in 1880 the French
Government was known to be considering plans for a Morocco–
Algerian railway. The small French colony in Morocco began to
press for a forward policy. Other foreign elements there began to
look towards France to take a lead in bringing pressure on Moulay
Hassan for an increase in their own privileges and for the promotion

[1] In the 1870s German trade links with Morocco began to develop alongside those
of England, France and Spain.
[2] A career diplomat of forceful and ambitious personality who had attracted
Gambetta's favourable notice. See J. L. Miège, *Le Maroc et l'Europe*, vol. 4, pp. 36, 37.

of local enterprises. Ordega at once proclaimed himself the champion of a forward policy. As a first step he sought to settle the boundary question in France's favour and clamoured, with Algerian support, for a French occupation of Figuig.[1] In order to bring pressure to bear on Moulay Hassan, he busily intrigued with the Sherif of Ouezzane,[2] who was one of the sultan's most formidable local opponents. Ouezzane, and his tribesmen were placed under French protection and, for a while, it seemed that unless Moulay Hassan was prepared to become a French puppet he might find himself replaced by Ouezzane. Thus menaced by Ordega, Moulay Hassan took refuge in prevarication, accompanied by appeals to the other Powers. Sir John Drummond Hay,[3] who on the whole enjoyed the support of growing German interests in Morocco, sympathised with some of Ordega's objectives but was not prepared to co-operate in bullying the Sultan to an extent which might lead to any dramatic crisis. The Italians, who hitherto had shown little interest in Morocco, were now smarting from what they regarded as the loss of Tunisia and were eager to block any French initiatives. Hence they too began to take an interest in Moroccan affairs. In these circumstances Moulay Hassan escaped Ordega's net. The attitude of the French Government towards Ordega had throughout been ambivalent and, as British, German and Italian complaints mounted, his policy was disavowed. In December 1884 he was withdrawn. French relations with the Sultan immediately improved; Ouezzane, deprived of French backing, made his own peace with Moulay Hassan. British influence, under Sir Drummond Hay's mild guidance, was in the ascendant. Moulay Hassan's plans, which depended on positive foreign aid for reform, collapsed. The difficulty was that he could not obtain aid from any one power without either sacrificing his independence, or promoting jealous reactions among the others. Though he manœuvred among the Powers with considerable dexterity his exertions enabled him merely to stand still.

[1] The Figuig oases might be described as Morocco's gateway to the Sahara. Control of Figuig was a long-standing objective of Algerian expansionists.

[2] Si Abdeslam, Sherif of Ouezzane. He was head of a powerful border tribe with followers on both sides of the Algeria–Morocco boundary. He had served as a useful instrument of French policy and he was proud to have been decorated with the Legion of Honour in 1876. See J. L. Miège, *Le Maroc et l'Europe*, vol. 4, note 3, p. 47.

[3] British Minister in Morocco until 1886.

After the failure of Ordega's bid for French supremacy Sir William Kirby Green,[1] who succeeded Sir Drummond Hay in 1886, began to press British interests with a renewed energy. Moulay Hassan, now on his guard against Great Britain, strove to obtain a revision of the treaties which were suffocating Morocco's struggling economy. Mutual suspicions between the Powers blocked the road. The Sultan, considering he had been let down by Great Britain, France and Spain, began to turn towards Germany for more disinterested support.

After 1889 France once again began to pursue a forward policy and, through Dr Linarès,[2] tried to regain the Sultan's confidence. In 1891 Sir Kirby Green died and was succeeded by Sir Charles Euan-Smith, a former Zanzibar imperialist. A period of sharp Anglo-French rivalry predictably ensued. It now seemed as if Great Britain was moving towards the establishment of a Protectorate. Moulay Hassan, always alert to immediate dangers, began to lean towards France. However with Gladstone's return to power in 1893, Smith was recalled and his forward policy was disavowed.

In 1894, frustrated in most of his endeavours and reduced to playing off one great Power against another, Moulay Hassan died. His son and heir, Abd-el-Aziz,[3] was a boy of sixteen. French influence, which had been in the ascendant at the time of Moulay Hassan's death, remained strong with the Grand Vizier, Bu Ahmed, who now sought to play the role of regent of the palace; his rivals proclaimed themselves 'reformers' and looked towards Great Britain to free them from French domination. As the power of the central government declined the extent of the areas under permanent revolt increased.

In October 1895 Sir Arthur Nicolson,[4] who had been appointed

---

[1] Sir William Kirby Green (1836–1891) had had long experience of service in Morocco as a Vice-Consul.

[2] Jean Léon François Ferdinand Linarès (1850–1938); appointed medical officer to the French military mission in Morocco in 1877, he was unofficially attached to the French legation in 1888 and remained in service there until 1901. See J. L. Miège, *Le Maroc et l'Europe*, vol. 4, note 6, p. 234.

[3] Sultan Abd-el-Aziz IV (1878–1943). He was forced to abdicate in 1908 after a successful rebellion led by his brother, Moulay Hafid.

[4] Sir Arthur Nicolson, subsequently Lord Carnock (1849–1928), Minister at Tangier 1895–1905; Ambassador at Madrid 1905–6 and at St Petersburg 1906–10; Permanent Under-Secretary 1910–16.

British Minister, arrived in Morocco. He came at a time when circumstances were most favourable for an extension of British influence; the leader of the reformers, the war minister Sid Menebhi Meheddi, was determined to seek British support. Kaid Maclean, who commanded the Moroccan forces and who had proved one of Moulay Hassan's most trusted servants, was in close touch with Menebhi and was a favourite with the young Sultan. Nicolson, however, was averse to playing power politics in Morocco.[1] He was prepared to use British influence for humanitarian purposes, for instance to secure prison reform, but not to make any take-over bids for Moroccan government. He despised the commercial greed of local British merchant adventurers and he was loth to cover their activities with his protection. He was well satisfied with his instructions which enjoined him to preserve the *status quo* and to avoid quarrels with France. He interpreted these instructions literally. There seems little doubt that a Cromer would have responded more actively to Moroccan appeals and would have become more closely identified with Moroccan government. A British Protectorate might then have gradually become a *fait accompli*.

But although Nicolson tried so hard to remain aloof he was unable to allay French suspicions. The role of Kaid Maclean and the fact that the young Sultan chose to surround himself with British servants convinced the French that Nicolson was playing a deep game. In fact Nicolson himself soon became convinced that reform from within was impossible and that intervention by some European power was eventually both desirable and inevitable. But he continued to wish to avoid that responsibility for England.

One of the results of Fashoda was the galvanisation of the African lobby[2] in the French Chamber of Deputies. Its press organ was the *Bulletin du Comité de l'Afrique française*[3] and this

---

[1] For Nicolson's career as Minister at Tangier see H. Nicolson, *Lord Carnock*, pp. 108–69.

[2] A small group of members of the *Comité de l'Afrique française*, led by Étienne, conceived the notion of securing compensation for French humiliation in Egypt by moving forward in Morocco. While joining in conventional anti-British attitudes they began privately to press on Delcassé their scheme for an Egypt–Morocco bargain. See C. M. Andrew, *Théophile Delcassé and the Making of the Entente Cordiale*, pp. 103–4.

[3] See p. 60 note 1.

E

periodical soon began to concentrate its attention on Morocco. The Government felt constrained to respond and in June 1899 plans were prepared for occupying Touat.[1] Negotiations on this vexed boundary question were therefore opened with the Sultan. French prestige in Morocco, now at a low ebb, was held to depend on the success of these negotiations. French pressure, however, met with irritating resistance from the Sultan for which British encouragement was blamed. In the light of this assumption and as French plans for unilateral action at Touat matured, Delcassé concluded that it would be wise to take a direct sounding of British reactions. Accordingly, on 15 May 1900 Cambon brought the matter up with Salisbury. He spoke of a British Press 'campaign' against France's military expedition in south-west Algeria and of the allegation that this constituted a threat to Morocco. 'Touat', he explained to Salisbury, 'had never been a part of the Moroccan Empire.' He expressed disquiet at 'the prospect of an appeal by the Sultan to other European Powers against France'.[2] Salisbury rejoined that Great Britain would not respond to such an appeal and Cambon concluded with satisfaction that 'the London Cabinet is very little preoccupied by what may happen between France and Morocco on the southern boundaries of that empire; only one point is of interest to them, that is Tangier...'.[3] Cambon's impressions were confirmed when, on 20 June 1900, Révoil,[4] reporting on British reactions to the Sultan's appeal over Touat, made it clear that Nicolson had given him no encouragement to resist the French.[5]

Delcassé's intention to follow a forward policy in Morocco, though still too tentative for the African lobby, was in the meanwhile pursued by secret Morocco–Tripoli agreements with Italy dated 14 and 16 December 1900 and officially transmitted by Barrère[6] to Delcassé on 10 January 1901.[7] Delcassé also initiated personal and highly secret discussions about Moroccan partition with León y Castillo,[8] the Spanish Ambassador; they were

[1] Touat was the most important of the Figuig oases. See p. 127 note 1.
[2] Cambon to Delcassé, 16 May 1900, *DDF* i, xvi, no. 143, p. 230.
[3] Cambon to Delcassé, 16 May 1900, ibid., p. 231.
[4] Paul Révoil, French Minister at Tangier.
[5] Révoil to Delcassé, 20 Jun 1900, *DDF* i, xvi, no. 189, pp. 285–6.
[6] French Ambassador at Rome; see p. 77.
[7] See *DDF* i, no. 17, pp. 20–3.
[8] León y Castillo, Marquis del Muni (1842–1918).

suspended in March 1901 as a result of a change of government in Spain.[1]

Cambon now sought to probe a little further in London. He hinted to Lansdowne that 'it might be desirable one of these days that we should arrive at an understanding as to certain boundaries which were still undecided'.[2] Lansdowne refused to be drawn. On 6 March 1901 Cambon, no doubt seeking to approach the question from another angle, reverted to an old Anglo-French bargaining formula and proposed that French rights in Newfoundland should be abandoned in exchange for Gambia.[3] Lansdowne rejected the proposal but took it sufficiently seriously to cast around for alternative territory to offer the French and thought that it might be found in the region of Sokoto. On 13 March 1901 Cambon reverted to Morocco and said that he assumed that British interests there were chiefly concerned with the coast.[4] Lansdowne, reporting this conversation to Chamberlain, described it as 'a proposal that we should be complaisant at the intended plundering of Morocco by the French'.[5] Chamberlain commented: 'If they and we are to discuss such a large question as Morocco please bear in mind that the Germans will have something to say – and both they and we will want compensation.'[6] At the same time he approved following up Cambon's Newfoundland hint and Lansdowne's tentative conclusion, stating that he had 'already thought of the Sokoto boundary as offering the possibility of a territorial compensation to France for the Treaty Shore'. Lansdowne, however, decided to let the matter drop for the moment.

In Morocco itself Nicolson was fighting a losing battle against Menebhi's[7] determination to lead a mission to London in search of urgent financial aid on the one hand and moral support against France on the other. He did, however, succeed in convincing the

[1] See C. M. Andrew, *Théophile Delcassé and the Making of the Entente Cordiale*, pp. 149–51.

[2] Lansdowne to Monson, despatch no. 16, 15 Jan 1901, F.O. 27/3531, quoted G. Monger, *The End of Isolation*, p. 38.

[3] See Monger, p. 39.

[4] Ibid., p. 38.

[5] Lansdowne to Chamberlain, 16 Mar 1901, Chamberlain MSS. Box JC11/4 quoted G. Monger, *The End of Isolation*, p. 39.

[6] Chamberlain to Lansdowne, 17 Mar 1901, quoted J. Amery, *Joseph Chamberlain*, vol. 4, p. 163.

[7] See p. 129. Since the death of Bu Ahmed in May 1900 Menebhi's influence with the young Sultan was in the ascendant.

Sultan that it would be politic also to send a mission to Paris. Révoil, who reported this with some satisfaction on 27 April 1901,[1] does not seem to have realised that the result was due to Nicolson's intervention. On the contrary he remained highly suspicious of British activity in Morocco. Cambon tried to reassure Delcassé, insisting on 11 June 1901 that there was no need to be too suspicious of Menebhi's mission to London.[2] 'The British', he argued, 'are watching us in Morocco, but they are at least as suspicious of the Germans. . . .'[3] In his opinion the British had no sinister designs of their own but they were obviously interested in Tangier. Although Cambon's conclusions were correct he found it difficult to maintain his own confidence when the mission arrived in England. A conversation with Lansdowne on 27 June 1901 left him somewhat uneasy.[4] The fact that Kaid Maclean, who accompanied the mission, was awarded a C.M.G. suggested that he was in high favour and this Cambon considered alarming. On 3 July Lansdowne tried to reassure him by insisting that Great Britain had gained no special advantages from the mission's visit but only promises which would benefit all European powers.[5] He added that the Sultan's representative had spoken of Moroccan fears of France and that he had advised him to avoid offending France by keeping a firm hand on their own border tribes. Cambon, in his turn, reassured Lansdowne about French designs. This reassurance was given point by Delcassé's declaration in the Senate in favour of the *status quo* in Morocco. On 10 July Lansdowne expressed his satisfaction to Cambon, who reported that Great Britain did not appear to wish to become further involved in Morocco.[6] Delcassé may have been further encouraged by a letter from Leriche, his Vice-Consul at Rabat, who reported that there were indications that Great Britain was moving towards acceptance of French predominance as inevitable and that the moment was opportune for pressing French claims.[7]

At all events, though wary of precipitating a crisis and anxious

[1] See Révoil to Delcassé, 27 Apr 1901, *DDF* i, no. 210, pp. 251–2.
[2] See Cambon to Delcassé, 11 Jun 1901, *DDF* i, no. 278, pp. 322–3.
[3] Cambon to Delcassé, 11 Jun 1901, ibid., p. 323.
[4] See Cambon to Delcassé, 28 Jun 1901, *DDF* i, no. 305, pp. 354, 355.
[5] See Cambon to Delcassé, 4 Jul 1901, *DDF* i, no. 315, pp. 374, 375.
[6] See Cambon to Delcassé, 10 Jul 1901, *DDF* i, no. 323, pp. 382, 383.
[7] See Leriche to Delcassé, 12 Jul 1901, *DDF* i, no. 324, pp. 383–6.

to pave the way gradually, Delcassé was by now set on a forward policy in Morocco. Saint-René Taillandier[1] had been designated to replace Révoil[2] and by this appointment Delcassé's intentions could hardly have been more heavily underlined. In his instructions to Taillandier, Delcassé urged him to increase French influence in Morocco, to be polite to the Spanish and generally to walk warily.[3] The approach to the prize must be cautious; but clearly the prize was to be won.

In London, setting Moroccan discussions aside, Cambon again mooted a Newfoundland bargain in a memorandum of 24 July 1901.[4] 'I do not see', Lansdowne wrote to Chamberlain on the same date, 'why a settlement should be unattainable – I wish they would ask us for a bit of hinterland somewhere or other.'[5] Accordingly, on 31 July 1901 Lansdowne, after reiterating to Cambon that Gambia could not be abandoned, hinted that alternatives might be found.[6] This attempt to leave the door open for further discussions did not meet with any positive French response.

Delcassé's resolve to press forward in Morocco was encouraged by the Paris visit of the Ben Sliman mission. Not only was agreement virtually reached on the boundary question but Ben Sliman seemed to have a healthy respect for the warning that, among European powers, France must be recognised as having a predominant interest in Morocco. No doubt largely as a result of representations from Ben Sliman, Menebhi was placed under arrest after his return to Morocco. Although in deference to British and German representations he was subsequently released, his authority was weakened and French influence appeared to be gaining ground.

The pace, however, was too slow for Saint-René Taillandier, and he found it far more difficult to establish his own paramount influence with the Sultan than had been anticipated immediately

---

[1] Georges Saint-René Taillandier, French Minister at Tangier 1901–6; he was known as an advocate of a forward policy. For his own account of his mission see G. Saint-René Taillandier, *Les Origines du Maroc français* (Paris, 1930).

[2] He was appointed Governor of Algeria.

[3] See Delcassé to Saint-René Taillandier, 27 Jul 1901, *DDF* i, no. 337, pp. 402–7.

[4] See G. Monger, *The End of Isolation*, p. 44.

[5] Lansdowne to Chamberlain, 24 Jul 1901, Chamberlain MSS. Box JC. 11/4, quoted ibid., p. 44.

[6] Ibid., p. 44.

following Ben Sliman's mission. On 11 January 1902 he reported that it was essential to combat British influence on the spot.[1] France, he maintained, must take the lead in promoting Moroccan reforms. Delcassé entirely concurred and on 17 January 1902 instructed Cambon to try to warn England against interference in Moroccan internal affairs.[2] Saint-René Taillandier further urged that Cambon should seek to pave the way in London for a French forward policy in Morocco.[3] Accordingly on 22 January 1902 Cambon saw Lansdowne and advised him that any special concessions for Great Britain in Morocco would be resented.[4] He insisted that France remained a champion of the *status quo* and he referred to persistent rumours of British Railway and Telegraph projects. Lansdowne replied that the rumours were exaggerated. He also deprecated French fears of excessive British influence, particularly where the role of Kaid Maclean was concerned, describing him as an old Scotsman employed to instruct Moroccan soldiers. He then referred to persistent rumours of French ambitions in Morocco but explained that, with Delcassé's assurances in mind, he refused to take any notice of these. From their conversation Cambon concluded that reports of British concession-hunting had been exaggerated but that some projects had certainly been under discussion.

After this endeavour to warn off Lansdowne, Saint-René Taillandier began to bring heavy pressure on the Sultan. On 12 February 1902 he reported to Delcassé that he had clearly warned the Sultan against taking advice from 'foreign' sources.[5] Delcassé rejoined by instructing Saint-René Taillandier that the Sultan must be made to understand that if he had recourse to any aid it must be French.[6] Though Saint-René Taillandier acted on this instruction he did not feel confident that his warnings were having the desired effect. He remained suspicious of British influences on the spot in spite of reassurances received in London.[7]

---

[1] See Saint-René Taillandier to Delcassé, 11 Jan 1902, *DDF*, II, no. 24, p. 25.
[2] See Delcassé to Cambon, 17 Jan 1902, *DDF*, II, no. 36, pp. 37, 38.
[3] See Saint-René Taillandier to Delcassé, 17 Jan 1902, *DDF*, II, no. 38, pp. 38, 39.
[4] See Cambon to Delcassé, 22 Jan 1902, *DDF*, II, no. 49, pp. 51–3.
[5] See Saint-René Taillandier to Delcassé, 12 Feb 1902, *DDF*, II, no. 83, pp. 92–5.
[6] See Delcassé to Saint-René Taillandier, 25 Feb 1902, *DDF*, II, no. 102, pp. 118, 119.
[7] See Saint-René Taillandier to Delcassé, 5 Mar 1902, *DDF*, II, no. 121, pp. 141–3.

In fact Lansdowne was genuinely anxious to avoid offending France by appearing as the Sultan's protector. This anxiety was fully shared by Nicolson, who carried out his instructions to the letter by repeatedly warning the Sultan against putting trust in England to help him resist the French, and by urging Kaid Maclean to try to 'limit the number of Englishmen employed at Court'.[1] While the *status quo* remained a favourite formula for Morocco, Lansdowne had no wish to combat the gradual extension of French influence. Indeed, as a prelude to improved Anglo-French relations, he was even disposed to encourage it. In this he was backed by Chamberlain. Although Eckardstein is not always a reliable witness it seems probable that he was correct when he claimed to have overheard Chamberlain and Cambon speaking confidentially about Morocco on 8 February 1902.[2] Soon afterwards Chamberlain submitted a memorandum to Lansdowne outlining the possibility of negotiating an agreement with France on Newfoundland, West Africa, the New Hebrides and Siam and suggesting that the general settlement might be facilitated by an understanding over Morocco.[3] In his reply, on 11 March 1902, Lansdowne spoke of 'the value of what we have to sell and its immense importance to the French'.[4] Talking to Cambon about the possibility of a Newfoundland–West African bargain, Lansdowne indicated that he had 'never excluded the idea of reasonable "give-and-take" arrangements in regard to their possessions in different parts of the world'.[5] Although there was no mention of Morocco the notion of bargaining on a wide scale was clearly present.

Delcassé, however, had some reasons in the early part of the year for deferring discussion about Morocco. On the one hand he wanted to give Saint-René Taillandier time to establish his own position there and on the other he wished to complete diplomatic negotiations projected with Italy and with Spain. The negotiations with Italy ended successfully on 30 June 1902 with an exchange

---

[1] See H. Nicolson, *Lord Carnock*, p. 145.

[2] At a banquet at Marlborough House. See Baron Eckardstein, *Ten Years at the Court of St. James*, p. 228.

[3] See J. Amery, *The Life of Joseph Chamberlain*, vol. 4, p. 181.

[4] Quoted ibid.

[5] Lansdowne to Monson, despatch no. 90, 30 Apr 1902, F.O. Print (West Africa), vol. 7996, no. 18, quoted G. Monger, *The End of Isolation*, p. 73.

of letters which constituted a formal agreement.[1] Negotiations with
Spain were not seriously resumed until August.[2]

It was perhaps the Italian agreement which influenced Delcassé
in favour of raising the Moroccan question with the British. But
he may also have been influenced by agitation on the part of the
Comité de l'Afrique française where accusations of weakness were
accompanied by renewed hints that a compromise with England
should be attempted. At any rate his decision to approach England
was implicit in a French Foreign Office Note on the Morocco
question dated 15 July 1902.[3] The Note stated that, although the
status quo for Morocco suited France, she must be prepared to
meet all contingencies. The agreements reached with Italy might
tempt the Italians to move into Tripoli. The Sultan might be led
to make unacceptable concessions to other powers. Spain, having
lost Cuba and the Philippines, was concentrating her ambitions
on Morocco.

Existing plans for an arrangement with Spain included (i) an
entente to preserve the *status quo*; (ii) agreement on zones of influence if the *status quo* were disturbed; (iii) a programme for
concerted diplomatic action after the agreement was reached.
British goodwill, which might be secured by promising neutralisation of Tangier, was essential and an approach to Great Britain
was therefore envisaged. Provided preparations to meet the possibility of a liquidation of Morocco had been completed, there would
be no danger in retarding such an event. Complete commercial
liberty could be promised to all Powers. This might not satisfy
Germany who would need to be compensated elsewhere in
Africa.

Action, apparently on Cambon's initiative, soon followed this
French Foreign Office appraisal. On 23 July 1902, at a meeting
with Lansdowne, he introduced the subject of Morocco by referring to the hostile attitude of Moroccan tribes on the Algerian

---

[1] See Barrère to Delcassé, 30 Jun 1902, *DDF*, II, no. 313, p. 375, and for texts of
letters 10 Jul 1902, *DDF*, II, no. 329, pp. 390–5.

[2] See C. M. Andrew, *Théophile Delcassé and the Making of the Entente Cordiale.*

[3] See *DDF*, II, no. 333, pp. 397–400. It is probably true as Dr Andrew argues
(C. M. Andrew, *Théophile Delcassé and the Making of the Entente Cordiale*) that Delcassé
wished to face Britain with a *fait accompli* over Morocco once he had concluded
agreements with Italy and with Spain. But this Note did give Cambon official justification for further probing of the ground in London.

border.[1] He complained of the unsatisfactory attitude of the Sultan and he suggested that this was due to British advisers who, unknown to the British Government, were pursuing a policy 'quite contrary to the spirit of *status quo*'. He spoke, once again, of the sinister role of Kaid Maclean. Lansdowne insisted that Maclean was simply an employee of the Sultan and that he was in no way a representative of Great Britain. Cambon replied 'that he was making no complaint, that he was noting a fact and that, since agreement in principle existed, namely maintenance of the *status quo* and the danger of raising the Moroccan question, it was necessary to have a frank explanation and to safeguard against any misunderstanding or incident'.[2] He added that although he had no precise knowledge of Delcassé's intentions he did know that he wished to discuss the matter and reach agreement with England. As far as he was aware England's only political interest in Morocco was Tangier. Europe would never allow England to control Tangier and England would never allow any other Power to do so. He emphasised the importance of an exchange of views on these questions and suggested that Siam might also be usefully discussed.[3] While Cambon promised to obtain Delcassé's permission 'to mention these subjects ... officially', Lansdowne declared himself 'perfectly ready to discuss them ... in the frankest possible manner'.[4]

Accordingly, after Cambon had verbally consulted Delcassé and Lansdowne had explained the situation to Balfour,[5] discussion was resumed on 6 August.[6] Referring first to Siam, Cambon indicated that French difficulties could probably be solved by direct negotiations with the Siamese Government. It was however important that the central zone of Siam, which had been excluded from the 1896 agreement over British and French zones of influence, should not become a 'closed field' where British and French agents

---

[1] For Cambon's account see Cambon to Delcassé, 9 Aug 1902, *DDF*, ii, no. 369, pp. 439, 440, and for Lansdowne's version see Lansdowne to Monson, 23 Jul 1902, *BD* ii, no. 321, pp. 263, 264.

[2] Cambon to Delcassé, 9 Aug 1902, *DDF*, ii, no. 369, p. 434.

[3] See Cambon to Delcassé, 9 Aug 1902, ibid., p. 440.

[4] Lansdowne to Monson, 23 Jul 1903, *DDF*, ii, no. 321, p. 264.

[5] He had succeeded Salisbury as Prime Minister on 12 Jul 1902.

[6] For Cambon's account see Cambon to Delcassé, 9 Aug 1902, *DDF*, ii, no. 369, pp. 440-3 and for Lansdowne's version see Lansdowne to Monson, 6 Aug 1902, *BD* ii, no. 322, pp. 264-6.

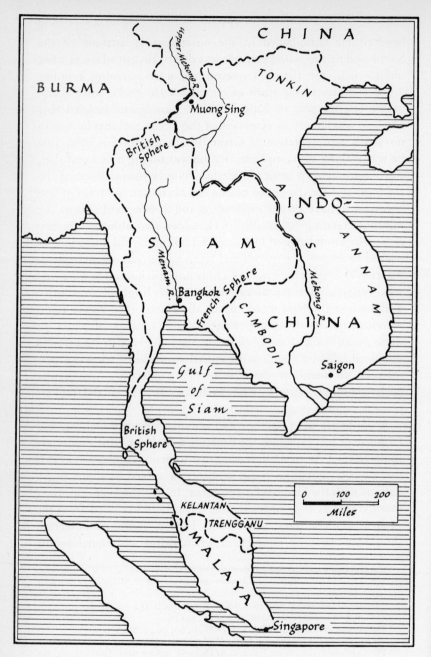

Siam

might clash and where, thanks to their misunderstandings, Germany might insinuate herself to mutual disadvantage. This danger could best be safeguarded by an extension of the 1896 Agreement. According to Cambon, Lansdowne seemed to favour this proposal and showed suitable interest by raising questions of detail.[1] On Morocco, after reiterating Delcassé's desire to preserve the *status quo*, Cambon stressed the importance of French interests. 'They are', he explained, 'of all kinds: they are economic and political. Morocco is, as it were, a prolongation of Algeria; it is the open door onto our African empire; we can at no price allow any authority to be established there which might escape our influence.'[2] British interests, he went on to argue, were, save for Tangier, purely economic. Neutralisation of Tangier and an area surrounding it should, in Delcassé's opinion, offer a satisfactory guarantee for England's political interest. 'As for her economic interests,' Cambon continued, 'M. Delcassé considers that, if in the future a solution of the Moroccan question was imposed and if France was led to establish her power or her effective influence there, it would be possible to allow England, for a period of time to be determined, full commercial liberty. Thus, all England's interests in Morocco would be safeguarded and she would have no cause for anxiety at the legitimate expansion of French influence.'[3] Then Cambon turned to Spain and, after recognising Spanish interests, he stated that Delcassé believed that 'it would be right to reserve for Spain a certain zone for expansion around her *présides* and to provide them with a hinterland adequate to meet the hypothetical case of a general liquidation of Morocco'.[4]

The word 'liquidation', which was to stick disturbingly in Lansdowne's mind, had thus been pronounced. It had, of course, been implicit throughout. According to Lansdowne's own account to Monson he took the opportunity to warn Cambon that 'any attempt to deal prematurely with the liquidation of Morocco would ... be sure to lead to serious complications'.[5] To soften the impression Cambon went on to explain that 'M. Delcassé hopes that this hypothesis will not for long be realised;

[1] See Cambon to Delcassé, 9 Aug 1902, *DDF*, II, no. 369, p. 442.
[2] Cambon to Delcassé, 9 Aug 1902, ibid., p. 441.
[3] Cambon to Delcassé, 9 Aug 1902, ibid., p. 442.
[4] Cambon to Delcassé, 9 Aug 1902, ibid.
[5] Lansdowne to Monson, 6 Aug 1902, *BD* II, no. 322, p. 266.

he wishes, for many generations, the maintenance of the *status quo*
and he will work to maintain it; but he considers that the best way
of preserving it is by frank exchange of views regarding the future
and by cutting short rivalries which might precipitate action.'[1]
Cambon reported to Delcassé that Lansdowne had listened with
close attention and had asked for his warm thanks to be conveyed
for a communication which he regarded as of 'extreme importance'. He had promised to speak of the matter at once to Balfour
but regretted that he would have no opportunity to consult the
Cabinet until 15 October, after the summer recess. This reaction
fully satisfied Cambon, who explained to Delcassé that he had not
pressed for any earlier resumption of discussions knowing that
he wished, in the meanwhile, to conclude his own negotiations
with the Spanish Government.[2] Cambon took it as encouraging
that Lansdowne should have reverted to the topic by insisting
that, in the event of neutralisation of Tangier, a zone around the
town must definitely be included, and by raising questions concerning the hinterland to be reserved for Spain. Further evidence
of Lansdowne's more general interest in pursuing conversations
was afforded when he proposed that the subject of Newfoundland
should also be included. To this Cambon replied that France,
as he had previously indicated, could not abandon her 'pretention
to territorial compensation' and was still awaiting a reply on this
point. 'I told you', Lansdowne rejoined, 'that we could not give
you Gambia; but that if you would be good enough to look about,
and ask for something else, we might see.'[3]

There seems little doubt that, although Lansdowne was alarmed
at any notion of precipitate liquidation in Morocco, he was
equally anxious to avoid offending French susceptibilities there.
Possibilities of settling the vexed Newfoundland question in
Britain's favour, of a mutually beneficial bargain over Siam and of
a guarantee for Tangier neutralisation were attractive. In these
circumstances Lansdowne, while careful to go slow over Moroccan
discussions, was certainly not disposed to rule them out of court
for the future.

---

[1] Cambon to Delcassé, 9 Aug 1902, *DDF*, 11, no. 369, p. 442. There is no mention
of this reassurance in Lansdowne's version of the conversation. Possibly Cambon was
not as explicit to Lansdowne as he claimed to have been in his report to Delcassé.
[2] See Cambon to Delcassé, 9 Aug 1902, ibid.
[3] Cambon to Delcassé, 9 Aug 1902, ibid., p. 443.

In the meanwhile, pending cabinet consideration, Lansdowne sought the opinion of the Service Departments. The Board of Admiralty was opposed to the acquisition of any territory by France on the seacoast of Morocco from Mazagan northwards and considered the neutralisation of Tangier a necessity in the event of any substantial absorption of Moroccan territory by France.[1] A memorandum from the Military Intelligence division of 9 September 1902 maintained that British interests could best be secured by preserving the *status quo*; if this proved impossible 'it will then be for England and Germany to decide whether they shall stake out claims before it is too late'.[2] The suggestion was added that, in the event of partition, France could take the east of the country, Britain the coastline from Tangier to Casablanca, and Germany the coast south of Casablanca. These views, calculated to increase Lansdowne's cautious proclivities, were nevertheless indicative of readiness to take the possibility of radical solutions seriously.

In Paris Delcassé was well satisfied with Cambon's report of Lansdowne's reactions. On 11 September 1902 he advised Saint-René Taillandier to proceed with patience and discretion in Morocco.[3] His own negotiations with Spain, he wrote, were almost complete.[4] Then he proposed to continue discussions with England, who seemed to have shown willingness to do so. For the present, therefore, it was essential to avoid a premature crisis.

Although Delcassé and Lansdowne desired, for different reasons, to proceed cautiously, their calculations were equally upset by the anxious activity of *The Times* Tangier correspondent, Walter B. Harris. On a visit to England during the summer he got wind of the Cambon–Lansdowne conversations and also of the interest in Morocco which was being taken by the Service Departments. He concluded that a bargain, favourable to French ambitions, had been struck.[5] Under this impression he hurried

---

[1] See G. Monger, *The End of Isolation*, p. 79.

[2] Memorandum by Forestier-Walker, 9 Sep 1902, F.O. 99/400, quoted ibid.

[3] See Delcassé to Saint-René Taillandier, 11 Sep 1902, *DDF*, 11, no. 394, pp. 473, 474.

[4] In fact Delcassé was somewhat prodigal in the concessions which he was prepared to make to Spain (particularly over possession of Fez). But Spanish dilatoriness and anxieties about possible British reactions prevented any formal conclusion Cambon was retrospectively jubilant that Delcassé had been saved, in spite of himself, from an unneccessary trap.

[5] See J. J. Mathews, *Egypt and the Formation of the Anglo-French Entente*, pp. 36, 37.

back to Morocco conveying alarmist reports to the Sultan and
confiding his fears to the German consular agent at Fez.[1] A flurry
of diplomatic agitation followed. Madrid pressed Paris for information. Dumba, the Austrian chargé d'affaires in Paris, acting on
inspiration from Berlin, warned Monson of Germany's interest
in Morocco and of the serious consequences of an Anglo-French
deal.[2] Kaid Maclean was dispatched to London, ostensibly to visit
his oculist, but in fact to endeavour to secure from Great Britain a
specific guarantee of Moroccan integrity against France.[3] Although
the Foreign Office might find Maclean a 'phenomenal bore'[4] and
although Lansdowne poured cold water on the notion of any
specific guarantee, the atmosphere, as far as further Anglo-French
talks on Morocco were concerned, had been seriously clouded.[5]

On 23 October Lansdowne informed Cambon that he had, as
agreed, reported their conversation of 6 August to his colleagues.
'But', he added, 'the Government is exclusively occupied at the
moment with the Education Bill, and there is no means of drawing
its attention to other matters; we must therefore resume our
discussions later.'[6] 'This preamble', Cambon commented to
Delcassé, 'did not seem to augur well.' He assumed that Lansdowne's altered attitude was due to the presence of Kaid Maclean
in London and he tackled Lansdowne on this point. Lansdowne
tried to play down the importance of Maclean's visit and said that
he was merely seeking a loan on the Sultan's behalf. He had been
advised that the Sultan should apply to France and to Germany
as well and that England would not consider unilateral aid with
all the responsibilities implied. Though somewhat reassured
Cambon could do no more than express willingness to return to
the subject of Morocco whenever Lansdowne wished to do so.[7]

While Moroccan discussions were thus suspended progress
towards agreement on Siam was proceeding satisfactorily. News
of the signing of a French treaty with Siam had provoked some

---

[1] See *Die Grosse Politik der europäischen Kabinette*, XVII, p. 344.

[2] See Monson to Lansdowne, 3 Oct 1902, *BD* II, no. 324, pp. 267, 268.

[3] See H. Nicolson, *Lord Carnock*, p. 148.

[4] Sanderson used the term in a private letter to Nicolson. See H. Nicolson, *Lord Carnock*, p. 147.

[5] For Cambon's suspicious reactions to Maclean's visit see Cambon to Delcassé, 4 Oct 1902, *DDF*, II, no. 421, pp. 514, 515.

[6] Cambon to Delcassé, 23 Oct 1902, *DDF*, II, no. 456, p. 559.

[7] See Cambon to Delcassé, 23 Oct 1902, ibid., p. 561.

hostile comment in the British Press. But Lansdowne, prompted by Chamberlain, had been proceeding with secret and parallel negotiations with Siam and he was prepared, in the light of his own previous discussions with Cambon, to welcome this development.[1] The proposed Siamese partnership seemed likely to pay good dividends. It suggested a model which, when circumstances permitted, might be followed elsewhere.

Immediately, however, Lansdowne was faced with a set of international problems which, while they encouraged avoidance of friction with France on the one hand, left him little leisure or relish to negotiate about Morocco on the other. Selborne, First Lord of the Admiralty, had on 17 October 1902 and for the first time in a cabinet memorandum, officially endorsed the growing naval opinion that the German Navy was 'being carefully built up from the point of view of a war with us'.[2] Although Lansdowne remained sceptical on this score, the mere existence of a powerful German Navy demanded a review of all previous strategic assumptions. Germany's hostile attitude to British Yangtze interests, which came to a head in October 1902, seemed to indicate a forewarning of future friction. With even the suspicion of such difficulties lying ahead, traditional fears of the Russian threat to the Indian Empire took on a new edge. The Committee of Imperial Defence, reorganised under the chairmanship of the Prime Minister, undertook a comprehensive reappraisal of the whole question of Indian security.[3] Fed by alarmist reports and commensurate military demands from India, the Committee concluded that any serious Russian challenge would be difficult to meet. Endeavours to strengthen British influence in Afghanistan and in Persia only served to underline local Russian advantages. As an alternative to vastly increased military and naval expenditure some sort of agreement with Russia on a bargaining basis seemed, as it often had done in the past, attractive. This line of thought was

[1] See Lansdowne to Monson, 22 Oct 1902, *BD* II, no. 327, pp. 271, 272. Further progress, however, Lansdowne explained, must depend on French ratification of the newly signed Treaty.

[2] Memorandum by Selborne, Naval Estimates 1903–4, 17 Oct 1902, Chamberlain MSS. Box JC 14/4, quoted G. Monger, *The End of Isolation*, p. 82. See also A. J. Marder, *British Naval Policy 1880–1905*, p. 464, where Selborne's words to the writer are quoted to the effect that in 1902 the Admiralty 'first became convinced that the German Navy was being built with a view to a naval war with England'.

[3] See G. Monger, *The End of Isolation*, pp. 95–9.

stimulated when, with trouble brewing in Macedonia, it became evident that Austria–Hungary was more anxious to avoid offending Russia than disposed to co-operate with Britain in protesting to Turkey against the recent passage of Russian warships through the Straits.[1] The conclusion tentatively reached by Salisbury in 1898 was now unequivocally drawn that, whatever the Russian provocation, British naval intervention via the Straits would not be contemplated. There remained the possibility that recognition of this fact might stimulate an improvement in Anglo-Russian relations and that Russian forbearance in Afghanistan and in Persia might be obtained by placatory rather than menacing attitudes. In any such approach to Russia, France, if well-disposed, could be useful. The notion of *rapprochement* with France as a road to better relations with Russia appealed to those members of the Cabinet who, like the Duke of Devonshire, had little relish for any bargaining with France on its own merits. Lansdowne, who deplored the deterioration of Anglo-German relations and looked forward to halting that trend, was certainly not the protagonist of any major diplomatic revolution. He did however recognise the advantage of coming to some kind of terms with Russia and he was in any case both committed and inclined to seek settlements, wherever possible, of Anglo-French colonial differences.

Although Lansdowne deprecated signs of Anglo-German misunderstanding there could be no doubt about the anti-German bias of the British Press. Writing to Delcassé on 11 November 1902 about the Kaiser's forthcoming visit to England, Cambon commented smugly that 'the English Press of all shades of opinion has expressed itself vigorously against any project of *Entente* with Germany' and added, as a specific example, an article in the *National Review* of 1 November underlining Anglo-German differences.[2] The pages of *Punch* were by now regularly padded with quips and cartoons of the Kaiser. Even if the Cabinet was slow to recognise any German naval menace, the Navy League, operating via the popular Press, openly denounced the enemy. Anti-German bias in England was becoming a factor which Cambon at any rate began to consider worthy of serious note in diplomatic calculation.

[1] See G. Monger, *The End of Isolation*, pp. 84–7.
[2] See Cambon to Delcassé, 11 Nov 1902, *DDF*, ii, no. 480, pp. 600–2.

While Cambon brooded, not without satisfaction, on symptoms of Anglo-German malaise the situation in Morocco itself was manifestly deteriorating. The young Sultan, partly as a result of his own incompetence and extravagance and partly because of the lethal effects of European rivalries, was losing the remnants of precarious authority which his father had bequeathed him. Serious troubles at Tetuan resulted in the dispatch of a British naval force to protect European lives and property. When Lansdowne and Cambon discussed the incident Lansdowne explained that the decision to send a naval force had been taken, as a matter of emergency, by the Governor of Gibraltar.[1] Cambon then spoke of rumours of the proclamation of a new Sultan, known as the 'donkey man', at Taza and of the Sultan's vulnerability in the face of this new threat. Lansdowne refrained from pointing out that there were suspicions in England that the Pretender's cause was being promoted by French agents. There was in fact no foundation for these suspicions because, as Saint-René Taillandier later reported to Delcassé, the present Sultan, for all his faults, was likely to prove a better instrument for French policy than the fanatical leader of a presumably popular rebellion.[2] But the threatened position of the Sultan and reports of general disorder combined with Britain's naval action resulted, not surprisingly, in the dispatch of a French naval force from Toulon to Tangier. It almost seemed as if Morocco was breaking up before the completion of Delcassé's projects for liquidation. Although internal disorders provided a justification for his long-term policy they could also be embarrassing in the short run.

His negotiations with Spain had finally resulted, on 8 November 1902, in the conclusion of a draft agreement.[3] Doubts about that agreement were however being expressed by Castillo, who now began to urge the need to obtain British approval and also complained of unfairness to Spain. On 3 December 1902 the Sagasta[4] Cabinet fell and Silvela,[5] believed to be the firmest protagonist

[1] See Cambon to Delcassé, 21 Nov 1902, *DDF*, ii, no. 500, pp. 624–6.

[2] See Saint-René Taillandier to Delcassé, 27 Dec 1902, *DDF*, ii, p. 678 note (i).

[3] See *DDF*, ii, no. 473, pp. 583–6.

[4] Práxedes Mateo Sagasta (1829–1903), veteran Spanish statesman and Leader of the Liberal Party.

[5] Augustino Francisco Silvela (1843–1905), Leader of the Conservative Party; while in opposition he had been conducting a propaganda campaign in favour of making a Moroccan agreement with France.

of agreement with France, succeeded him as Prime Minister. But surprisingly, Silvela refused to sign the draft agreement. This may have been due to the influence of his anglophile Foreign Minister Abarzuza.[1] At any rate the negotiations which had seemed complete in early November were now suspended. Delcassé was thus provided with a pretext for evading the generous concessions which had in fact been made to Spain. But, at the time, he could not see the event in that favourable light. On the contrary he still regarded agreement with Spain as a top priority and was dubious of the wisdom of pursuing negotiations with England until he held such an agreement in his pocket. Now, as the internal situation in Morocco worsened, he must either wait for the Spaniards to change their minds or, against his better judgement, tackle England in the absence of any prior compact with Spain. Pressed as he was by the Spaniards to seek British approval and anxious to avoid yet further delays, he moved rather reluctantly towards the second alternative.

On 17 December 1902 Cambon was given an opportunity to return to the subject when Lansdowne inquired what news he had of Morocco.[2] Cambon at once replied that the situation was dangerous and that Anglo-French agreement was urgently necessary. Lansdowne made no response. Cambon continued by arguing that although no treaty could be made it was surely possible to agree informally on maintenance of the *status quo* and on the steps which should be taken if the *status quo* was threatened. Lansdowne insisted that talks could only be informal and pointed out that neither he nor Delcassé might be foreign ministers when the crisis came. All the more reason, argued Cambon, to talk now. To Delcassé Cambon confided that 'Lord Lansdowne seemed anxious to enter into my views and at the same time held back by the fear of engaging himself too far. He was less open than in our talks of last August.'[3]

This moderately encouraging report of Lansdowne's reactions no doubt helped to diminish Delcassé's lingering doubts about approaching England. For that approach to be successful it was necessary to convince Lansdowne that France had no wish to

---

[1] Buenaventura Abarzuza y Ferrer (1841–1910), Foreign Minister 1902–3.
[2] See Cambon to Delcassé, 17 Dec 1902, *DDF*, II, no. 529, pp. 660–2.
[3] Cambon to Delcassé, 17 Dec 1902, ibid., p. 661.

precipitate a Moroccan crisis. A solution of the Sultan's immediate difficulties without French intervention was therefore to be desired. Although the rebels had gained recent successes against the Sultan, Delcassé remained opposed to intervention and, while endorsing Saint-René Taillandier's opinion that the Sultan's total defeat would be a blow to France, he refused to allow his minister to provide active aid.[1] He wrote to Cambon on 29 December 1902 explaining that French forces were ready at Toulon to intervene, if necessary, to preserve the *status quo*.[2] Lansdowne must be informed that France had no other designs than to end the present troubles. He further authorised Cambon to inform Lansdowne about his earlier conversations with Spain and reiterated the need to emphasise that the *status quo* represent French policy.

Accordingly, on 31 December 1902 Cambon spoke in these terms to Lansdowne, who readily agreed that the preservation of the *status quo* was a mutually desirable objective.[3] 'Once the present storm has passed', Cambon added, 'it would be useful to talk seriously about Morocco.' Reassured about the immediate present, Lansdowne was prepared to be more forthcoming about the future. He spoke of the interests of other powers. To his repeated enquiry about Italy Cambon insisted that he was quite certain that Italy had no interest in Morocco. Referring to Germany Cambon argued that England and France must have a prepared policy or else 'the Kaiser will pose as a champion of humanity'. 'That is also my feeling,' replied Lansdowne, and added: 'it is desirable that we should remain alone there; the less numerous we are the easier the business will be.'[4] He further remarked that Germany's possible interference was yet another reason why the *status quo* remained the best formula. The conversation ended with Lansdowne's promise to think over the whole question and discuss it with Balfour. In his report of this conversation to Monson, Lansdowne commented on the contrast between Cambon's present observations with those he had made in August. 'At that time', Lansdowne pointed out,

[1] See Delcassé to Saint-René Taillandier, 29 Dec 1902, *DDF*, II, no. 545, p. 678.

[2] See Delcassé to Cambon, 29 Dec 1902, *DDF*, II, no. 548, pp. 682, 683.

[3] For Cambon's account of this conversation see Cambon to Delcassé, 31 Dec 1902, *DDF*, II, no. 552, pp. 686–9 and for Lansdowne's see Lansdowne to Monson, 31 Dec 1902, *BD* II, no. 330, pp. 274, 275.

[4] Cambon to Delcassé, 31 Dec 1902, *DDF*, II, no. 552, p. 688.

the French Government seemed to contemplate with equanimity, if not with satisfaction, a 'liquidation' of Morocco, under which that country would be if not partitioned, at any rate divided into spheres of influence under the control of France, England and Spain. Today he made no reference to any such possibilities, and represented the French Government as the leading advocate of non-intervention and of the maintenance of the *status quo*.[1]

Monson interpreted this supposed change of attitude as confirmation of his own theory that Cambon had been pressing on ahead of his instructions over Morocco and that Delcassé was now imposing restraint.[2] In fact, in so far as there was any divergence between Cambon and Delcassé, it was not concerned with a forward policy in Morocco, which both cordially supported, but with the question of whether serious negotiations with England should follow or precede agreement with Spain. At this juncture Delcassé was beginning to rally to Cambon's point of view.[3] But Lansdowne, without understanding the situation, concluded more simply that the French were now no longer seeking to precipitate a Moroccan 'liquidation' crisis.

Thus reassured, he became better disposed to consider taking counsel with the French to meet the possible eventuality of a collapse of the *status quo* in Morocco. Provided that the contingency was reasonably remote it might profitably be explored. On this understanding Balfour gave qualified approval to Lansdowne's proposal that the Moroccan question should remain on the Anglo-French agenda. Cambon rightly concluded that the prospects for further conversations were favourable.

---

[1] Lansdowne to Monson, 31 Dec 1902, *BD* II, no. 330, p. 275.

[2] See Monson to Lansdowne, 9 Jan 1903, *BD* II, no. 334, pp. 277, 278.

[3] Cambon's conviction that Spanish dilatoriness was a blessing in disguise and his belief that he had successfully demonstrated this to Delcassé were expressed in a letter to his son Henri, then Third Secretary at Tangier, of 10 Jan 1903, *CC* II, pp. 67, 68. The letter as printed is in fact dated 1902 (see C. M. Andrew, *Théophile Delcassé and the Making of the Entente Cordiale*, p. 193 n. 3), but internal evidence makes it clear that this is incorrect.

8

The Royal Visit to Paris

CAMBON'S mood of optimism at the close of 1902 was soon to be strengthened by new evidence of Chamberlain's conversion to the cause of Anglo-French *rapprochement*. This evidence seems to have been deliberately planted, although not precisely in the way originally planned, by Chamberlain. Due to stop in Cairo on his way to South Africa in early December, he had apparently counted on a meeting prearranged by Cromer, with Raymond Lecomte, the French chargé d'affaires, to make a calculated revelation of his change of heart which was bound to reach Delcassé.[1] This plan misfired because bad weather delayed Chamberlain's arrival until the day when Lecomte was obliged to leave Cairo on official duty.[2] Unwilling to abandon what had obviously been a well-premeditated if somewhat crude manœuvre, Chamberlain provided Cromer with a statement of his views for transmission to Lecomte together with regrets that he had not been able to communicate directly.

In the circumstances Lecomte had no doubts about the authenticity of the message. 'Mr. Chamberlain', he dutifully reported to Delcassé,

said that once the experiences of recent years had convinced him that England would no longer take pride and draw profit from 'splendid isolation' and that he must henceforth look to a deal with one of the continental powers, his eyes had first turned towards Germany. However he soon realised that the violence of anti-British feelings aroused in Germany by the South

[1] For the way the meeting was arranged see Lecomte to Delcassé, 12 Dec 1902, *DDF*, II, no. 524, p. 653. Lecomte does not mention Cromer by name but speaks of a British official in Egypt who was a close personal friend of Chamberlain's. There seems to be no doubt, and Lecomte makes this very obvious, that it was in fact Cromer.

[2] He was committed to attend the opening by the Khedive of a new reservoir at Aswan.

African war, and nurtured by the jealous greed of rapid German commercial development, would render rapprochement with that power impossible for a long while. There remained Russia and France. From the former there was nothing to hope. . . . With France it was not the same. In France he believes government wishes are not opposed to a conciliatory policy, and public opinion, formerly so passionately hostile, seems to him to have returned to a measure of calm and quasi-neutrality which would permit prudent direction to infuse a new orientation upon it without too much protest. This evolution, which he does not regard as impossible in France, he feels quite confident of being able to promote in England with the spontaneous support of public opinion.

Convinced by experience of the need for foreign friendships and brought by logic to hope for that of France, he considers that the moment would be opportune to enter into negotiations or at least, if the wish for *entente* is reciprocal, to work towards its fruition by beginning with an exchange of 'down payments'. Although not the Foreign Secretary, he had made it his business to develop this theme among his cabinet colleagues. . . .[1]

In commenting on Chamberlain's views as thus presented, Lecomte pointed out that there was nothing sensationally new in English advocacy of *rapprochement* and he quoted a recent article in the *Manchester Guardian* in support of his argument. Public opinion in England, as far as he could judge, was favourable and it was not therefore in any way surprising that Chamberlain should have chosen to drop such a broad hint. It was, however, particularly significant in the light of Chamberlain's latest meeting with the Kaiser.[2] He was obviously anxious to make it clear that the reversal of his former attitude to Germany had not been modified by that encounter. 'I may add', continued Lecomte,

that while listening to these words and affirming my confidence in the dispositions of the British Cabinet towards our country I could not prevent myself from drawing attention to the discrepancy between these sentiments and Lord Lansdowne's speech at a Union Club dinner. My colleague pointed out to me that we knew nothing of the speech save for a telegram from the Reuter's agency, which is well known to be German-inspired and that at most it was not inadmissible that the

---

[1] Lecomte to Delcassé, 12 Dec 1902, *DDF*, II, no. 524, pp. 653–4.
[2] The Kaiser had been on a recent visit to Sandringham.

Foreign Secretary, while sharing Chamberlain's views and working in the same direction, should have judged it useful, in present circumstances, to restrain the opinions of his compatriots who were a little too prompt to take for established realities the programme of mutual concessions, no doubt hypothetical, which had been published by the British Press.[1]

While Lecomte's report was being studied in Paris, Chamberlain in South Africa was fretting about a rumour of Delcassé's impending resignation. 'I am sorry', he wrote to his son, 'to hear that Delcassé is likely to go. He seems to have done much to make possible an *Entente Cordiale* with France which is what I should now like. I wonder whether Lansdowne has considered the possibility of the King asking the President to visit England this year. . . .'[2] Although Chamberlain's zeal for new courses may not have had, at a distance, as much impact on the Cabinet as he might have hoped there was no doubt about the powerful effect of his Cairo conversation, as reported by Lecomte, on Cambon.

'It is certain', wrote Cambon on 22 January 1903 to Delcassé,

that he [Chamberlain] has suffered a deception where Germany is concerned. Having taken the friendly attitudes of Kaiser William II too seriously he dreamed of an Anglo-German alliance and talked rather loosely about it. He then came up against the basic and passionate hostility against England which has existed for some time among Germans and which came to light with typical Teutonic brutality during the South African War. Now there is a reaction and it brings him closer to us. I have confirmation of this from my own sources.[3]

Cambon went on to argue that, although Chamberlain lacked political principles, he was very sensitive to currents of public opinion and that opinion in England had now turned against Germany. 'She is disliked', he specified, with the Venezuela affair[4] as his example, 'even more as an ally than as a rival.'[5] In the

[1] Lecomte to Delcassé, 12 Dec 1902, *DDF*, II, no. 524, pp. 655–6.

[2] Chamberlain to Austen Chamberlain, 9 Jan 1903, quoted J. Amery, *Life of Joseph Chamberlain*, vol. 4, p. 206.

[3] Cambon to Delcassé, 22 Jan 1903, *DDF*, III, no. 37, pp. 47, 48.

[4] Venezuela's refusal to pay debts owed to British and German citizens had resulted, in early December 1902, in an Anglo-German naval blockade which culminated in the bombardment of San Carlos. Angry United States reactions stimulated widespread public indignation in England against association with Germany in this unpopular debt-collecting operation.

[5] Cambon to Delcassé, 22 Jan 1903, *DDF*, III, no. 37, p. 48.

light of this antipathy, Cambon concluded, Chamberlain's hints must be taken seriously. 'But', he warned, 'we must not count too much on the "down-payments" which he would be prepared to offer us; he is a realist, and if ever he were in a position to give us anything, we would obtain nothing from him except on a strict give and take basis.'[1]

This warning was intended to back up Cambon's own growing conviction that Egypt, although not yet directly mentioned by any responsible British statesman, was the clue to successful bargaining. Writing to his son on 3 February 1903 he expressed satisfaction that Delcassé now understood that his early dealings with Morocco had been precipitate, that Fez must be preserved for France and that, in these circumstances, England would require more compensation than the neutralisation of Tangier and guarantees of commercial liberty. 'He admits', Cambon rejoiced, 'what I had vainly repeated to him until now, that they will ask for territorial compensation or a linked settlement of the Egyptian question.'[2] In this latter connection he referred to an article in *The Times* of 2 February 1903 where the Madrid correspondent alleged that such a bargain had already been envisaged in recent conversations.[3] 'The essential character of these proposals', the Madrid correspondent had written, 'was that France and England should settle the Moroccan question in connection with the question of Egypt. In compensation for French official recognition of the British occupation of Egypt, France was to be allowed a free hand in dealing with Moroccan territory save on the North African coast line.'[4]

Cambon was strengthened in his own opinion about the need to introduce the Egyptian question when he met Lansdowne on 4 February 1903.[5] After a long and amicable discussion, which Lansdowne had initiated, about the question of projected loans to Morocco, Cambon recalled that, while France remained anxious to preserve the *status quo*, it had been agreed, in the light of

[1] Cambon to Delcassé, 22 Jan 1903, *DDF*, III, no. 37, p. 48.
[2] Cambon to Henri Cambon, 3 Feb 1903, *CC* II, p. 89.
[3] The article was in fact directly inspired by Cambon himself. See C. M. Andrew, *Théophile Delcassé and the Making of the Entente Cordiale*, p. 206.
[4] *The Times*, 2 Feb 1903.
[5] For Cambon's account of the meeting see Cambon to Delcassé, 4 Feb 1903, *DDF*, III, no. 63, pp. 85–8.

recent disorders, to take counsel about future contingencies. Explaining that he was not in any real hurry to tackle these questions, he reminded Lansdowne that he remained at his disposal. Delcassé, he added, was engaged in similar conversations with Spain. In reply to a request for further information from Lansdowne, Cambon specified that Delcassé was concerned with four main points: (1) Recognition of the hinterland of the Spanish possessions; (2) Neutralisation of Tangier; (3) Commercial freedom; (4) French influence south of the Spanish hinterland. 'All this', Cambon reaffirmed, 'has been the subject of numerous conversations between M. Delcassé and the Spanish Ambassador in Paris; but it is obvious that the exchanges of view must retain an academic character, so long as you are not associated with them and that, if any eventual agreement becomes possible, you must be called to take part in it. None of this prevents our policy from being in favour of the *status quo* and we sufficiently proved by our attitude of reserve, during recent events, that we were faithful to that policy. We are in no hurry, I repeat, but you will always find us ready to consider the future.'[1] From Lansdowne's reaction to this very cautious approach, Cambon contrived to draw highly significant conclusions. 'Lord Lansdowne', he reported,

> listened to me attentively; no doubt in order to avoid replying, he showed me the correspondence in *The Times* from Madrid and published on 2 February. He asked me if I knew where these false rumours might have originated. . . . I answered that I knew no more than he did about that, but the care with which *The Times* extract had been set aside and the minister's insistence on my reading it suggest an intention to demonstrate to me that the Moroccan question cannot be settled without England demanding massive compensation.[2]

Although Cambon's conclusion may have owed much to his own imagination, it was an effective method of preparing Delcassé to accept that, while the mood for general good understanding was becoming increasingly favourable in England, the price of a Morocco bargain would not be a light one. This warning came at a time when Delcassé was under heavy attack by the colonial group in the Chamber for lukewarmness in pressing

---

[1] Cambon to Delcassé, 4 Feb 1903, ibid., p. 88.
[2] Ibid.

colonial interests. His treaty with Siam[1] had been singled out for specific attack.[2] Finding the colonial group adamant in opposition, he abandoned his attempts to secure ratification and withdrew the treaty on 25 February 1903. Not satisfied with victory on this score one wing of the colonialist group continued campaigning against Delcassé by alleging that he was planning to buy a modest success in Morocco at the cost of recognising British supremacy in Egypt. Other champions of a forward policy in Morocco however were, on the contrary, becoming impatient with the lack of progress and reverted to the notion, which they pressed on Delcassé, that Morocco should have priority over Egyptian susceptibilities.[3] To these arguments Delcassé remained deaf and on 11 March, in a Foreign Affairs debate in the Chamber, he again proclaimed his faith in the *status quo* in Morocco and categorically denied the existence of any Moroccan bargain with England.

His declaration regarding the *status quo* was received with satisfaction in England while his denial of any bargain with England reassured the traditionalists among the colonial group.

While Delcassé played for time Cambon continued to report invitingly on the trend of British public opinion. Writing on 13 March 1903 of the favourable Press reaction to Delcassé's speech he concluded that 'the movement of English public opinion which these papers indicate is indubitable'.[4] In trying to explain this happy development Cambon suggested that preoccupation with the naval question and consequent mistrust of Germany was probably a preponderant factor. But, whatever the causes, evidence of his conclusion seemed to abound. Commenting on reactions to a speech which he had recently made at a Chamber of Commerce banquet he asked, 'Why did sentiments which I have already expressed so often this time arouse such an echo and create a rather exaggerated stir in the press?' 'It is', he insisted, 'because the situation has changed.'[5] But, he warned Delcassé,

[1] See p. 143.

[2] Opposition, which was led by Étienne, had been mounting since the treaty was signed in Oct 1902. A temporary rift in the close relations between Delcassé and Étienne resulted. See C. M. Andrew, *Théophile Delcassé and the Making of the Entente Cordiale*, pp. 198, 199.

[3] For the attitude of this group, directly under Étienne's wing, see ibid., pp. 197, 198.

[4] Cambon to Delcassé, 13 Mar 1903, *DDF*, III, no. 137, p. 184.

[5] Cambon to Delcassé, 13 Mar 1903, ibid., p. 185.

the improvement might not last nor, even if the situation were successfully exploited, would it mean getting something for nothing.

In thus reporting, Cambon was, of course, deliberately trying to promote a *rapprochement* policy. But there is no doubt that he was also reporting objectively. 'It is interesting to observe', he wrote to his son on 25 March 1903, 'that to be popular in England it is now necessary to show friendliness towards France.'[1] Pro-French attitudes certainly seemed to have become fashionable. This fashion was reflected soberly in *The Times*, *Spectator* and *The National Review*, and more crudely in the Harmsworth Press. Alfred Harmsworth[2] himself was supposed to have boasted that he would not allow 'the least thing that would injure France to appear in his papers'.[3] Evidence of the current mood, as Cambon correctly noted, abounded. Its causes cannot be so clearly diagnosed. Undoubtedly growing antipathy towards Germany helped to promote more friendly dispositions towards France. This antipathy, springing from a diversity of causes, was deliberately activated and emphasised by some leading navalists and by the Navy League, as part of a campaign for increased naval armament to offset the challenge which Tirpitz's[4] naval policy implied.

But friendliness towards France was not merely a reaction to anti-German agitation. There was a more positive aspect. Once England had won her Fashoda battle with France, and national pride had been satisfied, the way lay open for that friendly impulse of victors towards the vanquished which seems to stem from a very British amalgam of superiority and guilt. It was restrained by French animosity during the trials of the South African War but thereafter gathered momentum. The process was deliberately encouraged by a small but important group of English businessmen resident in France under the leadership of Thomas Barclay.[5]

[1] Cambon to Henri Cambon, 25 Mar 1903, *CC* II, p. 91.

[2] Then proprietor of the *Daily Mail*, *Evening News*, *Daily Mirror*, *Observer* and *Weekly Dispatch*.

[3] See J. J. Mathews, *Egypt and the Formation of the Anglo-French Entente of 1904*, p. 50.

[4] Grand-Admiral Alfred von Tirpitz, German Minister of Marine 1897–1916.

[5] Later Sir Thomas Barclay (1853–1941); he was not a businessman himself, but an international lawyer domiciled in Paris. For his own account of his efforts to improve Anglo-French relations see Sir Thomas Barclay, *Thirty Years of Anglo-French Reminiscences* (1914).

As President of the British Chamber of Commerce in Paris he conducted a formidable goodwill propaganda campaign. In 1900 he arranged for the visit of five hundred British merchants to the Paris Exhibition. This was a prelude to the organisation of further visits and return visits not only of businessmen but also of Members of Parliament. Apart from believing in the general benefit of such contacts Barclay, working in close contact with d'Estournelles,[1] was mainly concerned to mobilise support for his own favourite scheme, an arbitration treaty between England and France.[2] By 1903 twenty-seven British Chambers of Commerce, forty-one French Chambers of Commerce and thirty-five trade unions in England (representing 2,000,000 workmen), eighteen municipal councils and nineteen peace societies had given their support to the movement.[3] It had also been taken up by the Commercial Committee of the House of Commons.

In addition to political, emotional and commercial considerations there was also an intellectual and cultural aspect to the rising popularity of France. In the 1890's French writers, poets, painters and musicians provided a blaze of new inspiration. At the same time Paris became the Mecca, not only of artists and intellectuals, but also of smart society. Its admirers followed their betters. The Moulin Rouge was invaded by English tourists and adulating crowds flocked to the Great Exhibition of 1900. Paris was once again established as the capital of luxurious living. Small wonder, if luxury may be described as the trade-mark of social success in the Edwardian era, that it should have carried a French stamp.

Although the part played by society in shaping opinion – even in Edwardian England – was a nebulous one, its leadership was undisputed and its leader's personal influence unquestionable. During the long and politically barren years as Prince of Wales, Edward VII[4] had established himself as the doyen of luxurious

---

[1] Constant d'Estournelles (1852–1924), former diplomat and friend of Cambon. Now a leading political advocate of Anglo-French *rapprochement*, he mobilised the support of some 200 French deputies for an arbitration Treaty.

[2] See Monson to Lansdowne, 20 Jan, *BD* ii, no. 319, pp. 261, 262.

[3] For list of supporters see Sir Thomas Barclay, *Thirty Years of Anglo-French Reminiscences*, pp. 346–53.

[4] The official biography of Edward VII by Sir Sidney Lee, published in 1925, has provided a solid basis for subsequent studies; that of Sir Philip Magnus, *King Edward the Seventh* (1964), is the most recent.

living and the arbiter of fashion. Relentless in his pursuit of material pleasures he travelled with restless regularity abroad and with most evident relish to France. Biarritz and Paris were the favourite shrines of his annual social pilgrimage. The *gratin* of French society, existing in their idle self-inflicted estrangement from the masters of the Third Republic, welcomed him as a patron and as a friend; his membership of the Jockey Club symbolised the esteem in which he was held by the Faubourg-Saint-Honoré. Intimate links with the irreconcilable aristocracy did not prevent Edward VII, as Prince of Wales, from making some important contacts with leading personalities of the Third Republic; meetings with Gambetta[1] proved particularly successful and the friendly dispositions of the Prince of Wales were savoured by Gambetta's favourite disciples. His personal popularity in France, notwithstanding Anglo-French acerbities since 1882, was established and undisputed. The fact that the leader of English society was now King and that as Prince of Wales his pro-French proclivities and his personal popularity in that country were well known, set the seal on the pro-French trend in England.

Apart from this accidental contribution to the spread of pro-French attitudes Edward VII, as King, seems to have leaned quite deliberately, if not with complete consistency, towards a *rapprochement* policy. Although he had been systematically deprived by his mother of regular access to Foreign Office papers and although he lacked the temperament for study in depth he had, as Prince of Wales, maintained a considerable if amateurish interest in the conduct of foreign affairs. Like his mother he was vehemently and militantly patriotic, regularly favouring British intervention and the strong line. He admired Cecil Rhodes[2] as a man and as an imperialist. At the same time he mistrusted isolation and fully recognised the importance of cultivating friendships abroad. The pursuit of good understanding with France appealed both to his reason and to his personal inclination. But he was as ready as any Englishman to take up the challenge at Fashoda and to take umbrage at France's attitude during the South African War. His feelings towards Germany were ambivalent. Family

[1] For an account of these see Sir Sidney Lee, *King Edward VII*, vol. I, pp. 451-4.
[2] Cecil John Rhodes (1853-1902), founder of the De Beers Diamond Company and leading South African imperialist.

relationships and feuds cast a complicated shadow. His wife,[1] a Danish Princess who worshipped her parents, hated the Prussians with dutiful and obstinate Danish vehemence. In the early years of their marriage her attitude of uncompromising hostility to the Hohenzollerns was a frequent embarrassment to her husband, who, for family and state reasons, had every desire to avoid giving offence in that quarter. However, as the quarrel between his sister, the German Crown Princess,[2] and Bismarck deepened it became possible for him to sympathise with the prejudices of his wife and yet avoid the recriminations of his sister; condemnation of the policies of Bismarck gave equal pleasure to both. Although Edward VII was fully alive to the folly of indulging in any unnecessary quarrels with the German Government he did sometimes capitulate, in his attitudes, to the now combined pressure of his wife and of his sister. So long as Kaiser William I survived, the Crown Princess was powerless in her opposition to Bismarck; when he eventually died in 1888 her husband was also a dying man and the moment of political triumph of which she had dreamed never came. Although her son, who succeeded as Kaiser William II, soon dismissed Bismarck, it was not in any spirit of deference to the wishes of his mother whose influence he bitterly resented. Her rancour against Bismarck quickly turned against her own son and she did her best to prejudice her brother against his imperial nephew. It was not a difficult task. The young Kaiser was as tactless as he was talkative. He bored, as well as irritated, his uncle. But Edward VII was far too sensible and worldly a man to allow his own feelings towards his nephew to influence his conduct towards the German Emperor. On the contrary as far as it lay within his power he struggled, as Prince of Wales, both to propitiate the German Emperor and to stem the rising tide of anti-German feeling in England. However, although he was most circumspect in his public attitudes, it was assumed, not without cause, that he privately endorsed the popular conceptions of the Emperor which *Punch* cartoons reflected. Thus, in spite of his efforts, rumours of bad relations between the Prince of

[1] Queen Alexandra (1844–1925), daughter of King Christian IX of Denmark; her marriage to Edward VII took place in 1863.

[2] Victoria, Princess Royal (1840–1901) married to the German Crown Prince Frederick, who succeeded his father William I as Emperor Frederick III in 1888 and died in the same year.

Wales and the Emperor added spice to Anglo-German controversy.

At Queen Victoria's death family feuds were for a brief moment forgotten. The Kaiser, who hurried to her death-bed, behaved for once with exemplary tact. As King, Edward VII made every effort to be agreeable to his nephew and guest. The reopening of alliance negotiations which the Kaiser's visit had prompted, met with his entire approval. He blamed German policy for their failure but he tried to curb his own mounting irritation and was anxious to help Lansdowne, in so far as he was able, to moderate the violence of Chamberlain's furious reactions.

The King's apparent understanding of Lansdowne's wish to persevere in trying to promote better Anglo-German understanding, even when Chamberlain had become so quickly and awkwardly disenchanted, inspired the Foreign Secretary to seek further royal co-operation in his endeavours.[1] Accordingly he responded hopefully when the King, due to visit Germany for his sister's funeral, suggested that he should be provided with a brief for possible political discussion with the Kaiser. In the event, either because the opportunity did not arise or because the King was too upset to talk politics to his nephew, he simply handed over Lansdowne's hurriedly prepared notes to the Kaiser. William II forwarded them to the German Foreign Office as an official communication, not without some gibes about their contents. In reply to official German comments, Lansdowne was obliged to admit that the notes had been transmitted in error. This episode, although unimportant in itself, was an inauspicious prelude to the political conversations between Edward VII and the Kaiser which finally materialised at a luncheon at Wilhelmslöhe on 23 August 1901. The Kaiser was in a jocular mood and his jokes were at the expense of British foreign policy. In so far as Edward VII could be said to have undertaken a mission it had not been successful. He escaped, with relief, from his nephew to take the waters at Homburg.

Perhaps irritated by his failure as an ambassador Edward VII seems quite unfairly to have blamed Lansdowne for his own mistake in passing on his brief to the Kaiser. Henceforth at any rate the relationship between the King and his Foreign Minister was never to be a very happy one. Widely differing in their temperaments they would probably have found it difficult, in any

[1] See p. 118.

case, to establish any easy or congenial means of communication. Lansdowne could not, or perhaps would not, talk to the King about problems of foreign affairs in terms to engage his interest. The King's friends, notably Lord Esher[1] and Sir Ernest Cassel,[2] could. Possibly influenced by them he conceived it to be his duty to encourage a new generation at the Foreign Office. He became the patron of Hardinge[3] and of Bertie.[4] His sponsorship of these younger men was mildly irritating to Lansdowne. More annoying was the King's obstinate refusal to confer the Garter on the Shah of Persia when this honour had been deliberately planned as part of a campaign to counter Russian influence.[5] Equally trying was the King's persistent criticism of projected bargains with France over Siam.[6] It seemed as if he was trying to use his influence to block the one practical point of possible agreement with France. The only other comments which he ventured on foreign affairs were criticism of what he regarded as government weakness in meeting India's defence requirements. Even though these criticisms were discreetly voiced, Lansdowne was fully conscious of them. Assuming that he lacked the King's confidence and was sceptical of the King's judgement, Lansdowne was not disposed to rate Edward VII as more than a dubious asset in British diplomacy. Consequently, when in the early spring of 1902 the King expressed an inclination to visit Paris, Lansdowne refrained from any positive reaction. He raised no objections but he showed no enthusiasm. The initiative, quite clearly, lay with the King.

It can be explained by various considerations. Paris visits were, in any case, part of his routine of life. In 1900 he had cancelled an

[1] Reginald Brett, 2nd Viscount Esher (1852–1930); Secretary to H.M. Office of Works 1895–1902; appointed Lieutenant and Deputy-Governor of Windsor Castle in 1901 and Chairman of the War Office Reconstruction Committee in 1904. He repeatedly refused ministerial offices including the Secretaryship of State for War in 1903. In fact he became the King's unofficial political adviser and acted as a liaison officer between the King and the Cabinet.

[2] Sir Ernest Cassel (1852–1921); born in Cologne of Jewish origin, he settled in England where he was naturalised in 1880 and built up a spectacularly successful financial empire. From 1897 onwards he acted as Edward VII's financial adviser and became perhaps the closest of the King's friends. See Sir Philip Magnus, *King Edward the Seventh*, p. 258.

[3] See p. 161.   [4] See p. 119.

[5] See Sir F. Ponsonby, *Recollections of Three Reigns*, pp. 146–7.

[6] The King remained opposed to a bargain over Siam even when the *Entente* negotiations were seriously in train and, in one of his rare Minutes, indicated his disapproval. See *BD* II, p. 400.

official visit to open the Exhibition as a protest against the French
cartoon campaign against England's South African War. On his
accession to the throne he had wished to erase this impression by
a prompt visit to Paris. Ill-health obliged him to abandon the plan,
but it remained on his agenda of priorities. Apart from his personal
pleasure in visiting the French capital and his desire to repair a
former discourtesy he was, Siam notwithstanding, a protagonist
of Anglo-French *rapprochement*. His friends at the Foreign Office
were in favour on grounds of general policy. Sir Ernest Cassel
hoped it might prove a means of solving the Egyptian riddle.
Investment in Egypt was one of the cornerstones of his financial
empire. Close and mutually profitable friendship with Cromer had
been established in the process and Cromer was anxious that, if,
as he hoped, an opportunity to make a bargain with France was
presented, it should not be lost. Partly as a result of his friendship
with Sir Ernest Cassel and partly because of his instinctive
proclivity for proconsuls Edward VII became an admirer of
Cromer and of his work in Egypt. Although he surely never
analysed his motives in this kind of way, sympathy for Cromer's
cause was no doubt present among the reasons which prompted
the King to pursue his plans for a goodwill mission to Paris. More
obviously the visit was in line with his established inclinations and
with the trend of public opinion.

The organisation of foreign tours was an exercise which
appealed strongly to the King. He liked to supervise all the details
and he also liked to pick a carefully chosen company of friends.
At the outset, on this occasion, he indicated to Lansdowne that
he did not wish a cabinet minister to be in attendance and that,
as an official Foreign Office aide, he wanted the company of
Charles Hardinge,[1] then Assistant Under-Secretary of Foreign
Affairs.[2] Although Lansdowne complied with this request it
seemed to emphasise the cloud of mild misunderstanding which
persisted between the King and himself. Without indicating any
special interest he instructed Monson to discover whether the
projected visit would be welcomed by the President of the

---

[1] Later Lord Hardinge of Penshurst (1858–1944).
[2] He was appointed Minister Plenipotentiary for the occasion. For his own account
of the appointment and of Lansdowne's delaying tactics see Hardinge of Penshurst,
Old Diplomacy, p. 85. See also Sir F. Ponsonby, *Recollections of Three Reigns*, p. 154.

F

Republic and on 13 March Monson furnished a positive reply.[1]
On the same day Lansdowne mentioned the matter in the course
of a conversation with Cambon.[2] Cambon reported to Delcassé
that the King was aware of Loubet's projected visit to Algeria and
that he was anxious to arrange a meeting which would not interfere with these plans. Cambon noted this royal tactfulness as a
good augury, and advised Delcassé to respond with alacrity to the
King's initiative. The visit, he explained, is 'recommended by the
English Press and by Public Opinion'.[3] He drew that conclusion
from various newspaper articles which had appeared early in
March. But, warned Cambon, it was important that there should
be no premature publicity about the visit in France; Edward VII
liked to preserve his own freedom of action until the last moment.

Delcassé had no hesitation in accepting his Ambassador's advice.
By the end of March arrangements had been quietly concluded
for Edward VII to pay a state visit to Paris at the end of his April
Mediterranean cruise.

Although Lansdowne did not regard the visit as likely to prove
of major diplomatic significance he was ready to recognise that
any consequent boost to the current trend of improving Anglo-
French relations would be welcome. This he felt more particularly
as new storm-clouds began to gather early in April in the Far
East. Indications that Russia intended to go back on her promises
to evacuate Manchuria provoked violent reactions in Japan. The
consequences of Anglo-Japanese Alliance were awkwardly and
alarmingly apparent. While Lansdowne had been hoping to meet
Russian pressures by amicable agreement and compromise, he was
now being plaintively urged by Japan to show firmness. In this
dangerous and delicate situation the value of good understanding
with France was at a premium.

Appreciation of this fact no doubt contributed to the enthusiasm
which greeted official news of the King's forthcoming visit to
Paris. As Cambon happily reported on 23 April, an allusion to the
visit was applauded in the Commons.[4] In the Press reactions were
generally favourable; in the *Spectator*, Cambon noted, it was

---

[1] See Lord Newton, *Lord Lansdowne*, p. 275.
[2] See Cambon to Delcassé, 14 Mar 1903, *DDF*, iii, no. 138, p. 186.
[3] Ibid.
[4] See Cambon to Delcassé, 23 Apr 1903, *DDF*, iii, no. 192, p. 259.

affirmed that 'in spite of difficulties and past quarrels, the French Nation has never been really unpopular on this side of the channel'.[1] Cambon stressed particularly that 'in some circles where an improvement of relations with Russia is warmly desired, it is thought that France could render service in that direction'.[2]

While Cambon thus indicated confirmation of his own previous reports of the changing temper of English public opinion towards France, Delcassé no doubt also drew satisfaction from the comment by his chargé d'affaires in Berlin that news of Edward VII's visit had been received there with 'badly concealed ill-humour'.[3] 'The Emperor's uncle', Prinet added, 'has not yet officially visited Berlin since his coronation; it is therefore not surprising that some bitterness should be felt here.'

As publicity on his forthcoming visit to Paris began to focus the King was already engaged, during his Mediterranean cruise, in private and useful preparation. While stopping at Lisbon he had made a speech to the Portuguese Chamber of Peers in which he contrived to combine a compliment to his hosts with a friendly reference to France. This was duly noted by Rouvier, the French Ambassador, who also reported to Delcassé on the particular courtesy which Edward VII had manifested towards Mme Rouvier.[4] These indications of goodwill were confirmed, Rouvier explained to Delcassé, by the Marquis de Soveral,[5] who expanded on how anxious Edward VII was for the success of the Paris visit and how popular he believed the cause of Anglo-French *rapprochement* to be in England. Thus, by his own tact and deftly via Soveral, Edward VII made his point. It was not lost on Delcassé.

After Lisbon the King visited Gibraltar, Malta, Naples and Rome. On 30 April he left Rome by train and was joined by Monson on 1 May in the morning at Dijon. The President of the Republic was waiting to receive his royal guest in the early afternoon at the

[1] Cambon to Delcassé, 23 Apr 1903, ibid., p. 260.
[2] Cambon to Delcassé, 23 Apr 1903, ibid., pp. 261, 262.
[3] Prinet to Delcassé, 25 Apr 1903, *DDF*, III, no. 201, p. 277. 'The German newspapers', *Punch* declared, 'show such absurd annoyance when commenting on Edward's visit to France that one can only suppose that, in their opinion, they and their country should control everyone.' *Punch*, 29 Apr 1903.
[4] See Rouvier to Delcassé, 12 Apr 1903, *DDF*, III, no. 178, pp. 244–6.
[5] Marquis Luis Maria Pinto de Soveral (1853–1922), Portuguese Ambassador to London and for many years a leading member of Edward VII's private circle of boon companions.

The Chain of Friendship, 29 April 1903

Bois de Boulogne station and accompanied him, in a vast procession with cavalry escort, to the British Embassy. As they moved through the crowded Champs-Elysées the cheers, according to Ponsonby,[1] who travelled in one of the last carriages, 'had become jeers. There were cries of *Vive Marchand!* and *Vive Fashoda!*, *Vivent les Boers!* and occasionally *Vive Jeanne d'Arc!*'[2] Half an hour after their arrival the King paid an official visit to President and Mme Loubet. Then he addressed the British Chamber of Commerce. In the evening, after dinner at the British Embassy, he attended a performance at the Théâtre-Français. His reception at the theatre was rather cold. But, to the consternation of the police, he insisted on wandering around the foyer during the interval. Noticing Mlle Jeanne Granier, the actress, he walked up to her, kissed her hand and said, 'Mademoiselle, I remember applauding you in London where you represented all the grace and spirit of France.'[3] This little incident immediately made a favourable impression and the story quickly enjoyed wide publicity.

On the morning of 2 May the King attended a military review at Versailles. Monson reported on the signs of increased cordiality among the crowds.[4] Afterwards on his arrival at the Hotel de Ville the King was cheered. He replied briefly and in French saying: 'I will never forget my visit to your charming town and I can assure you that it is with the greatest pleasure that I return to Paris, where I have always felt as if I were at home.'[5] His frequent visits to Paris as Prince of Wales and the ties of friendship which he had then established gave a ring of sincerity to this otherwise somewhat obvious compliment. The effect, both on the spot and in subsequent reports, was considerable. The King's past associations with Paris were beginning to pay dividends.

A further bonus was provided in the afternoon when the Jockey Club arranged a special race-meeting at Longchamps in his honour. In theory the Jockey Club was welcoming, not the King of England, but its own most distinguished member. At any rate an

[1] Sir Frederick Ponsonby (1867–1935), 1st Lord Sysonby; Assistant Private Secretary to Edward VII 1901–10.

[2] See Sir F. Ponsonby, *Recollections of Three Reigns*, p. 170.

[3] See letter in *The Times*, 10 May 1922, quoted Sir Sidney Lee, *King Edward VII*, vol. 2, p. 238.

[4] See Monson to Lansdowne, 5 May 1903, *BD* VI, appendix 1(*a*), p. 762.

[5] Quoted Sir F. Ponsonby, *Recollection of Three Reigns*, p. 170.

opportunity was provided for the King to be seen by vast crowds on an informal occasion. With Ponsonby's help he managed to escape, for a good while, from the presidential box, and to renew acquaintance with his old Jockey Club friends.[1]

In the evening there was a state banquet at the Elysée Palace. In reply to the President's toast, the King made an excellent speech in French which carried clearly to all ends of the table and contrasted very favourably with the nervous mumbling of the President.[2] After dinner there was a gala performance at the opera. The temper of the crowds was by now unmistakably friendly. Next day, when the King emerged from the Embassy to walk to the English Church and later to attend a luncheon at the Quai d'Orsay, he was greeted with cheers of *Vive Edouard! Notre Bon Edouard!* On the following morning, with the President in farewell attendance, the crowd at the station was so dense that, in Monson's ponderous account, 'passage for the party was not easily gained'.[3]

The visit, to the King's satisfaction and to Delcassé's relief, was proving a huge success. No doubt part of this success was fortuitous. Good republicans could worship foreign royalty with a clear conscience. They set to the task with relish. The tide of feeling against England was in any case beginning to turn. Friendly attitudes in the Press on the other side of the Channel had been too marked not to cause some response. But, allowing for all this, it would be foolish to dismiss the part played by the King himself. Starting with the advantage of his own genuine appreciation of Paris and of the French and of his erstwhile popularity in Paris, he made the most of every opportunity. Altogether larger than life, he was splendidly equipped to play the role of a visiting King. Years of training lay behind the superb performance of this master of public relations. His command of the banalities of public speaking and his display of royal informality were the work of an artist.

While it would be an exaggeration to say that the royal visit to Paris caused a revolution in French public opinion towards

---

[1] See F. Ponsonby, *Recollections of Three Reigns*, p. 171.

[2] Ibid., pp. 172–3.

[3] For Monson's detailed account of the whole visit and of its success see Monson to Lansdowne, 8 May 1903, *BD* VI, appendix 1(*b*), pp. 763–8.

England, there seems little doubt that it did contribute materially to an improvement already in train. This result was of particular importance to Delcassé who could now rely on some degree of enthusiasm in France for the President's return visit to London. The City had already expressed eagerness to receive him and Delcassé lost no time in raising the matter with Monson. At first it seemed as if there might be some difficulty about immediate arrangements and Lansdowne advised Monson that the King favoured delay. Monson, however, was under pressure from Delcassé and warned that any reluctance might cause offence. On 19 May 1903 Lansdowne informed Monson that the King had reconsidered his attitude[1] and arrangements for a return visit in early June were then speedily concluded. To Delcassé the visit clearly represented an opportunity to move forward, as Cambon advised, with his own plans for pursuing negotiations with England. He began discreetly to pave the way within the French diplomatic hierarchy. On 11 May he sent a circular letter to all French embassies.[2] Referring to the King's visit he insisted that the initiative had come from Edward VII and that the visit did not imply any change in the direction of French foreign policy. On the other hand he explained that it represented 'a current of opinion which we must note with satisfaction'. England and France, he pointed out, had many common and many conflicting interests. These could degenerate into quarrels unless the two governments were conciliatory and sympathetic.

This hint of his future intentions was particularly destined for Bompard,[3] the French Ambassador in Russia. Though a pupil of Cambon, whom he recognised as his master, Bompard clung to prejudices against England and was fearful of any Anglo-French *rapprochement* which might endanger the Russian alliance. It was therefore gratifying to Delcassé to learn from Bompard, in a dispatch dated 21 May, that the King's Paris visit was provoking favourable comment in Russia where it was regarded as a snub to the Kaiser.[4] Furthermore, according to Bompard, there were signs of improving Anglo-Russian relations. Lamsdorff, the

---

[1] See G. Monger, *The End of Isolation*, p. 128, note 1.
[2] See *DDF*, iii, no. 237, pp. 321–3.
[3] See p. 95.
[4] See Bompard to Delcassé, 21 May 1903, *DDF*, iii, no. 255, pp. 343–4.

Foreign Minister, was relieved that England had avoided en-
venoming the Manchurian quarrel and satisfied that British support
for the Baghdad Railway had apparently been abandoned. These
indications that England was anxious not to irritate Russian susceptibilities were equally welcome in St Petersburg and in Paris.
Delcassé was well aware of the risk of attempting Anglo-French
rapprochement against a background of Anglo-Russian hostility.

To Lansdowne the problems posed by Russian ambitions in the
Far East and on the Indian borders were more urgent than the
prospect of negotiations with France over the various questions
which had been under preliminary discussion with Cambon.
Although alarm aroused by the April crisis over Manchuria had
subsided the danger was not yet past. Prospects of a general
agreement with Russia, though slightly more hopeful, remained
extremely dubious. And yet it was to this end that Lansdowne
felt he must mainly apply his energies. A firm declaration on
Persia[1] was intended as a warning to secure Russian forbearance
on this sensitive point. But agreement with Russia, however
difficult, remained Lansdowne's prized objective.

In this direction little support was forthcoming from the
popular Press which remained suspicious and hostile where
Russia was concerned. Anglo-French *rapprochement*, on the other
hand, seemed increasingly popular. The success of Edward VII's
visit produced a new wave of enthusiasm and the merits of *Entente
Cordiale* were heavily canvassed. The English atmosphere was
obviously congenial for negotiations with France. Even though
Lansdowne might regard them as of secondary importance compared to his projects for conjuring the Russian problem, he could
not fail to appreciate that a settlement, quite apart from its own
merits, would bring badly needed popularity to a government
now obviously afflicted by division and decay. In this mood he
may have been particularly receptive to an appeal from Cromer.
'We must', Cromer wrote on 29 May 1903, 'make a serious effort
to get rid of the *Caisse de la Dette*.'[2] The method he proposed was
a bargain over Morocco. Lansdowne answered on 8 June acknow-
ledging the importance of eliminating the *Caisse* and hinting at the

---

[1] On 5 May 1903.
[2] Cromer to Lansdowne, 29 May 1903, Lansdowne MSS., vol. VIII, quoted
G. Monger, *The End of Isolation*, p. 128.

possibility of accommodating both the French and the Spaniards in Morocco provided Germany were excluded.[1] The possibility of using the Moroccan question to Egyptian advantage had, as Cambon suspected, by now taken firm root.

The British Press, in the meanwhile, was beginning to take note of significant developments in the attitude of some members of the French colonial group. The rift with Delcassé which had culminated in their compelling him to abandon his Siamese treaty was gradually healing. Articles in *La Dépêche coloniale* appeared on 13 and 19 May advocating negotiations with England.[2] Delcassé, who had only recently suffered violent criticism for his supposed efforts in that direction, was now receiving direct encouragement. *The Times* at any rate concluded that one of the main barriers to Anglo-French *rapprochement,* the intransigence of the French colonial group, was in the process of disappearing.

The atmosphere on both sides of the Channel was more favourable in June 1903 for friendly conversations than at any time since Fashoda and possibly since 1882.

While Lansdowne could contemplate this situation with satisfaction his anxieties concerning the Far East were reviving in acute form. There were signs that Japan was losing patience with Russia and on 3 July 1903 Hayashi informed Lansdowne that a policy of forbearance could no longer be pursued.[3] His Government now intended to make a direct approach to Russia for settlement of their grievances in Manchuria and in Korea. Ominously he added that 'the Imperial Government would be glad to know what steps the British Government proposed to take in defence of their threatened interest'.[4] It has been argued that Lansdowne, under the impulse of this threat of Russo-Japanese war, immediately reassessed his attitude to Anglo-French *rapprochement*. From being a mild protagonist he became an impatient advocate, ready to snatch at any opportunity which Delcassé's

[1] See Lansdowne to Cromer, 8 Jun 1903, Lansdowne MSS., vol. VIII, quoted ibid., p. 128.
[2] The articles were in fact inspired by Étienne and, as has been seen, he had long been in favour of such negotiation. But hitherto his views and those of his friends on the *Comité de l'Afrique française* had been pressed privately on Delcassé. It had been assumed that, like the majority of the colonial party which he led, he was resolute in opposition to Anglo-French collaboration.
[3] See Lansdowne to Macdonald, 3 Jul 1903, *BD* II, no. 237, pp. 206–7.
[4] Lansdowne to Macdonald, 3 Jul 1903, ibid., p. 207.

F2

forthcoming presence in London might present. In fact there does not seem to have been any dramatic change in Lansdowne's attitude. As has been seen *rapprochement* with France was a very long-standing item on the Foreign Office agenda. The prospect of a bargain over Morocco had already been carefully mulled. As will be seen Lansdowne discussed the possibility of a general settlement with Étienne two days before Hayashi's supposedly decisive warning.[1] Even though French negotiations may not have been a top priority their value was clearly understood and recognised by Lansdowne. The threatened crisis in the Far East might endow them with a new significance but there was no need for a sudden reappraisal. The file on Anglo-French colonial difference, and the arguments in favour of settlement, were too well-worn to admit the suggestion of any flurry to negotiate. On the contrary it was with ponderous deliberation and with roles carefully rehearsed that bargaining was to begin. The business was serious but, since Edward VII's Paris visit, it also promised to be popular even in France.

[1] See pp. 173–6.

9

The Bargaining Opens in London

'I AM no partisan of these presidential visits',[1] wrote Cambon to his son on 6 June 1903. A president, Cambon explained, was not a sovereign but merely a temporarily elected magistrate; if he returned all state visits, he would constantly be on tour during his term of office; this, to the cautious Cambon, represented a dismal prospect of unnecessary diplomatic hazards. Apart from his disapproval on principle of presidential visits, Cambon had little relish for the role of host. It was therefore with relief that he abandoned plans to receive the President and his suite at the Embassy when an invitation, which could not be refused, eventually arrived offering royal hospitality at 'gloomy' York House instead.[2] 'I will only have Delcassé if he comes and', Cambon confided with satisfaction, 'I am sure that he will come.'[3] The prospect of Delcassé's presence in London, unlike that of the President, was, for Cambon, a matter of major importance. In his general plan of campaign for Anglo-French *rapprochement* a private meeting between the English and French Foreign Ministers now seemed opportune. The ground had been sufficiently prepared to permit Delcassé to open a way for the next stage of more serious negotiations. As Cambon later commented: 'He [Lord Lansdowne] never takes the initiative and it is necessary to force his hand a little in order to make him more communicative.'[4] That, obviously, was to be Delcassé's London assignment.

In the meanwhile Cambon was forced to concentrate on detailed arrangements for the President's visit. To him, although he

---

[1] *CC* II, p. 93.
[2] See Cambon to his son, 6 Jun 1903, *CC* II, p. 93.
[3] Ibid.
[4] Cambon to Delcassé, 6 Aug 1903, *DDF*, III, no. 393, p. 520

savoured the humorous side, they seemed irrelevant and boring. To Edward VII they were a matter of professional pride. He explored and supervised every ramification of the official programme, constantly arranging and re-arranging.[1] On 18 June 1903 a telegram was sent to Paris at his request announcing that a review of troops had been scheduled for Wednesday, 8 July, after a visit to Walmer Castle. 'We had hoped to be spared this trial,'[2] wrily commented Cambon. The King, however, took particular interest in planning this military occasion, bombarding the general in command at Aldershot with instructions, including directions to the band about the playing of the *Marseillaise*, until the very last moment.[3] The most awkward aspect of royal intervention proved to be the question of knee-breeches.[4] The King, in conversation with Cambon and officially with Lansdowne, tried to prescribe this *ancien régime* formal dress for the President and for Delcassé at the Buckingham Palace state banquet to be held on 6 July. The President and his Foreign Minister, loyal to the revolutionary tradition which they claimed to represent, lodged formal objections and the King was eventually compelled to rescind his knee-breeches edict. Cambon concluded that Edward VII had only been joking, but the King's fanaticism on matters of dress was such that, initially at least, he may have been quite serious in his effort to impose conformity. Fortunately, however, he was not prepared to press the point against Delcassé's threat to cancel his projected visit to London altogether.

In this comic-opera atmosphere Cambon struggled to concentrate on essentials. As July approached he emphasised to Lansdowne that 'the visit of the King to Paris and that of the President to London would have no meaning unless they led to exchanges of view between the two governments on all matters which might interest them', and that it was important that Delcassé 'should be able to have a serious discussion with him'.[5] According to Cambon, 'he [Lansdowne] had seemed to share this opinion, but, with his usual reserve, he had guarded his freedom to consult the Prime Minister and doubtless the King about the subject'.

[1] See Cambon to his son, 18 Jun 1903, *CC* II, p. 93.
[2] Ibid.
[3] See Sir Sidney Lee, *King Edward VII*, vol. 2, p. 245.
[4] See Cambon to his son, 18 Jun 1903, *CC* II, p. 93.
[5] Cambon to Delcassé, 1 Jul 1903, *CC* II, p. 95.

On 1 July 1903 Cambon reverted to his theme and he found Lansdowne much 'warmer'.[1] They agreed that it would be impossible to hold serious talks in the midst of banquets and official celebrations. It was therefore decided that Delcassé should call on Lansdowne at the Foreign Office at 9.30 in the morning on Tuesday, 7 July, and that they might then talk at leisure.[2] It has been suggested that because arrangements for this private meeting were made so late and then on Cambon's initiative, Lansdowne had not been prepared for any serious confrontation; but in the light of constant amendments and re-amendments of the royal programme, definite arrangements could hardly have been made sooner. The fact that the initiative came from Cambon was entirely in keeping with the whole trend of the *rapprochement* manœuvre. In view of his own previous conversations with the French Ambassador, Lansdowne could hardly have been unaware of the probable significance of a meeting with the French Foreign Minister.

Once Cambon had arranged the private meeting between Lansdowne and Delcassé he turned his attention to ensuring that the French Foreign Minister should also have an opportunity of talking, at some point, with Chamberlain. For Chamberlain, he argued, 'is now the government of England. I know that, disgusted with the Germans, he wants to turn towards us.'[3] Therefore Cambon proposed that, in spite of protocol, Delcassé should be seated between Lansdowne and Chamberlain at the French Embassy dinner arranged for 7 July. 'In such circumstances', Cambon smugly advised, 'protocol must be sacrificed to policy.'[4] 'Chamberlain', he added, 'is pride incarnate; he proclaimed the necessity of an Anglo-German alliance after half an hour's conversation with Emperor William, who deluged him with compliments. I think you could talk to him more usefully than the Emperor.'[5]

After these calculated preparations Cambon was glad to find support from a quarter which he professed to find unexpected. Étienne, now Vice-President of the Chamber of Deputies, had just arrived in London on a goodwill mission. The recent appearance of an article in *The National Review* in which Étienne had

---

[1] Ibid.   [2] Ibid.
[3] Ibid.   [4] Ibid.   [5] Ibid.

outlined the possibility of a settlement of Anglo-French colonial differences on the basis of wide-ranging bargains had impressed, not only Cambon,[1] but the Paris correspondent of *The Times*. 'M. Étienne', he declared, 'speaks on colonial matters in France with an authority which can be compared to that of Mr. Chamberlain in England, and his views on such subjects are generally endorsed by all parties in the country.'[2]

In Cambon's opinion Étienne had finally rallied to the sensible conclusion that his forward colonial policy was unviable if he remained England's implacable adversary.[3] 'Is it not curious', he remarked to Delcassé, 'that M. Étienne should decide to adopt your policy? It is the finest compliment which could be made to you.'[4] In fact it was the policy which Cambon had been pressing on Delcassé that Étienne had decided to adopt and, in any case, his conversion was not as sudden as Cambon indicated.[5] Indeed it was probably Étienne's prompting which helped to bring Delcassé round to the notion of taking a major diplomatic initiative. Étienne's advocacy of *rapprochement*, which Cambon affected to find surprising, was in no way unexpected by Delcassé. On the contrary the manœuvre was carefully concerted. Either Cambon underestimated his chief or else, to mask the success of his own planning, he was being deliberately disingenuous.

At any rate, with Étienne's disposition now clearly revealed, Cambon was glad to learn from Lansdowne that he was expecting a visit from him on 2 July and that he also wished to include him in the official Foreign Office dinner party arranged for 8 July, provided neither Delcassé nor the President had any objections. Cambon hastened to assure Lansdowne that none existed.[6]

On 2 July Lansdowne and Étienne met at the Foreign Office as arranged. 'He told me', wrote Lansdowne to Monson, 'that he was paying a short visit to this country in the hopes of promoting a good understanding between the two governments. There seemed to him to be no really serious points of divergence

---

[1] Cambon to Delcassé, 2 Jul 1903, *CC* II, p. 96.
[2] *The Times*, 2 Jul 1903.
[3] See Cambon to Delcassé, 2 Jul 1903, *CC* II, p. 96.
[4] Ibid.
[5] See p. 169 note 2.
[6] See Cambon to Delcassé, 2 Jul 1903, ibid.

between them, and the moment appeared to be particularly propitious for such a *rapprochement* as he suggested.'[1] After this
friendly opening Étienne 'passed in view the various political
questions which have lately occupied the joint attention of the
British and French Foreign Office'.[2] It was in fact a dress-rehearsal
for much of the *Entente* negotiations. On Morocco Étienne made
it clear that France must have a preponderant influence, but he
reassured Lansdowne that 'he did not contemplate that that
country, or any part of it, should be annexed to France'.[3] He
recognised British interests on the Moroccan seaboard and in the
freedom of trade.

Lansdowne responded by accepting without question the
'special interests' of France but 'deprecated the idea of bringing
on a premature partition of Morocco'.[4] To this Étienne 'observed
that the Sultan's government appeared to be on the point of
falling to pieces and that it seemed provident to provide for the
event of its complete collapse'. This probing prompted Lansdowne
to warn 'that these Eastern monarchies often managed to survive
in spite of apparent decay and seemingly insurmountable difficulties. A premature attempt to define new spheres of influence
was, moreover, likely to arouse the susceptibilities of the Powers
who conceived they had an interest in Morocco. Spain, for
example, not without reason, had considerable pretensions in
that country.'[5] The point was readily admitted by Étienne, who
then turned to the Newfoundland question, which he felt sure
was 'capable of adjustment'; to the New Hebrides, where he
tentatively proposed partition; and to Siam, where he affirmed
that, although France had once looked forward to ultimate
annexation, her pretensions had now been abandoned and no
reason for differences seemed to remain. After speaking briefly
on these matters, Étienne 'dwelt at greater length and with considerable earnestness upon the necessity of a rearrangement of the
frontier in the region of Sokoto. That frontier, he said, was
agreed to when neither Power was aware of the local conditions,
and the arrangement had resulted in confining the French to a
barren and waterless region which they were obliged to traverse,
and by a circuitous route, whenever they desired to pass from their

---

[1] *BD* II, no. 356, p. 292.   [2] Ibid.
[3] Ibid.   [4] Ibid.   [5] Ibid.

western possessions to their posts on the side of Lake Tchad.[1] It
was only equitable that we should agree to revise the boundary:
France did not wish for any large accession of territory, but only
to be allowed to come down to a region in which water could be
obtained for the use of French convoys.'[2] Lansdowne replied
that he saw no reason why there should not be discussion of 'a
transaction of which some such concession might form a part',
but added that 'the country within the Sokoto "semi-circle" was,
however, ours and we could not be expected to part with it except
for a consideration'.[3] The interest which Étienne had shown in
Sokoto obviously impressed Lansdowne and, as will be seen later,
he concluded somewhat over-optimistically that concession on
this point would be a very valuable bargaining card.[4]

Étienne's desire for an accommodation and his relative moderation on the Moroccan question could not have failed to make a
powerful impact on Lansdowne. Even though, with sensible and
characteristic caution, he thought it 'inadvisable to express during
the above conversation any definite ideas of my own as to the
manner in which the different questions upon which M. Étienne
had touched might be treated', he did assert that nothing would
give him 'greater satisfaction than to promote a reasonable "give
and take" arrangement between the two Governments'.[5] 'At the
conclusion of our conversation', Lansdowne recorded, 'M. Étienne
expressed his belief that the most serious menace to the peace of
Europe lay in Germany, that a good understanding between
France and England was the only means of holding German
designs in check, and that if such an understanding could be
arrived at, England would find that France would be able to
exercise a salutary influence over Russia and thereby relieve us
of many of our troubles with that country.'[6] Lansdowne did not
volunteer to Monson any information about his own reactions
to these last inducements towards a *rapprochement*. It may be suggested that the prospect of a bridge to Russia appealed more
strongly to him than that of a barrier to Germany. But it is
significant that Étienne's reference to Germany was made and
that it passed without protest from Lansdowne. Whatever his
reservations on that score, it seemed that a general settlement with

France, ranging over questions widely divergent in importance but all susceptible of generating some kind of friction, was within sight of achievement. Apart from the direct benefits of such a settlement, Lansdowne could hope that it might lead to the establishment of a better *modus vivendi* with Russia, and to the building up of a new insurance against the danger, which in his view some navalists and some of his own Foreign Office staff tended to exaggerate, of the growing German Navy.

While Lansdowne judicially contemplated *rapprochement* there was no doubt about the powerful movement of public opinion in England. The President's visit proved a splendid occasion for outward manifestation. As Cambon later remarked to Delcassé: 'that coldness, that reserve which ordinarily characterises the English had for a moment disappeared. . . . Never, for fifty years, has the head of a foreign state been the object in this country of such ovations and, if the fact was striking in London, it seemed to me all the more significant in a small quiet provincial town such as Dover, where the whole population emerged from habitual calm to demonstrate warm sympathy towards France and its representative.'[1] With the public and, as Cambon jubilantly noted, also the Press so responsive, the visit was an unqualified success. In this achievement Edward VII's solicitude paid dividends. The complicated arrangements which he had supervised worked without a hitch. The crowds played their part by turning out night and day to cheer 'Long live Loubet! Long live Delcassé! Hip Hip Hooray!' The gala at the Opera, which had been transformed into a bower of roses,[2] the dinners at Buckingham Palace, the French Embassy and the Foreign Office, even the Aldershot review with 150,000 troops on display, all met with Cambon's fastidious approval.[3] The 'tiring solemnities' from the arrival on 6 July to the President's departure on the cruiser *Quichen* on 9 July passed without the suspicion of an untoward incident. It was an auspicious backcloth for the more serious business so meticulously plotted by Cambon and so happily introduced by Étienne.

[1] Cambon to Delcassé, *DDF* III, no. 384, p. 502.
[2] *Punch*, reporting on 'A Very Grand Opera Night', with 'Loubet among the Roses and Royalties', found him looking 'prim, spry and as pleased as is proverbially *Mr Punch*; which is the supreme expression of perfect contentment.' See *Punch*, 15 Jul 1903.
[3] See Cambon to his son, 12 Jul 1903, *CC* II, p. 97.

Friends, 8 July 1903

On Tuesday, 7 July at 9.30 a.m. Delcassé called on Lansdowne at the Foreign Office as arranged. Both statesmen had been studying their parts for some time, and the dialogue flowed easily, as is clear from the full account which Lansdowne rendered on the same day to Monson.[1] It was Lansdowne who, as befitted the host, opened the discussion. After expressing pleasure at having this opportunity to learn Delcassé's views at first hand, he referred to his own previous discussions with Cambon about 'Newfoundland, Siam, the New Hebrides and other parts of the world.' These discussions, he pointed out, had not led to any definite results. They had, however, been 'useful in clearing the ground' and they had 'certainly' led him 'to the conclusion that the points at issue between the two Governments were few in number, and by no means incapable of adjustment'.[2] Lansdowne could hardly have gone further in encouraging Delcassé to follow his own chosen road. Not surprisingly, 'Delcassé expressed his entire agreement, and added that this view now prevailed in the French Chamber, which was inclined to take a reasonable, not to say friendly, line in regard to all such questions. As for the French Government, they had ceased to desire a wide extension of their Colonial possessions, and were intent, not upon adding to them, but upon consolidating them, and removing all sources of future trouble within them and upon their borders.'[3] Lansdowne replied that 'his Government were influenced by very similar sentiments' and that 'the opportunity was in every way propitious for a frank exchange of opinions between the two Governments'.[4]

After this round of unusually significant compliments Lansdowne raised the Newfoundland question. The discussion followed lines which had already become familiar and which were to be re-echoed as a leitmotive throughout the *Entente* negotiations. Delcassé said 'that the question of the supply of bait, so indispensable to the French fishermen, was that which had most importance for France'. He also stressed that 'the considerations which had had to be taken into account by the French Government were largely of a sentimental character. There was a feeling that the fish which had of late deserted the French shore might

---

[1] See Lansdowne to Monson, 7 Jul 1903, *BD* II, no. 357, pp. 294–7.
[2] Lansdowne to Monson, 7 Jul 1903, ibid., p. 294.
[3] Ibid.   [4] Ibid.

some day return there, and any surrender of French rights would be resented unless it could be shown that sufficient compensation could be secured.'[1] Lansdowne claimed that he too must take sentimental considerations into account but that, as far as Great Britain's Colony of Newfoundland was concerned, there was much more at stake than sentiment. The French system of bounties to fishermen and particularly to the fishermen of St-Pierre and Miquelon, enabled them to compete on terms which were 'ruinous' to the fishermen of Newfoundland. The Newfoundland people, on their side, 'were masters of the situation so far as supply of bait was concerned, and naturally felt that this was a trump card which they were entitled to use to the best effect.'[2] Lansdowne continued by reminding Delcassé that he had discussed with Cambon the possibility of 'a settlement on the basis of the withdrawal of the French from the French Shore with compensation to the persons engaged in the fishing industry, while the French fishermen would receive facilities for obtaining a free supply of bait on the Newfoundland Coast'.[3] Cambon 'had suggested that France was entitled to territorial compensation as well as compensation in money', and, although 'surprised at this demand', he had not 'altogether excluded the idea' but, as he had made clear to Cambon, the giving up of Gambia could not be considered; 'there might however be other quarters in which a concession might perhaps be made to France'[4] and he invited Delcassé to make suggestions in due course. There was no comment from Delcassé on this point and he reverted instead to the question of bounties which he described as 'a matter of domestic concern to the French Government' and one on which it would be difficult to give way. Lansdowne reiterated that the question was of prime concern to the Colonial Government of Newfoundland and pressed Delcassé to give further study to the problem. This rather sterile discussion was cut short by Delcassé, who observed 'that the possibility of coming to an understanding as to the Newfoundland question really depended upon our attitude with regard to French interests in Morocco. If we could come to terms as to that country, all other difficulties would disappear, or become

---

[1] Lansdowne to Monson, 7 Jul 1903, *BD* II, no. 357, p. 294.   [2] Ibid.
[3] Lansdowne to Cambon, 7 Jul 1903, ibid.
[4] Lansdowne to Cambon, 7 Jul 1903, ibid., p. 295.

comparatively easy to deal with.[1] Having emphasised the
importance which France attached to Morocco, Delcassé then endeavoured to allay British anxieties on lines which had already become familiar. 'The French Government had no desire to get rid of
the Sultan or to annex his country. They wished on the contrary to
maintain the Sultan's rule. Such a system was much more convenient than French administration pure and simple. . . . Nor,
again, had the French Government any desire to force the pace.'[2]
As evidence of this Delcassé pointed to French 'moderation' in
dealing with the tribes on the Algerian frontier. But, he argued,
it was becoming obvious 'that the authority of the Sultan
was waning rapidly, and that it was insufficient to maintain
order in the country, and the French Government could not
regard with indifference the prevalence of chronic disorder in
Morocco, or admit that it was the business of any other Power
than France to undertake the task of regenerating the country.
In these circumstances what they desired was a reasonable
assurance that their policy would not be obstructed by Great
Britain.'[3]

Lansdowne accepted his cue and firmly grasped the Morocco
nettle. 'I said', he reported to Monson, 'that we had shown by
our conduct during the last two years that we had no desire to
call in question the right of the French Government to take
measures for the pacification of the Franco-Moorish border, and
we had readily accepted the assurances of the French Government that the operations in which they had lately been engaged
were to be of a strictly defensive character, nor did I think it likely
that this country would ever take a leading part in the pacification
of the interior of Morocco, should there be a collapse of the
Sultan's authority, followed by a condition of confusion and
anarchy.'[4] Lansdowne then poured scorn on French suspicions
of the alleged intrigues of Sir Harry Maclean, insisting that official
advice to the Sultan had been 'of the soundest description' and
adding that 'there was nothing in it to which the French Government could take exception. On the other hand,' he affirmed, 'we
could not be indifferent to the fate of Morocco.'[5] There were

[1] Lansdowne to Monson, 7 Jul 1903, ibid.
[2] Ibid.   [3] Ibid.
[4] Ibid.   [5] Ibid.

three points of major concern: the Mediterranean seaboard and particularly Tangier and the neighbouring coast, Spanish interests, and British trade in Morocco.

Delcassé declared himself confident of being able to offer satisfaction on these three points. Already well primed by Cambon, he envisaged the 'neutralisation' of Tangier and its neighbouring seaboard. A satisfactory compromise with Spain was, he assured Lansdowne, in any case a French policy requisite. The 'open-door' for trade would present no problem.[1] Thus while Delcassé could congratulate himself that Lansdowne seemed well disposed towards a Moroccan settlement, Lansdowne could take comfort that no immediate Moroccan crisis seemed imminent and that in any agreement British trade interests could be safeguarded and British obligations to Spain honoured without too much difficulty.

However, it was no doubt with some relief that the Foreign Secretaries turned from Morocco to the far less controversial question of Siam. Here Delcassé came straight to the point and stated that 'the position of France and Great Britain had virtually been determined by the Agreement of 1896 which involved the recognition of the claims of France in the valley of the Mekong and of Great Britain in the Malay Peninsula'.[2] Although this bargain was by now quite acceptable to Lansdowne, he could not endorse anything so crude and simple without some reference to the past and some reservation for the future. He reminded Delcassé that 'Lord Salisbury had expressly guarded himself against this interpretation of the Agreement'.[3] Delcassé showed his appreciation of this diplomatic refinement by laughing and insisting that 'there was, however, no resisting the conclusion that the two Powers when they guaranteed the centre of Siam, had by implication admitted that they were free to deal with the external portions of the Kingdom'.[4] In a spirit almost of banter, he pointed out that Great Britain's recent conduct in Kelantan showed that the British considered themselves at liberty to do what they pleased in the Peninsula. Lansdowne denied that Kelantan had been occupied by a British force and referred to British rights in the Mekong Valley which 'the Franco-Siamese draft treaty had

---

[1] See Lansdowne to Monson, 7 Jul 1903, *BD* ii, no. 257, p. 296.
[2] Ibid.   [3] Ibid.   [4] Ibid.

seemed to ignore'.[1] Delcassé immediately appreciated that British trade interests were involved and explained that there was no wish 'to encroach' upon the British most-favoured-nation treatment. France was merely concerned to establish a preference in possible railway construction. Lansdowne rather pompously declared that he 'had no reason to suppose that British capital was likely to be forthcoming for railway construction in the Mekong Valley', and that 'the British had no desire to obstruct French railway enterprise in that part of the world'. An open door for commerce was Great Britain's only concern. Delcassé gave the necessary assurance and the problem, reduced to this dimension, had clearly been resolved.[2]

No greater difficulties, at this stage, emerged over the question of the New Hebrides. Lansdowne referred to Étienne's partition proposal and said that he anticipated opposition from Australia. Delcassé declared himself open to any British suggestions and added that if they could come to terms over Morocco the New Hebrides could surely be settled with 'the utmost ease'.[3]

After this generous hint Delcassé turned to Sokoto and while admitting that, according to the Convention of 14 June 1898, Great Britain was 'entitled to the territory comprised within the arc of the 100-mile circle of which Sokoto was the centre', he felt there was occasion for revision of arrangements reached 'in ignorance of the local conditions' and compelling 'French convoys, when proceeding from the French possessions on the Niger to those in the neighbourhood of Lake Tchad, to follow a circuitous and waterless route'.[4] Lansdowne, after his conversation with Étienne,[5] scented a good bargaining card and observed that if any revision were contemplated Great Britain would require a substantial concession elsewhere. He took the opportunity to declare that he was 'in favour of a comprehensive settlement between the two Governments, and that possibly a concession at this point might form an element in a general settlement'.[6] It had become, for him, the territorial compensation which the French were demanding for Newfoundland. But he did not, at this point,

---

[1] Ibid.　　　　　　　　　　[2] Ibid.
[3] See Lansdowne to Monson, 7 Jul 1903, ibid, p. 297.
[4] Ibid.　　　　　　　　　[5] See p. 176.
[6] Lansdowne to Monson, 7 Jul 1903, *BD* II, no. 357, p. 297.

declare his hand. Instead, having spoken of a comprehensive settlement, he moved with dexterity to his own chief concern: the Egyptian question. 'In the event of such a settlement being reached', he claims to have specified,

> we should also have to take stock of the situation in Egypt. No one, I supposed, for a moment believed that we were likely to retire from that country, and I learned with pleasure from Lord Cromer that the French representatives in Egypt were on excellent terms with ours; but I was under the impression that it might still be possible for France, if she chose, to give us trouble in matters of detail, and we should certainly have to consider this point if a general settlement were to be attempted.[1]

According to Lansdowne, Delcassé replied 'that he was entirely in favour of a comprehensive settlement and that the Egyptian question formed part of the larger African question which could, he felt sure, be disposed of satisfactorily if only we could come to an agreement as to the position of France and Morocco'.[2] It is only at this point, as will be seen later,[3] that any serious difference occurred between Lansdowne's and Delcassé's versions of their discussion. In the meanwhile Lansdowne evidently thought that he had made himself quite clear about the Egyptian question and that it was safely on the agenda of the negotiations. This he regarded as a cause of major satisfaction.

It was therefore in a cheerful frame of mind that he turned to a very minor cause of difficulty: the treatment of British firms in the French Congo. Lansdowne was obviously inspired by fear of awkward questions in Parliament. Delcassé answered, good-humouredly, that 'it was extremely difficult to moderate the ardour of Colonial Courts, and that we had probably experienced similar difficulties in dealing with ours'.[4] He promised, however, to bear the matter in mind.

In concluding his account of the meeting to Monson, Lansdowne confirmed 'the immense importance' which the French Government attached to their predominance in Morocco. Provided this was recognised Delcassé was ready to accept

---

[1] Lansdowne to Monson, 7 Jul 1903, *BD* II, no. 357, p. 297.
[2] Ibid. [3] See p. 193.
[4] Lansdowne to Monson, 7 Jul 1903 ibid.

Off Duty, 12 August 1903

specific British conditions over Morocco and to be most accommodating elsewhere.[1] Lansdowne was quite correct in his assumption about the importance which Delcassé attached to Morocco
and shrewd in his judgement that a good bargain for Britain was
available. On the other hand there is no sign that he appreciated
the wider vision which surely dominated Delcassé. Quite apart
from the merits of the Moroccan bargain, his sights were set on
the European impact of the *rapprochement* which, he calculated,
must follow the settlement. Hesitant about timing and ready to
deviate for tactical or concrete advantage, his purpose was an
article of faith. Patriotic necessity, in the long run, imposed
Entente Cordiale. However he might tackle the bargain its achievement loomed larger than its terms. These must be debated but, in
the meanwhile, his own wishes were reflected in the optimistic
assertion in *Le Temps* that 'the Anglo-French *rapprochement* is an
accomplished fact'.[2]

[1] Lansdowne to Monson, 7 Jul 1903, *BD* II, no. 357, p. 297.
[2] *Le Temps*, 11 Jul 1903.

10

The First Misunderstanding

ON 15 July Lansdowne and Cambon had their first private meeting since the President's visit. 'The French Ambassador', Lansdowne recorded, 'told me that the President had been much pleased with his reception in this country, and that which he had met with on his return to Paris showed that the French people appreciated the goodwill which had been shown him in London, and approved of the friendly relations which had been created between the two nations.'[1] Discussion then turned to the Lansdowne–Delcassé conversations of 7 July and to procedure for pursuing the negotiations. There seems to have been some confusion in Cambon's mind about what the two Foreign Ministers had proposed.[2] He asked whether he could expect a *pro memoria* giving British views. Lansdowne replied that an exchange of memoranda, which could then be compared, had been contemplated. Cambon insisted that he believed that the next step was simply to have been a British statement of views on the Moroccan question. Lansdowne replied that 'he did not think that the Moroccan question could be discussed except in connection with other matters of interest to both Governments'.[3] He further reminded Cambon that any Moroccan settlement depended on three conditions: commercial freedom, freedom of the Strait and agreement with Spain. He also referred to Newfoundland and insisted that the bounty question was vital as far as the Colony's Parliament was concerned.[4] Cambon judiciously avoided any comment. The meeting ended without any definite decision on

---

[1] Lansdowne to de Bunsen, 15 Jul 1903, *BD* II, no. 358, p. 298.
[2] See Cambon to Delcassé, 22 Jul 1903, *DDF*, III, no. 363, p. 473.
[3] Lansdowne to de Bunsen, 15 Jul 1903, *BD* II, no. 358, p. 298.
[4] See Cambon to Delcassé, 22 Jul 1903, *DDF*, III, no. 363, p. 474.

future procedure, although Cambon did get the impression that Lansdowne was prepared for an immediate exchange of memoranda on Morocco; Lansdowne, on the other hand, seems to have gathered that a summary of French views ought 'to begin with, be prepared' for his 'private information'.[1]

Cambon evidently felt it necessary to see Delcassé in order to clear his own mind. He therefore travelled to Paris and they met on 18 July. Delcassé seems to have admitted that he had agreed, with Lansdowne, 'to a general examination of questions interesting the two Governments, including Morocco',[2] proposing to include in the French memorandum all matters where France was seeking concessions and leaving Great Britain to take the initiative on other points. Following this conversation Delcassé summarised his own version of his 7 July discussion with Lansdowne in a telegram, dated 21 July, claiming that, on the Egyptian question,

> faced by my extreme reserve he [Lansdowne] did not touch on the political aspect. He only spoke of financial obstacles which he might meet. I replied [continued Delcassé] that he knew my spirit of conciliation and that it would be easier for me to show it without provoking public opinion in France, if that opinion, which watches with jealous care over affairs in Morocco, could feel that our action in Morocco could be exercised not only without the opposition, but with the favour of England.[3]

In reply to Lansdowne's proposal of a comprehensive settlement, Delcassé confirmed that he had welcomed this initiative and expressed willingness to respond. 'But', he emphasised, 'the first step is the settlement of Morocco according to the views of France.'[4] According to Delcassé Lansdowne replied 'that he understood my reservation and that he would submit to you [Cambon] a pro memoria giving his views'.[5]

Delcassé's latest communication and their conversation of 18 July still left Cambon undecided and anxious about the best means of pursuing the negotiations. Accordingly when on 21 July he again saw Lansdowne, ostensibly to discuss the

[1] Lansdowne to de Bunsen, 15 Jul 1903, *BD* II, no. 358, p. 298.
[2] See Cambon to Delcassé, 22 Jul 1903, *DDF*, III, no. 363, pp. 474–5.
[3] Delcassé to Cambon, 21 Jul 1903, *DDF*, III, no. 362, p. 472.
[4] Ibid.   [5] Ibid.

Arbitration Treaty project,[1] he merely confirmed that he had been under some misapprehension about the tentative agreements on procedure but did not pursue the matter any further. Instead he confided the reasons for his hesitancy to Delcassé. 'It is very difficult', he wrote,

> to be precise on the questions where we are demanding and where we are on the defensive. In Newfoundland only can it be said that we are in exclusive possession of rights recognised by Treaties and for which it is up to England to propose a purchase price. But in the New Hebrides, in Siam, in Nigeria, interests are mixed, rights reciprocal and pretensions more or less well defined. Is it possible in a friendly discussion on these points at the outset to take any definite position as in a legal case on a precise and limited point? Is it even prudent to mix these questions with the Moroccan question? Because that is the essential point, and we run the risk of obscuring it by mixing it with others and subordinating it to controversies of all kinds.[2]

With some diffidence Cambon expressed the opinion that Great Britain, fearing German intervention in a matter which should be settled exclusively between France, Great Britain and Spain, positively desired a Moroccan settlement. Spain itself, he argued, was temporarily in a more favourable mood. Therefore he recommended that the first step should be an exchange of unofficial memoranda between England and France on the Moroccan question. Once agreement had been reached definitive memoranda could be submitted to the Spanish Government and, once Spanish agreement had been secured, declarations could be exchanged between the three Governments. After that the other questions at issue could be considered in the following order: Siam, Nigeria, Newfoundland and New Hebrides.[3]

This certainly would have been a tidy way of proceeding. But Cambon was over-sanguine in assuming that Lansdowne was in any hurry to settle the Moroccan question or that he would be prepared, in any circumstances, to treat it in isolation. One of the reasons for Cambon's optimism was that he was still under some delusion about what at least Lansdowne believed to have

[1] See p. 156.
[2] Cambon to Delcassé, 22 Jul 1903, *DDF*, III, no. 363, p. 473.
[3] Ibid.

transpired at his meeting on 7 July with Delcassé. Feeling the need for further consultation with his own chief, Cambon returned to Paris to discuss his own latest suggestions.

The result of this meeting was a note by Delcassé dated 27 July and apparently taken down in Cambon's hand.[1] The note, which was to serve as a basis for Cambon's next conversation with Lansdowne, represented something of a compromise. The principle of a comprehensive settlement was accepted and there followed draft declarations of agreement on Morocco, Newfoundland, New Hebrides and Siam. There was no mention of Egypt.

While Cambon had been consulting with Delcassé, Lansdowne had received powerful encouragement and a good deal of unsolicited advice from Cromer. In a long letter[2] which Lansdowne received on 27 July Cromer expressed gratified but cautious surprise that Delcassé should have shown himself so forthcoming. For France, Cromer concluded, the main question was manifestly Morocco. Siam seemed to present no problem. Some concession on Sokoto, he thought, could buy counter-concessions in Newfoundland. He admitted ignorance about the New Hebrides. But on Morocco he strongly recommended, as he had previously advised, the advantage of making concessions in return for counter-concessions in Egypt, urging, however, that this should be done 'with our eyes open to what it means'. This meaning he somewhat brutally exposed. Referring back to Lansdowne's comment to Étienne that 'Eastern Monarchies often managed to survive in spite of apparent decay and seemingly innumerable difficulties', he continued:

> this is perfectly true, but the reason is also obvious. It is that the agony of these decadent Oriental States such as Turkey and Persia is prolonged owing to the dissensions and rivalries among possible heirs to the succession . . . if once the French succession were secured the agony of Morocco would not be of long duration . . . the question therefore to my mind is this: have we any objection to Morocco becoming a French province? Personally, I see none, provided always (1) that we had an adequate quid pro quo in Egypt and elsewhere; and (2) that the French comply with your three conditions as regards

---

[1] *DDF*, III, no. 373, pp. 485–6, and note, p. 485.
[2] Cromer to Lansdowne, 17 Jul 1903, *BD* II, no. 359, pp. 298–301.

Morocco . . . I base my opinion on the following considerations: (1) that there appears to be no particular reason why we should endeavour to prolong the existence of a bad native government in Morocco; (2) that that country is manifestly destined to fall within the sphere of influence of some European Power; (3) that, under these circumstances, it is necessary, and under present circumstances, desirable to decide which of the European Powers should exercise a predominating influence; (4) that we certainly do not wish to be burdened with the government of the interior of Morocco; (5) that M. Étienne is right in saying that the Spaniards are quite incapable of dealing with the question; and (6) that therefore the French had better be allowed a free hand in the matter.[1]

After this forthright declaration Cromer urged that Great Britain's attitude towards Morocco should be defined before the proposed visit of Sir Eldon Gorst[2] to Paris in the autumn 'with a view to sounding the French as regards their attitude to the Conversion of the Egyptian Debt and the abolition of the Caisse de la Dette'.[3] His mission, Cromer warned, would be foredoomed to failure unless Morocco could be used as a bargaining counter. 'In all diplomatic negotiations', Cromer advised, 'there is always a danger of moving either too fast or too slow. In the present case the danger lies rather on the side of moving too slow.'[4] Provided the British Government could agree that there was no objection to French predominance in Morocco the opportunity seemed clear. Details of British counter-concessions in Egypt, which would require 'very careful consideration', could be postponed until that policy decision had been definitively taken.

No doubt gratified by Cromer's plain speaking, Lansdowne had a long and important meeting with Cambon on his return from Paris, on 29 July. Cambon's account to Delcassé is, not surprisingly, more detailed than Lansdowne's to Monson; but there is substantial agreement about what transpired. Cambon opened the proceedings by declaring that 'it seemed to M. Delcassé that we were virtually in agreement',[5] and continued by reading out

---

[1] Cromer to Lansdowne, 17 Jul 1903, ibid., pp. 299–300.
[2] Financial Adviser to the Egyptian Government 1898–1904, and Cromer's eventual successor as Consul-General.
[3] Cromer to Lansdowne, 17 Jul 1903, *BD* II, no. 359, p. 300.
[4] Ibid.
[5] Cambon to Delcassé, 31 Jul 1903, *DDF*, III, no. 381, p. 497.

Delcassé's note of 27 July.[1] Lansdowne just commented on the form of the Morocco declaration, objecting to the term 'the High Contracting Parties' because it suggested the existence of a treaty. He preferred an exchange of notes.[2] This was typical of Lansdowne's general caution and does not seem to have had any deep significance. Lansdowne then enquired whether any approach had yet been made to Spain. Cambon replied that proposals had been made but no reply received.[3] He explained that the question of giving satisfaction to Spain, on which both Governments were agreed, would be settled by direct negotiation between France and Spain. As soon as agreement had been reached the terms would be communicated to Great Britain. According to Cambon, Lansdowne acquiesced in this procedure.[4] On the question of the freedom of the Strait, Lansdowne pointed out that Great Britain was not interested merely 'in that part of the Moroccan coastline which abutted on the Straits of Gibraltar'. Cambon readily agreed that the neutralised zone should be extended, and confided to Delcassé that he assumed that Lansdowne was concerned about a former German plan to establish a coaling station or possibly even a naval base on the Mediterranean in the region of the Spanish *présides*.[5] In fact, as will be seen later,[6] Lansdowne was more directly anxious to exclude the possibility of any French military establishments on that coast. Delcassé, however, took up Cambon's point and noted that that was the reason why in his own previous negotiations with Spain he had sought to include a proviso preventing Spain from alienating any Moorish territories which she might acquire without French permission.[7] On Newfoundland Lansdowne again referred to the bounty question without drawing any comment from Cambon. On the New Hebrides Lansdowne remarked that there were serious difficulties in the way of partition and Cambon suggested that other solutions might be sought.[8] Lansdowne then asked for a copy of Delcassé's

[1] *DDF*, III, no. 372, pp. 485–6; and see p. 190.
[2] See Cambon to Delcassé, 31 Jul 1903, *DDF*, III, no. 381, p. 497.
[3] See Lansdowne to Monson, 29 Jul 1903, *BD* II, no. 363, p. 304.
[4] See Cambon to Delcassé, 31 Jul 1903, *DDF*, III, no. 381, p. 498.
[5] Ibid.
[6] See p. 205.
[7] See *DDF*, III, no. 381, p. 498 n.
[8] Ibid., p. 498.

note of 27 July. Cambon explained that the document was not an official one, but readily agreed to furnish Lansdowne with a personal letter summing up Delcassé's views so that this could be shown to the King.[1] 'I thought', wrote Cambon, 'that the negotiation was thus most satisfactorily engaged when Lord Lansdowne pointed out to me that you had made no allusion to the Egyptian question. Nevertheless' he added, 'I spoke about it to M. Delcassé; he must have told you so.'[2] Cambon admitted that, according to Delcassé, Egypt had been mentioned on 7 July, but claimed that the reference had been a passing one and that, at his own recent meeting with Delcassé, the subject had not been raised. 'I did speak of Egypt', Lansdowne insisted, 'and M. Delcassé did not seem unwilling to examine our situation in the Nile Valley. No settlement of questions interesting France and England would be understood here unless Egypt were included.'[3] Cambon answered that he had no authority to proceed in this matter, that its examination implied many points which interested other powers, such as the neutrality of the Suez Canal and the international institutions and that it did not seem as if Egypt could therefore be linked with the questions which could be dealt with between their own two Governments.[4] According to Lansdowne Cambon did, however, add that an arrangement on the basis of existing institutions, citing particularly the interest of France in Egyptian archaeological researches, might be considered.[5] Lansdowne for his part insisted that there never would be a more favourable moment to tackle the Egyptian question, that Lord Cromer was shortly expected in England, that his presence would be useful in helping to seek a solution and that in any case the matter should be recalled to Delcassé's attention.[6] After pressing this point Lansdowne concluded the discussion by observing that he would 'have much pleasure in repeating Cambon's observations to his colleagues', admitting that 'they seemed to be useful as a basis for further discussion' but warning that there were

[1] Ibid.   [2] Cambon to Delcassé, 31 Jul 1903, ibid., pp. 498–9.
[3] Cambon to Delcassé, 31 Jul 1903, ibid., p. 499. In Lansdowne's account of this to Monson he claims to have repeated to Cambon the version of Delcassé's words which he had originally given to Monson on 7 July. See *BD* II, no. 363, p. 305.
[4] See Cambon to Delcassé, 31 Jul 1903, *DDF*, III, no. 381, p. 449.
[5] See Lansdowne to Monson, 29 Jul, *BD* II, no. 363, p. 303.
[6] See Cambon to Delcassé, 31 Jul 1903, *DDF*, III, no. 381, p. 499.

many points which would require to be examined very carefully before further progress could be made.[1]

From this discussion Cambon rightly concluded that Egypt was, from England's point of view, the vital factor; it is difficult to see how he could have thought otherwise unless positively misled by Delcassé's version of the conversations of 7 July. At any rate he now tried to make the position quite clear to his own chief. Egypt could not be excluded if negotiations were to proceed and it was now up to Delcassé to decide whether 'the question which has weighed for twenty years on the relations between the two countries' should now be tackled. 'But', advised Cambon, 'if we do consent to recognize the British occupation of Egypt it would not be enough . . . to obtain guarantees for the international institutions and for the French services established in Cairo; we should show ourselves more demanding in Morocco or elsewhere.'[2]

'Of course', noted Delcassé, 'that is why I showed so much reserve when Lord Lansdowne spoke to me of Egypt.'[3] Delcassé may have thought that Cambon, in assuming that the stakes would need to be raised, was stating the obvious and failing to understand that this had been his own objective throughout. But, in that case, Delcassé was doing less than justice to Cambon's appreciation of the true position. Once the Egyptian question had been posed – and Delcassé's claims to have evaded it at his meeting with Lansdowne do not carry much conviction – it would have been better to stress the magnitude of the proposed concession at once rather than to try to strike a better bargain later. Most of the difficulties of the subsequent negotiations centred on the problem of where and how France could show herself more 'demanding' while Lansdowne, believing that France's demands had already been clarified, was particularly loth to make any further concessions. Once he had sketched out to his colleagues the possibility of a settlement on certain terms, it is hardly surprising that he should have been reluctant to present them with the need for any substantial modifications. Cambon, either because Delcassé was genuinely confused or because he had tried to be

---

[1] See Lansdowne to Monson, 29 Jul 1903, *BD* II, no. 363, p. 305.
[2] Cambon to Delcassé, 31 Jul 1903, *DDF*, III, no. 381, p. 499.
[3] Ibid., p. 499 n.

too subtle, was in the weak position of seeking to improve on a bargain which had already been outlined. His professional pride was such that he could relish the task; but he was forced repeatedly to take the offensive against a stubborn British defence.

Authority to include Egypt in the negotiations was provided almost immediately by Delcassé, but before doing so he tried, none too successfully, to indicate that there was no inconsistency in his attitude. He repeated his version of the original conversation with Lansdowne which he had already communicated to Cambon.[1] His views, he insisted, remained unchanged. 'I do not', he continued, 'therefore refuse to examine Lord Lansdowne's suggestions about Egypt: but it is clear that the concessions which, for our part, we could be brought to make on this point, would demand equivalent concessions elsewhere.'[2] Perhaps, he suggested, France's liberty of action in Morocco might be more definitely stressed; a limit, say twenty-five or twenty years, might be set to the proposed guarantee of commercial liberty; some provision might be made for dealing with the unlikely possibility of total Spanish intransigence; if partition in the New Hebrides proved unacceptable, territorial compensation for France would be required in addition to that envisaged for Newfoundland.[3]

Thus briefed, Cambon joined, on 5 August, in what was to prove a marathon session with Lansdowne.[4] Cambon opened the proceedings by confirming that, where Morocco was concerned, Delcassé was in agreement with Lansdowne over the question of commercial liberty, negotiation with Spain and freedom of the Strait. On the latter point he concurred that the part of the Moorish coast to be neutralised should be determined after a report from the British Admiralty. German aims were discussed and Lansdowne agreed that these had now turned from the Mediterranean to the Atlantic. Cambon endeavoured to fan British fears by claiming that he had information that the German Embassy in Tangier was on the look-out for some concession at

---

[1] See Delcassé to Cambon, 2 Aug 1903, *DDF*, III, no. 387, p. 511; and see also p. 188.

[2] Delcassé to Cambon, 2 Aug 1903, ibid.

[3] Ibid.

[4] Cambon's report to Delcassé is fuller than Lansdowne's to Monson, but there are no substantial differences save in the order of topics discussed. See *DDF*, III, no. 392, pp. 516–20, and *BD* II, no. 364, pp. 306–7.

Rabat or Casablanca. Lansdowne then enquired about Spain. Cambon explained that an informal agreement with Spain had been reached the previous August.

'Yes, I remember', replied Lansdowne, 'you seemed even more satisfied with Spain's response to M. Delcassé's overtures than with our own.'[1] Cambon pointed out that, due to constant Spanish cabinet crises, the negotiations had lapsed but that they could be reopened and that they were based on concession to Spain of 'a considerable slice of the Moorish coastline in the neighbourhood of her existing possessions with a certain amount of adjoining hinterland'.[2] Lansdowne remarked that this concession could only take effect in the case of general liquidation and recalled that maintenance of the *status quo* remained the basis of agreement. Cambon readily concurred but pointed out that Spain should not be hindered in her action in areas eventually destined to fall to her. 'Just as you assume', rejoined Lansdowne, 'that you will meet with no interference in the rest of Morocco, or be obstructed in your commercial enterprises or in the advice which you would feel obliged to give to the Sultan.'[3] 'Precisely', concluded Cambon. Lansdowne then explained that his purpose in raising the matter was to be able to reply to probable questions from the Spanish Ambassador about rumours of an Anglo-French agreement over Morocco. He proposed to reply that Morocco had been discussed but that nothing would be done without the knowledge of Spain. Cambon demurred at this, pointing out that it might lead to constant questioning on Spain's part, but suggesting instead that Lansdowne could confirm that nothing would be done unless Spain was satisfied. Lansdowne agreed.[4]

He then referred back to the question of commercial liberty, urging that agreement in principle was not enough and that there must be a clear definition of what the principle entailed. Cambon, presumably because he wished to reserve the question for future bargaining as suggested by Delcassé, answered that as the basis was agreed the form could easily be settled. Moving to the attack on an easier front Cambon then asked what territorial compen-

[1] Cambon to Delcassé, 6 Aug 1903, *DDF*, iii, no. 392, p. 517.
[2] Lansdowne to Monson, 5 Aug 1903, *BD* ii, no. 364, p. 307.
[3] Cambon to Delcassé, 6 Aug 1903, *DDF*, iii, no. 392, p. 517.
[4] Ibid., pp. 517–18.

2

sation Lansdowne was proposing for Newfoundland. Lansdowne parried by speaking of bounties and by indicating that, if France could give some appearance of satisfaction to the Newfoundlanders on this point, the rest [presumably territorial compensation] would be facilitated.[1] While on the subject of territorial compensation Cambon indicated that, where the New Hebrides were concerned, although Delcassé favoured partition, he would be prepared to accept territorial compensation elsewhere instead. According to Cambon this raised a smile from Lansdowne, who answered: 'Another territorial compensation . . . I wonder where it could be found, perhaps in the region of Sokoto.' 'Would you give us Sokoto?', enquired Cambon with some eagerness. 'Oh no, the Colonial Office would never consent to that.' 'Then let us speak of it no more; for we would not be content with some barren bit of the Sahara to the north of your Niger possessions.'[2]

After this mildly probing exchange main business could no longer be avoided. But, in approaching the Egyptian question, Cambon began by resorting to fencing tactics. Delcassé, he said, recalled discussing Egypt but only in relation to financial questions. 'I did not intend only to speak of financial questions',[3] insisted Lansdowne. 'I wanted to initiate an examination of the Egyptian question as a whole. My Cabinet colleagues consider as I do that we cannot settle the questions which interest us without including the Egyptian question.'[4] Cambon repeated the objections which he had raised at a previous meeting and added: 'Whether we were wrong or right not to intervene with you in 1882 is not the question . . . you went into Egypt alone promising that you would move out again; your occupation is therefore precarious, and its end, as far as French opinion at large is concerned, is still awaited.' 'I know', recognised Lansdowne, 'that our situation is not quite regular, and we would wish to regularise it.' 'That is to say', interjected Cambon, 'that you expect from us recognition of your occupation, a consolidation of the present state of affairs. I know of nothing more difficult to make France accept. I know that M. Delcassé has a sincere desire to settle with

[1] Ibid., p. 518.

[2] Cambon to Delcassé, 6 Aug 1903, ibid. This part of the conversation was not reported by Lansdowne to Monson.

[3] But Delcassé noted on this report: 'He did not do so.' Ibid., p. 518 n.

[4] Cambon to Delcassé, 6 Aug 1903, ibid., p. 518.

you all questions at issue, even, if possible the Egyptian one; I think he is courageous enough to put himself above popular clamour; but if I may use a slang expression he will need great guts [*estomac*] to assume responsibility for a settlement of the Egyptian question.'[1] At last Cambon had come round openly to the point which Lansdowne had assumed to have been reached on 7 July. 'Do you think', he parried, 'that we do not need guts to abandon Morocco to you?' 'It is not the same thing', replied Cambon and significantly added, 'You would have given us full freedom of action long ago in Morocco, if we had supported your establishment in the Nile Valley.'[2] After this dialectic success Cambon returned to present realities and confirmed that, while all now depended on the British Government's interpretation of an Egyptian settlement, Delcassé was prepared to consider what-ever proposals might be made. The initiative lay with England. 'That', answered Lansdowne, 'leaves me with work to do during the coming recess.'[3] The Cabinet, he informed Cambon, was not due to meet again before the end of September but by then British views on Egypt could be formulated and means could be sought to settle all problems. In order to pave the way for his future offensive Cambon reiterated that a new element had been brought into the discussions and argued that 'if France was so obliging as to extract "this big thorn" from the foot of Great Britain, she would look for "une grosse compensation". It might take the shape of greater liberty of action in Morocco – something less remote and conjectural ("moins hypothétique") than she had yet asked for.'[4] Thus, at last and with a prospect of hard bargaining ahead, the seal was set on the substance of the original Lansdowne–Delcassé conversations.

Following this progress Lansdowne could go ahead with the preparation of concrete proposals for a settlement of the Egyptian question. A memorandum from Cromer, who had arrived in London for consultations, facilitated the task. 'I assume', wrote Cromer, 'that we do not wish to go as far as to annex Egypt, but that our main objects are (1) to acquire a political *status* which

---

[1] Cambon to Delcassé, 6 Aug 1903, *DDF*, III, no. 392, pp. 518-19.
[2] Cambon to Delcassé, 6 Aug 1903, ibid., p. 519.
[3] Ibid.
[4] Lansdowne to Monson, 5 Aug 1903, *BD* II, no. 364, p. 306.

will be recognized by the French Government and (2) to obtain
as much freedom of action as possible in the administration of the
Country.'[1] He warned that 'complete freedom of action, such as
would enable the Capitulations to be abolished, cannot, save by
annexation, be obtained without the consent of all the Powers of
Europe', and he advised 'limiting ourselves to what may be obtained by an understanding with France alone'.[2] The first and
essential point was recognition by France of the permanent
character which British occupation had acquired. The second was
to obtain complete liberty of action in financial matters. As far as
the Capitulations were concerned he advised leaving matters alone
for the present, arguing that even with a completely free hand it
would be difficult to put forward solutions, that 'the most trifling
change would require the consent of all the Powers' and that once
financial liberty had been secured and the permanency of the
British occupation recognised, 'time' would 'eventually bring
about a solution of all other points'. He did, however, suggest
that it might be wise to insert into any agreement a clause to the
effect that Great Britain reserved the right at a future date to
propose the abolition of the Capitulations and that France would
not raise objections in the event. Finally Cromer referred to the
position of the Consul-General and English Heads of Departments. He thought that it might be necessary to make provision
for their presence at the Council of Ministers and at the same time
to convert the Council of Ministers into a real governing body.
These changes were, however, for future consideration and he
saw no reason to mention such possibilities to the French.[3] The
burden of Cromer's message was simple. Once financial freedom
had been secured and the permanency of British occupation recognised Egypt's sovereign rights could be recovered at leisure and
methods of Anglo-Egyptian government could be reorganised
gradually and deliberately.

While British demands concerning Egypt were thus in process
of formulation Delcassé authorised Saint-René Taillandier to proceed with negotiations for a new Moroccan loan.[4] He indicated

[1] Memorandum by Cromer, 7 Aug 1903, *BD* II, no. 365, p. 307.
[2] Ibid.
[3] See Memorandum by Cromer, 7 Aug 1903, ibid., pp. 308–9.
[4] See Delcassé to Saint-René Taillandier, 8 Aug 1903, *DDF*, III, no. 394, p. 522.

that, if the Anglo-French negotiations were successful, there would be full British recognition of French rights to 'watch over the tranquillity of Morocco and to provide aid for necessary financial, administrative and economic reforms'.[1] It was now, therefore, Saint-René Taillandier's task to prepare the local approaches for the exercise of such rights.

Even before this encouragement to Saint-René Taillandier his activities, taken in conjunction with the obvious opening of *Entente* negotiations, had aroused the suspicions of the Spanish Government. To their enquiries, via Durand,[2] Lansdowne now felt obliged to make some kind of reply. Durand was authorised to admit that conversations about Morocco had been in progress. In those conversations opposition to any proposals for partition had been declared and it had been emphasised that 'should such a partition become inevitable . . . the interests of Spain would receive adequate recognition'.[3] Explicit assurances had been given by the French that they had 'no desire to annex Morocco or to bring about the removal of the Sultan'.[4] On the other hand, as the Sultan was not likely to hold his own for long without assistance and advice, and as he must turn for advice to France, the French assumed that they would 'as a logical consequence thereby acquire a predominant position at the Moorish Court'.[5] Discussion of questions of detail had not yet commenced. They were bound to be difficult and Great Britain's 'task' would be 'greatly facilitated by a full knowledge of the views of the Spanish Government'.[6] Thus, while Lansdowne had accepted France's argument that it would be best for France to approach Spain directly and in her own time, he left the door open to the Spanish Government to keep him informed of their reactions. In fact Lansdowne's communication strengthened Spanish suspicions but did not produce the obvious corollary that Spain should seek at once for the best terms they might yet obtain from the French. The vacillation which had prevented final conclusion of a bargain with France while England's attitude was uncertain continued to paralyse Spanish policy even when British intentions were correctly interpreted.

[1] Delcassé to Saint-René Taillandier, 8 Aug 1903, *DDF*, III, no. 394, p. 522.
[2] Sir M. Durand, British Ambassador at Madrid.
[3] Lansdowne to Durand, 11 Aug 1903, *BD* II, no. 366, p. 309.
[4] Ibid.   [5] Ibid.   [6] Ibid.

Speculation about the outcome of the Lansdowne–Delcassé conversations was, of course, not confined to Spain. German displeasure at signs of Anglo-French *rapprochement* was tempered by confidence that no real accommodation could be achieved without disruption of the Franco-Russian Alliance.[1] No pains were spared to exploit Russian suspicions. Reporting from St Petersburg on 31 July 1903, Bompard warned that, although Russia had initially welcomed signs of increasing cordiality between London and Paris, recent effusions of goodwill had provoked some doubts. Any major change in the direction of French policy towards England might induce the Russians to seek reinsurance elsewhere. That opportunity was eagerly awaited by Germany.[2] In replying to Bompard Delcassé made it quite clear that a real settlement with England was intended but insisted that the Franco-Russian Alliance remained a pivot of French foreign policy.[3] His belief that the Alliance could be combined with Anglo-French *rapprochement* was strengthened by a report from Cambon that Benckendorff,[4] the newly appointed Russian Ambassador, was anxious to open friendly discussions with Lansdowne but, as yet, was nervous about how to begin.[5] Cambon, who confessed himself somewhat mystified by Russian motives, reassured Benckendorff about British dispositions, but warned him that with Lansdowne it was always necessary to take the initiative.[6]

In fact, as Cambon well knew, one of the arguments which Lansdowne used with his colleagues in favour of an Anglo-French understanding was that it might lead to an improvement of Anglo-Russian relations. The main preoccupation of the Committee of Imperial Defence continued to be the question of the defence of India. Indian vulnerability to Russian attack was repeatedly stressed, and the financial liabilities of increased military preparedness gloomily recognised. Suggestions that the Japanese Alliance might be adapted to help meet this threat were

---

[1] See Bihourd to Delcassé, 18 Jul 1903, *DDF*, III, no. 359, p. 463.

[2] See Bompard to Delcassé, 31 Jul 1903, *DDF*, III, no. 383, pp. 501–2.

[3] Delcassé to Bompard, 12 Aug 1903, *DDF*, III, no. 397, pp. 527–8.

[4] Count Benckendorff, Russian Ambassador at London 1903–17.

[5] See Cambon to Delcassé, 6 Aug 1903, *DDF*, III, no. 393, pp. 520–1.

[6] In fact Lansdowne had already thrown out a broad hint to Benckendorff. See Lansdowne to Scott, 31 Jul 1903, *BD* II, no. 242, p. 212.

rejected, partly because of the increased commitments towards Japan which might be involved, and partly because of the unwillingness of the Indian Government to contemplate any Japanese involvement in Indian defence. The cheapest and best way to defend India, therefore, seemed to be by accommodation with Russia, thus reducing, if not eliminating, the Russian threat. The most immediate obstacle in the way of any *rapprochement* with Russia, apart from Russian reluctance, was the Manchurian question. After violent Japanese alarms[1] in early July and the failure of Lansdowne's endeavours to persuade the Japanese to seek American support, there had been a project for a Russo-Japanese agreement based on a Manchuria–Korea bargain. Lansdowne had regarded this with little relish but, while indicating British reserve, obviously could not prevent the main parties concerned from making the attempt.[2] Lansdowne feared the consequences of a Russo-Japanese agreement or of its failure. Agreement would leave England isolated in the Far East; its failure might end in war between Russia and Japan. In the meanwhile, much as Lansdowne might desire improved relations with Russia, Manchuria was obviously a very delicate topic for discussion, although he did indicate to Benckendorff his willingness to examine the question.[3] The situation was further complicated in August when Vice-Admiral Alexeiev was appointed by the Tsar Vice-Regent of the Far Eastern Provinces.[4] Rightly Sir Charles Scott,[5] in spite of reassurances from Count Lamsdorff, had 'misgivings'.[6] The champions of a forward policy in the Far East were now virtually independent of any Russian Foreign Office control. The danger which this situation implied magnified the value, and increased the difficulty, of achieving Anglo-Russian *rapprochement*.

Preoccupied mainly during the summer with Far Eastern anxieties, Lansdowne gradually prepared the way for a resumption of his negotiations with Cambon. The reactions of the

[1] See p. 169.
[2] See Lansdowne to Macdonald, 13 Jul 1903, *BD* II, no. 238, p. 208; Memorandum to Hayashi, 16 Jul 1903, *BD* II, no. 239, p. 209 and Macdonald to Lansdowne, 17 Jul 1903, *BD* II, no. 240, p. 210.
[3] See Lansdowne to Scott, 31 Jul 1903, *BD* II, no. 242, p. 212.
[4] On 13 Aug.
[5] British Ambassador at St Petersburg, 1898–1904.
[6] See Scott to Lansdowne, 27 Aug 1903, *BD* II, no. 244, p. 213.

Passive Assistance, 5 August 1903

Service Departments to the prospect of an *entente* with France were initially unenthusiastic. Their objections were based entirely on the strategic implications of a French Morocco. In a memorandum of 10 September Lansdowne pressed the advantages of an *entente* with France on his cabinet colleagues and argued that 'a good understanding with France would not improbably be the precursor of a better understanding with Russia'. Undoubtedly this argument, in the light of the Far Eastern situation, carried weight. On the other hand, as has been seen, Lansdowne had been ready to negotiate an Anglo-French settlement on it own merits. The situation in the Far East provided him with an added argument, in the Cabinet, in its favour. At least as far as he was concerned it was not the decisive argument. No new incentives were needed to urge him on a road on which he had already travelled so far. Once his interpretation of Delcassé's willingness to include the Egyptian question had been confirmed by Cambon, he had no thoughts of turning back.

11

The Question of Territorial Compensation

ON 1 October Lansdowne wrote to Cambon informing him that he had now consulted his colleagues about the proposed settlement and that, with their approval, he was able 'unofficially and confidentially' to submit a statement of Great Britain's conditions.[1] The statement was divided into eight headings: Morocco, Egypt, Newfoundland, Siam, New Hebrides, Nigeria, Zanzibar and Madagascar. As regards Morocco, while clearly recognising the preponderance of influence which France claimed, Lansdowne reasserted, with some important modifications, the three conditions which he had raised in previous discussions. On the question of commercial liberty he reiterated the importance of the general principle, emphasised that Great Britain currently enjoyed the lion's share of Moroccan trade and specified the rights which had been obtained in the 1856 Moroccan Treaty and must be guaranteed. Where the neutralisation of the Moroccan seaboard was concerned, Lansdowne, influenced perhaps by the Service Departments, made a definite and at the same time rather more sweeping claim than previously indicated.[2] The portion to be included was from the Algerian frontier to Mazagan including that port. As for Spain, Lansdowne, while repeating the need for giving satisfaction, explicitly capitulated to the French insistence on unilateral negotiation. He indicated, however, that Great Britain assumed that territories immediately adjoining existing Spanish possessions would be assigned to the Spanish sphere of influence. More significantly he proposed that

[1] See *BD* II, no. 369, pp. 311–17.　　　　[2] See p. 192.

'in the event of a complete collapse of the Sultan's authority'
Spain 'should be entrusted with the duty of administering the
seaboard now in the possession of Morocco from the Algerian
frontier to Mazaghan',[1] adding that Spain must then be precluded
from fortifying this portion of the coast or alienating it, or any
other of her existing possessions in Morocco, to any other power.
Thus while recognising the liquidation of Morocco on the one
hand, Lansdowne was seeking to use the satisfaction of Spanish
interests as an insurance policy to cover British strategic anxieties.

Turning to Egypt, Lansdowne made it absolutely clear at the
outset that any 'understanding' over Morocco was dependent on
an 'understanding' over Egypt. Great Britain's terms followed
Cromer's advice to the letter.[2] The permanency of British occupation must be recognised. The Egyptian Government must be
freed from financial fetters and consequently France must agree
not to oppose the abolition of the *Caisse de la Dette* and the
reorganisation of the Railways Administration. As for the Capitulations no immediate proposals would be made but their eventual
abolition was envisaged. In return for eventual French acquiescence, Great Britain would be prepared to back similar proposals
for Morocco should the circumstances arise. Once again, the
liquidation of Morocco was clearly implied, thus encouraging
France to pursue a forward policy and at the same time presenting
that encouragement as a bargaining concession. With Egypt and
Morocco exactly equated Lansdowne was not prepared to be
generous on other points at issue. As far as Newfoundland was
concerned France had stipulated that she would surrender her
Treaty rights in return for (1) an indemnity to those engaged in
the pursuit of the fishing industry on the French shore; (2) territorial compensation; (3) a guaranteed right to catch or buy bait.
The question of an indemnity did not seem to present any problem
as it could be decided either by mutual agreement or by reference
to The Hague Tribunal. Concerning territorial compensation,
however, Lansdowne was very guarded. It must be conditional
on 'a satisfactory arrangement being arrived at in regard to the
other points at issue'.[3] He then tried to minimise the value of the

---

[1] Lansdowne to Cambon, 1 Oct 1903, *BD* II, no. 369, p. 313.
[2] See pp. 198–9.
[3] Lansdowne to Cambon, 1 Oct 1903, *BD* II, no. 369, p. 314.

French fishing rights, arguing that the yield of recent years had been insignificant and that these rights were therefore of 'sentimental' rather than 'substantial' importance. British concession on the bait question, he insisted, must be made dependent on French abandonment of bounties to the fishermen of the islands of St-Pierre and Miquelon. He was, however, prepared to concede that bounties to fishermen from Metropolitan France might continue.

Over Siam Lansdowne was able to confirm that no difference of opinion existed; however he tried, but obviously without much hope of carrying conviction, to imply that this was somehow a concession to the French point of view.[1] On the New Hebrides he again pronounced against partition.[2] Under the heading Nigeria he referred to the Sokoto boundary as fixed by the July 1898 Treaty, and here he offered to provide territorial compensation for Newfoundland rights. This compensation would give France access from her Niger possessions to those in the region of Lake Tchad. In return France would be expected to give up the two Niger enclaves which she had received in 1898.[3] Here then, perhaps inspired by his conversation with Étienne,[4] was Lansdowne's version of territorial compensation.

On the assumption that all points of friction were to be removed, Lansdowne then introduced the question of Zanzibar, where remnants of French influence, particularly the existence of a French post office, constituted a minor grievance. The implementation of previous French promises concerning its closure was now requested.[5]

Finally Lansdowne made reference to Madagascar. British protests against French annexation and its consequences had been made in 1896, 1897 and 1898. There had been no French reply. Lansdowne now offered 'as part of a general settlement of pending questions, to withdraw . . . claims and protests'.[6] He was obviously, as Cambon was not slow to indicate, scraping the barrel where so-called concessions were concerned.

---

[1] See Lansdowne to Cambon, 1 Oct 1903, *BD* ii, no. 369, p. 315.
[2] Ibid.
[3] See Lansdowne to Cambon, 1 Oct 1903, ibid., pp. 315–16.
[4] See pp. 175–6.
[5] See Lansdowne to Cambon, 1 Oct 1903, *BD* ii, no. 369, p. 316.
[6] Lansdowne to Cambon, 1 Oct 1903, ibid., p. 317.

In Paris Delcassé and Cambon studied Lansdowne's letter together. On Cambon's return to London he called on Lansdowne on 7 October and they embarked on a preliminary but very characteristic discussion.[1] After admitting that Delcassé regarded Lansdowne's letter as 'worthy of consideration' Cambon first pointed out that Delcassé had raised one relatively minor objection. France could not draw distinctions where bounties were concerned between fishermen from Metropolitan France and from St-Pierre and Miquelon. But, Cambon explained, Delcassé was chiefly concerned with the Egyptian and Moroccan questions. Here Great Britain was asking for immediate and concrete advantages in return for mere hopes. Lansdowne tried to turn this argument by claiming that Great Britain was in fact proposing the recognition of an existing situation in Egypt while offering, by abandoning positions held, to meet repeatedly expressed French wishes in Morocco.[2] Cambon countered that France would still have to consider other Powers, including Spain, in Morocco. She might also have to face German pretensions. French concessions in Egypt could perhaps be phased according to French progress in Morocco. Lansdowne claimed that he had already suggested this solution over Capitulations. Cambon then proposed that settlement of the Egyptian debt question should proceed *pari passu* with developments in Morocco. Lansdowne demurred and insisted that in any case an immediate 'Yes' or 'No' answer was required about the permanency of the British occupation of Egypt. He also pointed out that Great Britain would have other Powers to deal with over Egypt just as France anticipated the need for negotiation with other Powers over Morocco. After this exchange Cambon expressed general agreement on British reservations regarding Morocco but lodged a preliminary objection to the extent of seaboard which Lansdowne had allocated, in the event of eventual liquidation, to Spain. Lansdowne's reply suggested some room for manœuvre.

Before closing the interview Lansdowne explained that, while fully appreciating that Delcassé needed time to consider his proposals, he was anxious for an early reply. 'The public', he

[1] See Cambon to Delcassé, 11 Oct 1903, *DDF*, III, no. 7, pp. 15, 16.
[2] See Lansdowne to Monson, 7 Oct 1903, *BD* II, no. 370, pp. 317–18. This and the following details of the conversation were not reported by Cambon to Delcassé.

declared, 'was beginning to get wind of the negotiations, and if they were prolonged until the meeting of Parliament, we should certainly have some troublesome questions with regard to them.'[1] It seems likely, in this instance, that Lansdowne was less worried by public opinion than eager to conclude a bargain on British terms.[2] Indeed one of the interesting features of these negotiations is that each side only invoked the necessity for speed when making a considered offer or raising a specific demand. Of course they were influenced by outside and wider considerations, but these played a very marginal part in the tactical game. At this stage Lansdowne had proposed what he regarded as a sound and sensible bargain. Cambon, for reasons previously discussed, was anxious to improve on it. However valuable British friendship in a European context might be there was no reason, according to Cambon, why particular arrangements should not be patriotically defensible in their own right. As a professional diplomat he was determined to strike the best possible bargain. As a believer in Anglo-French *rapprochement* he was anxious that such a bargain should be seen in France to be a good one. Delcassé, although less concerned with detail, had great confidence in his Ambassador and was quite willing to play the diplomatic game. If in his first conversation with Lansdowne he had, in spite of his own denials, too easily conceded a major point,[3] he was now prepared to explore every avenue of recovery.

Lansdowne's eagerness to conclude was again in evidence when he received Cambon on 14 October for the signature of the Arbitration Treaty.[4] In reply to information that Cambon was leaving that afternoon for talks with Delcassé in Paris, Lansdowne repeated to him that it was 'of the utmost importance that we should arrive at a decision upon the points at issue with as little delay as possible'.[5] Monson made the same point in Paris to

[1] Lansdowne to Monson, 7 Oct 1903, *BD* II, no. 370, p. 318.

[2] It is true that at this time Lansdowne was preoccupied over the situation in Macedonia and that Anglo-French *rapprochement*, as a step towards improved Anglo-Russian relations, seemed particularly attractive. See Monger, *The End of Isolation*, p. 138. But although this made an agreement generally more desirable, Lansdowne, in arguing speed, was pressing acceptance of British terms. He was not climbing down to accommodate the French.

[3] See p. 194.

[4] See p. 156. For text of treaty see *DDF*, IV, no. 10, pp. 18, 19.

[5] Lansdowne to Monson, 14 Oct 1903, *BD* II, no. 371, p. 319.

Cogordon[1] and indirectly to President Loubet on 21 October.[2] On the same date Cambon attended Lansdowne's formal weekly reception and Lansdowne immediately took the opportunity to ask whether Delcassé had yet expressed any opinions on the British proposals.[3] Cambon replied that Delcassé had been very busy with the King of Italy's visit and that he had not yet had time to formulate his views precisely. He was however equally anxious to conclude a settlement before the end of the year. Although Cambon thus evaded any definite reply he used the opening in order to prepare for future bargaining and, for Lansdowne's benefit, thus summed up Delcassé's reactions:

> According to his letter Lord Lansdowne seems, notably in what concerns Egyptian affairs, to consider matters from an exclusively British point of view, without taking French interests into account. We are allowed freedom of action in Morocco, that is to say we are put in a position to face all the difficulties of penetration into a new country, without institutions of any kind. In exchange we are asked to abandon in Egypt a situation which is perfectly defined and existing interests, some of which are considerable.
>
> In a word England, who possesses nothing in Morocco, gives us what she has not got and France, who has sure and tangible advantages in Egypt, is begged to abandon them. Exchange on these terms would not be acceptable to French opinion and M. Delcassé could not consent to recognise a privileged position for England in the Valley of the Nile unless he could put into the balance equivalent advantages on other points.[4]

French concessions in Egypt, Cambon hinted, must be related more closely to French progress in Morocco. He then passed quickly over the other questions but insisted that Gambia alone could be regarded as satisfactory territorial compensation for Newfoundland. Lansdowne could not let that pass and argued that such a claim would doom the whole negotiations to failure. Cambon held his ground with familiar arguments about the uselessness of Gambia to Great Britain, and Lansdowne once more

---

[1] See Note of 21 Oct 1903, *DDF*, IV, no. 27, p. 37.

[2] See Monson to Lansdowne, 22 Oct 1903, *BD* II, no. 372, p. 319.

[3] See Cambon to Delcassé, 22 Oct 1903, *DDF*, IV, no. 30, pp. 42–5. There is no account of this meeting in the *British Documents*.

[4] Cambon to Delcassé, 22 Oct 1903, *DDF*, IV, no. 30, p. 42.

pressed for speed[1] in formulating an official French reply. After this sparring match Lansdowne turned to a point on which he was on very strong ground. He confided to Cambon that British financiers were being heavily pressed to grant a new loan to Morocco; the City would be guided by the Government. Cambon replied that as France was shortly to be recognised as the privileged lender it seemed useless to involve British financiers. But, claimed Lansdowne, the matter was urgent. The Sultan was bankrupt; current negotiations might last weeks, possibly months. Would it not be wise to agree to share a loan at once? Cambon answered that he must consult Delcassé. He strongly advised Delcassé to accept. Premature chaos in Morocco was not a French interest; the situation might easily be exploited by Germany. Delcassé, thus briefed by Cambon, did not hesitate and wired back immediately approving that a new loan of £300,000 should be raised in England and in France.[2] The indication of British goodwill was obvious and by this move Lansdowne effectively increased French confidence in Britain's ultimate intentions.

On 24 October Delcassé sent Cambon instructions, which they had prepared together, for an official reply to Lansdowne.[3] In his covering letter Delcassé significantly confided to Cambon that where Egypt was concerned 'time had worked against France, that little by little England had transformed the precarious possession which military occupation assured into a disguised protectorate, that evacuation, formerly regarded as a probable eventuality, could not now be envisaged save as the consequences of a lost war'.[4] It was therefore manifestly a French interest to negotiate the renunciation of rights and privileges which were each year becoming more theoretic. But while freely granting to Cambon that France's bargaining position in Egypt was a dwindling asset, he was, as his instructions confirmed, still determined to sell at the highest price.

---

[1] In a private letter to Delcassé dated 23 Oct Cambon explained that the reason why Lansdowne was in such a hurry was because of the precarious situation of the Cabinet. He feared that he would not be included in a Cabinet reconstruction. Perhaps, Cambon suggested, he regarded a settlement with France as a means of consolidating his own position. 'Any way', he concluded, 'we have every interest in fortifying and maintaining him for who knows if we could get on with another?' *CC* II, p. 99.

[2] See *DDF*, IV, p. 45, note 1.

[3] See Delcassé to Cambon, 24 Oct 1904, *DDF*, IV, no. 36, pp. 50–1.

[4] Delcassé to Cambon, 24 Oct 1903, ibid., p. 51.

That price was officially conveyed to Lansdowne by Cambon on 26 October in the form of comments on Lansdowne's proposals concerning Morocco, Egypt, Newfoundland, Siam, New Hebrides, Niger, Zanzibar, Madagascar.[1] On Morocco Lansdowne's conditions about commercial freedom and British rights according to her 1856 treaty with Morocco were accepted without reservation; as far as neutralisation of the seaboard was concerned, Delcassé proposed that the portion should extend from Melilla to the heights about the right bank of the river Sebou: this was an important modification. He also suggested that, apart from the consequences of the present arrangement, the territorial *status quo* should be guaranteed for a radius of 500 miles around the Strait of Gibraltar. He recognised that the neutralised seaboard, according to his own amended proposal, should be included in the eventual Spanish sphere of influence. He also agreed that in French negotiations with Spain, guarantees would be obtained that Spain could not alienate any part of her sphere of influence and that she should adhere to provisions respecting freedom of trade and the Gibraltar Strait.

On Egypt, Delcassé accepted the general proposition that France 'should not interfere with British action . . . or ask that a limit should be fixed on British occupation'.[2] He also agreed that eventual abolition of the Capitulations would be favourably considered by France in return for a similar promise on Great Britain's part regarding Morocco. On the other hand he objected to the complete financial freedom which was proposed. The *Caisse de la Dette* must be preserved and while he was ready to adhere to some immediate reforms, adherence to others should be held in abeyance until they could proceed *pari passu* with similar French operations in Morocco. Control of railways administration was quoted as a case in point. Commercial liberty must be guaranteed and the free passage of the Suez Canal, as per the 1888 Treaty, reaffirmed.

On Newfoundland, Delcassé recalled the three French conditions for abandonment of the French shore: pecuniary indemnity, territorial compensation and freedom to acquire bait. He accepted that the indemnity question should be referred to The Hague

[1] See *DDF*, IV, no. 40, pp. 55–60; also *BD* II, no. 373, pp. 320–3.
[2] *DDF*, IV, no. 40, p. 56; *BD* II, no. 373, p. 321.

Tribunal. But, where territorial compensation was concerned, he rejected Lansdowne's proposition that the French were being asked to give up rights in Newfoundland which only had a sentimental value. Those rights, he insisted, were hallowed by solemn treaties and conventions. Furthermore the value of the fishing off the French shore could not be determined by its present yield but by its productivity in the past and its likely productivity in the future, 'if the cod, which formerly frequented the vicinity of Newfoundland and which had deserted those shores, returned as it had already been established that they were tending to do'.[1] Thus stressing the potential value of the French shore, Delcassé claimed that Gambia must be offered in fair exchange as territorial compensation. Somewhat maliciously he then argued that Gambia was only of sentimental value to Great Britain since it was now completely surrounded by French possessions. To the British suggestion that freedom to acquire bait should depend on abolition of bounties to the fishermen of St-Pierre and Miquelon, Delcassé replied that no discrimination could be made against colonists; he pressed Lansdowne to drop this condition.

On Siam Delcassé expressed satisfaction that Lansdowne concurred with French proposals. Over the New Hebrides he regretted that partition was rejected, but declared willingness to continue to seek for some means of settling local difficulties. Regarding the Niger he noted Great Britain's desire to modify the 1898 Convention respecting the two French enclaves and indicated that the French Government would not be unwilling to consider British proposals when the French railway in construction from Dahomey had reached the Niger. He made no mention of Lansdowne's Sokoto proposals, thus seeking to emphasise that Gambia was the only territorial compensation which he thought worth considering. Concerning Zanzibar he confirmed that France was prepared to abandon her consular jurisdiction and postal privileges but put responsibility for speeding up proceedings on Great Britain. As for Madagascar he permitted himself a short historical lecture. French annexation had, by universally accepted practice, entailed the lapse of all Madagascar's previous treaties. France therefore could not recognise any British rights. As for the importance of British interests Lansdowne's opinion on this

---

[1] *DDF*, IV, no. 40, p. 58; *BD* II, no. 373, p. 322.

matter was not generally held in England; and he quoted Lord Salisbury to illustrate his point. Having ruled out of court Lansdowne's attempt to use the waiving of British grievances over Madagascar as a bargaining counter, Delcassé rather pompously concluded: 'The Government of the Republic nevertheless respects the sentiment which has inspired Your Excellency with the idea of profiting from the general arrangement now in preparation to withdraw protests which the Foreign Office had thought it ought to formulate after the annexation of Madagascar.'[1]

During the course of Lansdowne's meeting with Cambon on 26 October he took the opportunity, after receiving confirmation that Lamsdorff was shortly expected on a visit to Paris, to indicate his anxiety about the Manchurian situation and the importance of obtaining a clarification of Russian policy.[2] Cambon stressed the difficulty of Lamsdorff's position since the creation of the new Far Eastern Vice-royalty, but promised to report the substance of Lansdowne's remarks to Delcassé. Accordingly when Delcassé did meet Lamsdorff he told him that 'the British Government was far from desiring to follow a provocative policy' and 'suggested that a little more frankness was desirable and would be calculated to smooth difficulties'.[3] Lamsdorff promised to give instructions to Benckendorff to be more forthcoming. This, in fact, proved the prelude to Anglo-Russian discussions which encompassed a wide range of problems. While thus using Anglo-French *rapprochement* as a bridge towards Russia, Lansdowne tried at the same time to bolster Japan and, by adopting a firm stand over Afghan and Tibetan problems, to indicate that any negotiation with Russia would be conducted from a position of strength.[4]

Although Lansdowne was glad to be able to use French good offices as a means of promoting better communications with Russia, he now showed no hurry in following up the Anglo-French negotiations. In fact he did not reply officially to Delcassé's comments on his proposals until 19 November.[5] His sense of

---

[1] *DDF*, IV, no. 40, p. 60; *BD* II, no. 373, p. 323.
[2] See Lansdowne to Monson, 26 Oct 1903, *BD* II, no. 250, pp. 217, 218.
[3] Lansdowne to Monson, 4 Nov 1903, *BD* II, no. 257, p. 221, and also *DDF*, IV, no. 45, p. 68, where Delcassé noted that he had advised Lamsdorff: 'Talk to Lord Lansdowne, it is probable that many misunderstandings can be dissipated.'
[4] See G. Monger, *The End of Isolation*, pp. 142, 143.
[5] See Lansdowne to Cambon, *BD* II, no. 376, pp. 324–7.

urgency was far less in evidence now that his own proposals had received an unpalatable French gloss. When Cambon visited him on 28 October he found him suffering from flu' and anxious to postpone any serious discussion for a week.[1] After claiming an invalid's privilege Lansdowne added that, on a first reading, Cambon's letter of 26 October gave him the impression that an arrangement would be very difficult, that French pretensions were rather excessive, that the cession of Gambia was out of the question and that the progressive abandoning of French advantages in Egypt was not satisfactory. He added that he would in due course submit his objections in the form of a memorandum. Cambon answered that when Lansdowne had had an opportunity to study the French proposals more carefully he would appreciate that they were not excessive, 'that he now had in his hands a means of definitely resolving the thorniest of questions', and 'that it would be wise to hurry, for the lost opportunity might not recur'.[2] After this warning Cambon urged surrender on Gambia and added, with all the persuasiveness that he could muster:

> as for Egypt, we deliver it to you, we leave you the freedom of occupation, we give you the reserves of the Debt. These are considerable advantages. As for the rest we virtually admit concession, but against equivalent compensation. In a word, we give you Egypt in exchange for Morocco; you win on the deal. You may be sure that no politician in France, save M. Delcassé, will have the courage to settle the Egyptian question.[3]

To this flood of eloquence Lansdowne gave no reply but merely nodded his head, 'seeming', Cambon concluded, 'convinced'. But influenza and tactics, rather than acquiescence, more probably explained Lansdowne's silence.

Discussion was resumed on 4 November.[4] In the meanwhile Lansdowne had heard from Cromer, who was engaged in a reappraisal of the financial aspects of the Egyptian question. He advised against hurrying 'to make detailed proposals to the French before the bases of negotiation are more definitely settled'.[5] He

---

[1] See Cambon to Delcassé, 28 Oct 1903, *DDF*, IV, no. 46, p. 69.
[2] Ibid.   [3] Ibid.
[4] See Cambon to Delcassé, 4 Nov 1903, *DDF*, IV, no. 59, pp. 83, 84.
[5] Cromer to Lansdowne, 30 Oct 1903, *BD* II, no. 374, p. 323.

also suggested that it might be worth trying to make the whole arrangement 'dependent on satisfactory settlement of the Egyptian questions with or without consent of other Powers'. Cromer's uneasiness on that particular score was often to be in evidence. For the moment, however, he was chiefly preoccupied with the financial questions and anxious that Lansdowne's reply should be delayed until he had had an opportunity of co-operating in the drafting. This object was achieved.

Further encouraged towards dilatory tactics by Cromer's plea for time, Lansdowne was not very forthcoming when Cambon returned to the attack fresh from a recent visit to Delcassé.[1] Egypt and Gambia, he insisted, were the two points for discussion. Once again he urged that Delcassé was the only French minister who could take responsibility for settling the Egyptian question. 'Yes', replied Lansdowne, taking his cue from Cromer, 'but who can assure us that once you have agreed to certain arrangements we shall not meet with objections from other Powers?'[2] Cambon argued that French backing would almost certainly ensure that of several other great Powers and that the rest would follow. On the other hand if France refused all concessions, and supported by Russia and Germany sought to create difficulties, England's position would be most awkward. 'I think', said Lansdowne, 'that for Egypt it will be possible to find some arrangement; but I always told you that we would never abandon Gambia.'[3] Cambon noted with satisfaction that Lansdowne seemed to be weakening a bit on Egypt; but until his official reply, there was no means of being certain.

Two days before its dispatch, Cambon had another brief conversation with Lansdowne.[4] 'My impressions', he confided to Cogordon, 'are rather mixed and on the whole bad. Lord Lansdowne told me that it was not easy to find anything practical for Egypt, but that he hoped nevertheless to reach a satisfactory formula. As for Gambia', he added, 'I have always told you that we could not cede it to you. On Newfoundland we ask for the suppression of bounties. You reject it; you ask us for Gambia; we cannot give it to you. The two demands cancel out and we

---

[1] See Cambon to Delcassé, 4 Nov 1903, *DDF*, IV, no. 59, pp. 83, 84.
[2] Cambon to Delcassé, 4 Nov 1903, ibid., p. 84.   [3] Ibid.
[4] On 17 Nov 1903.

could settle on that.'[1] The exasperation, which Cambon may have concealed from Lansdowne, was ironically conveyed in his comment to Cogordon: 'this method of suppressing territorial compensation will no doubt seem admirable to you. It is very British; you must know that at the Foreign Office matters are transacted as in a City merchant's office.'[2] Sensing rejection of France's territorial claim, Cambon was already taking up a new attitude. Having tried to impress on Lansdowne the need for speed when considering French proposals, he was now preparing to go slow in the face of Lansdowne's probable reply. 'I am of opinion', he advised Cogordon, 'to yield on nothing, to take our time, *not to show ourselves in any hurry*. We have a right to be difficult; the British have a greater interest in accommodation with us over Egypt than we have to settle with them over Morocco. They will become intractable if they feel we are too eager to finish.'[3]

As Cambon had surmised, Lansdowne's reply, while moving in some directions to meet the French, was in others simply a restatement of intransigence.[4] Over Morocco Lansdowne was prepared to accept Delcassé's limitation of the neutralised seaboard provided it was extended twenty miles south of the Sebou River to include the port of Rabat. The only other problem he raised was to query 'the proposal that the two Governments should agree to maintain the *status quo* within a radius of 500 miles from the Straits of Gibraltar', pointing out that this would 'extend beyond the boundaries of Morocco and include part of Algeria'.[5]

Passing to Egypt he noted Delcassé's willingness to undertake that France would not 'obstruct the action of Great Britain in Egypt' and would recognise the 'permanency' of British occupation; he also noted that Delcassé was prepared to agree that 'the economies resulting from the debt conversion of 1890, which were now under the control of the "Caisse", *shall be used in Egyptian interests as, for instance, in the construction of railways or other large public works*',[6] and that Delcassé accepted the principle of reciprocity 'in regard to modification in the régime of the

[1] Cambon to Cogordon, 18 Nov 1903, *DDF*, IV, no. 89, pp. 115–16.
[2] Cambon to Cogordon, 18 Nov 1903, ibid., p. 116.   [3] Ibid.
[4] See Lansdowne to Cambon, 19 Nov 1903, *BD* II, no. 376, pp. 324–7.
[5] Lansdowne to Cambon, 19 Nov 1903, ibid., p. 325.
[6] Passages printed in italic indicate Cromer's amendments to the original draft.

Capitulations in Egypt and Morocco respectively'.[1] On the other hand he objected to Delcassé's refusal to undertake that France should withdraw 'from her part in the financial control, *from the right claimed by the French Government to oppose the conversion* of the Egyptian debts, or from the administration of the Egyptian Railways'.[2] Nor was he prepared to accept Delcassé's suggestion that the abandonment of financial control by France in Egypt 'could be considered only *pari passu* with the acquisition of financial control by France in Morocco'.[3] As a compromise solution however he submitted the following proposals:

1. That the *Caisse de la Dette* should be maintained, but that its function should be strictly limited to receiving *the sum necessary* for the service of the debt, with a right to sue the Egyptian Government in the Law Courts should that sum not be punctually paid.

An essential part of the arrangement would be that the railways, telegraphs and port of Alexandria should cease to be governed by a Mixed Administration.

2. That the French Government should agree to join with us in addressing the other Powers for the purpose of securing their assent to these proposals, and it would be understood that, should the consent of the other Powers be refused, France would not oppose any steps which His Majesty's Government may hereafter find it expedient to take for the purpose of *giving effect to the agreement which the French and British Governments will have arrived at.*

3. That the French Government should not object to the Egyptian Government exercising its right to convert the Egyptian debts *whenever an opportune moment for effecting this operation may occur.*[4]

Thus Lansdowne, with Cromer's approval, was ready to make a concession in preserving the *Caisse de la Dette*. But its functions were to be drastically curtailed and the reality of financial freedom secured. Furthermore Cromer's point about securing French co-operation *vis-à-vis* other powers was added to British demands.[5] Concluding his comments on Egypt Lansdowne, as Delcassé had requested, accepted the principle of maintaining commercial

---

[1] Lansdowne to Cambon, 19 Nov 1903, *BD* II, no. 376, p. 325.
[2] Ibid.   [3] Ibid.
[4] Lansdowne to Cambon, 19 Nov 1903, ibid., pp. 325, 326.
[5] See p. 216.

liberty in Egypt and the guarantee of free passage of the Suez Canal in accordance with the 1888 treaty, '*but without specific observance of Article VIII of that Convention, which is incompatible with the necessary consequences of the British occupation*'.[1] The article in question provided (1) for meetings of the Canal Commission upon special occasions when the neutrality of the Canal might appear to be menaced and (2) for an annual meeting of the Commission under the presidency of a representative of the Sultan. This reservation was made by Lansdowne at Cromer's particular request[2] and was designed to prevent the possibly awkward consequences of the presence of a presiding Turkish Commissioner in Egypt if only for an annual and formal occasion.

While Lansdowne was prepared with Cromer's agreement for some measure of compromise on Egypt, over Newfoundland he proved quite unyielding. He ruled Gambia out of the question as territorial compensation and again offered readjustment of Nigerian boundaries in the region of Sokoto as the only possible alternative. If the French were adamant in refusing to abolish bounties then free purchase of bait could not be conceded. It would then become necessary 'to consider whether any modified arrangement' was possible. . . . 'With this object', he added, 'we are willing to confer with the Newfoundland Government as to the possibility of an arrangement, confined to the Treaty Coast, of the following kind: . . . The right of the French to fish for any kind of fish, whether bait fish or others, or to purchase bait on the Treaty coast might be continued, but they would give up their right of using the shore for the purpose of drying fish. If such an arrangement were come to, we should be prepared to compensate the owners of existing French establishments, but in that case no claim for territorial compensation could be admitted.'[3] Thus, as Cambon had already inferred, was territorial compensation to be eliminated.[4]

Having dealt, to his own satisfaction, with 'the more important questions', Lansdowne remarked reassuringly that 'the remaining points do not seem likely to give rise to any difficulty.[5] He could

---

[1] Lansdowne to Cambon, 19 Nov 1903, *BD* II, no. 376, p. 326.
[2] See ibid. note 8.
[3] Lansdowne to Cambon, 19 Nov 1903, ibid., pp. 326, 327.
[4] See p. 217.
[5] Lansdowne to Cambon, 19 Nov 1903, ibid., p. 327.

not, however, resist a riposte over Madagascar and insisted that
the grievance which he had offered to waive was 'a very substantial
one'. Furthermore the French claim that annexation entailed the
suspension of existing engagements could conceivably prove a
dangerous precedent in relation to the proposed Egypt–Morocco
arrangements. He therefore desired it to be put 'on record that,
should either Power at any future time find itself compelled, by
the force of circumstances, to modify its policy in this respect
[viz. annexation] any engagements into which that Power had
entered as to commercial equality shall remain intact, and that if
either side should in any way depart from those engagements, the
other side will be at liberty to do the same'.[1] Clearly Lansdowne
relished his tit-for-tat over Madagascar.

Cambon and Lansdowne met again on 20 November; while
declaring that it would be premature to discuss Lansdowne's
letter of the 19th, Cambon nevertheless volunteered some comments upon it.[2] To include Rabat in the neutralised zone was, he
argued, somewhat excessive. He admitted 'that there must be a
mistake in the French stipulation that the *status quo* should be
maintained within a radius of 500 miles from the Straits of
Gibraltar'.[3] Turning to Spain, where he promised to remind
Delcassé of Lansdowne's particular preoccupation, he took the
opportunity to remark that 'the Spaniards are a difficult people to
pin down, they do not know how to reach a conclusion, they have
the kind of mentality which prefers, to a tangible but limited
reality, unrealisable but limitless hopes . . . Must our agreement',
he urged, 'depend on their dreams and would we not do well to
fix between ourselves a time limit after which we should go
ahead?'[4] To Cambon's satisfaction Lansdowne did not reject this
possibility. As far as Egypt was concerned Cambon indicated that
while the maintenance of the *Caisse de la Dette* was satisfactory its
remaining powers must be studied in more detail. France could
hardly be expected to bring pressure on other Powers in support
of British plans; to ask for more than benevolent neutrality would
be to create embarrassment. On Newfoundland Cambon insisted

[1] Lansdowne to Cambon, 19 Nov 1903, *BD* II, no. 376, p. 327.
[2] See Lansdowne to Monson, 20 Nov 1903, *BD* II, no. 377, p. 328, and Cambon to
Delcassé, 22 Nov 1903, *DDF*, IV, no. 98, pp. 127–31.
[3] Lansdowne to Monson, 20 Nov 1903, *BD* II, no. 377, p. 328.
[4] Cambon to Delcassé, 22 Nov 1903, *BD* II, no. 98, p. 128.

that failure to provide territorial compensation was a major difficulty. Lansdowne then expressed a hope that he might have an answer before 15 December as the last cabinet meeting before Christmas was scheduled for 18 December.[1] Lansdowne summed up his own impressions of the conversation by commenting to Monson: 'I noticed with satisfaction that M. Cambon's tone was by no means severely critical; indeed he went so far as to say that there seemed to him to be the materials for a compromise in the proposals which I had laid before him.'[2]

He would have been less sanguine had he known the advice which Cambon was giving to Delcassé.[3] He concentrated on three points: the Egyptian debt, France's new position in Morocco, and Newfoundland. On the debt question the absence of the effective controls which Lansdowne's proposals seemed to imply might create a panic among French bondholders. This would entail opposition which could render fruitless the whole negotiation. The matter ought to be studied very seriously. 'I appreciate', he added, 'that he [Lansdowne] is in a hurry to conclude, but it is little use concluding if the result is not acceptable to French opinion and above all to the bondholders. It is better to delay, better to break up the negotiations than to accept an arrangement for which Your Excellency would be responsible and which France would not ratify.'[4] British financiers and Lord Cromer himself, he explained, were so anxious for a solution that they were bringing pressure on the British Government. 'They are', he insisted, 'in a greater hurry than we are; they are more in need of an immediate solution. The correct attitude in such a situation is to maintain a certain reserve.'[5]

This was all the more recommendable because the Morocco counterpart was not immediately realisable. French freedom of action there depended on the co-operation of the Sultan and his court. True it would be an advantage no longer to be faced by hostile British influences. But other potentially hostile outside influences must still be considered. For instance he argued: 'If it pleases a German syndicate to buy the Sheikh el Menebhi with an

---

[1] See Lansdowne to Monson, 20 Nov 1903, *BD* II, no. 377, p. 328.
[2] Lansdowne to Monson, 20 Nov 1903, ibid.
[3] See Cambon to Delcassé, 22 Nov 1903, *DDF*, IV, no. 98, pp. 129–31.
[4] Cambon to Delcassé, 22 Nov 1903, ibid., p. 129.
[5] Ibid., p. 130.

adequate bribe or even if the fears of the Sultan about our
aggressive intentions are awakened, we would find all the concessions which we might ask for refused. Experience shows all
too well that with oriental governments there are only two
resources, money or threats. Consequently it will be necessary to
bribe the Sultan's entourage, and that takes time, or to make the
point of our sword felt on the Moroccan border, and all the
speeches which echo in the French Chamber of Deputies illustrate clearly that the Government would not be supported if it
wanted to use force. In any case England's withdrawal in Morocco
will not put us here and now in the possession of advantages
equal to those which she would acquire in Egypt by the complete
annihilation of debt control; this needs further study.'[1] In the
meanwhile he recommended preparing the way in Morocco so
that concrete benefits could be secured if and when agreement
with Great Britain was concluded. On Newfoundland he warned
that the British were trying to 'drown' the territorial compensation condition. They would probably remain obstinate over
Gambia. For, as he admitted to Delcassé, 'they have too great an
interest in conserving the only good harbour on the West Coast
of Africa'.[2] Therefore, he concluded, 'we must ask for something
else' or offer more Newfoundland concessions and repeat the
Gambia demand. Finally Cambon, while recognising that Lansdowne was sincerely in favour of reaching agreement, warned
once more against hasty conclusions. 'I consider it prudent', he
declared 'only to advance step by step.'[3] He was to repeat this
theme and later, in letters to his son, he claimed credit for having
put a brake on Delcassé, who otherwise, in pursuit of his own
grand design, might have been tempted to settle too easily
and might then have found it difficult to get his agreements
ratified.[4]

Support for Cambon's caution on the Egyptian question was
forthcoming from de la Boulinière, the French Consul-General in
Cairo, who on 25 November sent a long report to Delcassé sum-
marising the existing situation in Egypt and the French interests,
financial and otherwise, which would be affected by a settlement

---

[1] Cambon to Delcassé, 22 Nov 1903, *DDF*, IV, no. 98, p. 130.
[2] Ibid.   [3] Ibid., p. 131.
[4] See *CC* II, 10 Dec 1903, p. 101 and 26 Dec 1903, p. 104.

on British lines.[1] He followed this up by a letter dated 3 December in which he recognised that Lord Cromer had become somewhat less sweeping in his demands but warned that his objectives remained the same.[2] Safeguards for French interests and against accelerated changes must be sought. This in the long run would benefit Anglo-French relations, and they must be 'sheltered' from 'certain temptations' which would be 'dangerous' to all Egypt's creditors.

Before receipt of that letter Delcassé, after discussions with Cambon, had prepared a set of preliminary comments on Lansdowne's proposals. Cambon was authorised to transmit informally to Lansdowne for his observations and, in the light of them, Delcassé proposed to make his own official reply.[3]

Accordingly on 9 December Cambon visited Lansdowne and, reading from Delcassé's notes, volunteered a lengthy commentary.[4] Apart from objecting to the inclusion of Rabat in the neutralised seaboard zone and making a rather vague reference, in reply to Lansdowne's query about the 500 miles radius of neutralisation, little was said about Morocco, although Cambon did mention possible German designs. On the other hand, the Egyptian question was subjected to a detailed analysis, particularly in relation to Lansdowne's proposal that the French Government should abandon its right to oppose any conversion of the Egyptian debts. Security for the French bondholders was presented as Delcassé's main concern. Their interest in the Administration of the Railways was stressed because that Administration had in fact been set up to ensure the service of the privileged debt. In effect Delcassé was asking that there should be a strengthening of the guarantees, already outlined by Lansdowne, for the bondholders. With regard to the proposal 'that the French Government should join . . . in asking other Powers to assent to the agreement that might be arrived at on the subject of the Debt, M. Delcassé could only leave His Majesty's Government to take the initiative in the matter; it was, of course,

---

[1] See *DDF*, IV, no. 105, pp. 136–41.
[2] See *DDF*, IV, no. 114, pp. 157–9.
[3] See Delcassé to Cambon, 6 Dec 1903, *DDF*, IV, no. 117, pp. 162–8.
[4] See Lansdowne to Monson, 9 Dec 1903, *BD* II, no. 378, pp. 329–32 where the account of the meeting is much fuller than that given by Cambon to Delcassé on 10 Dec 1903, *DDF*, IV, no. 119, pp. 169–71.

understood that the Government of the Republic would place no obstacle in the way'.[1] Replying to Lansdowne's point that freedom of trade in Egypt and Morocco should be mutually guaranteed, even in the event of annexation, Delcassé accepted the general principle but proposed that a term of 'say, fifteen or twenty years' with option for renewal should be agreed. He also made a special point of the need to safeguard the interests of French employees in Egyptian government service. On the Suez Canal question Delcassé asked for clarification about why Lansdowne considered Article VIII of the 1888 treaty as incompatible with the occupation.

While Delcassé's responses on the Egyptian question could be regarded, from Lansdowne's point of view, as reasonably satisfactory, it was equally clear that he intended to make a major issue of the Newfoundland territorial compensation problem. In Delcassé's view 'the question of territorial compensation remained untouched', but, as Lansdowne concluded, 'territorial compensation seemed to M. Delcassé indispensable'.[2] As a compromise Delcassé now proposed that Great Britain should cede Gambia but without the island and town of St Mary Bathurst. In that case, however, the French expected to be offered 'some advantage in regard to the delimitation of their possessions on the Niger'.[3] 'Yet another concession',[4] Lansdowne exclaimed and added that the cession of Gambia, even without St Mary Bathurst, would not be acceptable to the Cabinet. Almost inevitably he then went on to speak of the declining value of the French fisheries while Cambon argued that a reverse trend was now in evidence. At the end of the meeting Lansdowne promised to bring Delcassé's observations to the notice of the Cabinet. From the meeting he gained the impression that Cambon seemed 'to desire earnestly that we should come to terms'.[5]

In Lansdowne's opinion Delcassé's attitude over the Egyptian question was now definitely encouraging. He was, therefore, not inclined to take very seriously criticisms which had been emerging in some sections of the Press about the presumed Morocco bargain.

[1] Lansdowne to Monson, 9 Dec 1903, *BD* ii, no. 378, p. 330.
[2] Ibid., p. 331.
[3] Ibid.
[4] Cambon to Delcassé, 10 Dec 1903, *DDF*, iv, no. 119, p. 171.
[5] Lansdowne to Monson, 9 Dec 1903, *BD* ii, no. 378, p. 332.

'I have told Balfour', he reassured Cromer, 'that he must make up his mind to be told by the *Spectator* and critics of that kidney that we have given away the Western Mediterranean and betrayed the interests of the Empire at other points. We must make up our minds to face that sort of music, I don't want a Baghdad Railway fiasco.'[1] Lansdowne's reassurances to Cromer were matched by Cromer's enthusiastic reception of the news of Delcassé's latest response. 'I think', he wired on 11 December, 'that the French answer is very satisfactory.'[2] He felt confident that requisite guarantees to placate French bondholders could be made and advised that 'the negotiations on details should now be continued by Sir E[ldon] Gorst[3] in Paris.[4] Judging from what the French Consul-General says to me', he continued, 'I gather that the two points to which they attach importance are firstly, that the Caisse de la Dette should still preserve such funds as not to render them ridiculous, and secondly the railways. The first point is fairly well met by our detailed proposals, and I hope that we may deal with the second by removing the railways from pledged revenues.

'We can afford to be very generous as regards French employés. . . .

'As regards the Suez Canal I think that we may yield, save on one point. I do not like the permanent presence of an Ottoman Commissioner here. . . .'[5]

On Friday, 11 December, after a Cabinet meeting, Lansdowne again received Cambon and conveyed to him the Cabinet's reactions to Delcassé's proposals. In the light of these Cambon reported at length to Delcassé listing nine major points:[6]

(1) *Neutralisation of the Moroccan seaboard to the heights of the right bank of the river Sebou*
The Cabinet insisted that Rabat must be included in the neutralised zone. Cambon had pressed French objections but, as he explained to Delcassé, 'the question remains in suspense'.

---

[1] Lansdowne to Cromer, 7 Dec 1903, quoted Newton, *Lord Lansdowne,* p. 287. In the same letter Lansdowne expressed gratification that, thanks to Cromer, Fashoda had been rechristened Kodok.

[2] Cromer to Lansdowne, 11 Dec 1903, *BD* II, no. 379, p. 332.

[3] See p. 191, note 2.

[4] Cromer to Lansdowne, 11 Dec 1903, *BD* II, no. 379, p. 332.

[5] Ibid., p. 333.

[6] See Cambon to Delcassé, 11 Dec 1903, *DDF,* IV, no. 120, pp. 172–5.

(2) *Maintenance of the* status quo *in a radius of 500 miles around the Gibraltar Straits*

The Cabinet still regarded this precaution as excessive. It included part of Spain, the Balearic Islands, part of Algeria and the Sahara. 'It would', explained Lansdowne, 'go beyond the scope of our agreement to introduce a clause of this kind.' 'You may wish to consider', Cambon advised Delcassé, 'whether you ought not to modify your proposal on this point. It seemed to me, from the way in which Lord Lansdowne spoke of the Balearic Islands, that the Cabinet understood that we feared the Germans less than the British themselves in this direction.'

(3) *Railways and Ports*

French rights of control in Morocco would be recognised in the same measure as France recognised those of Great Britain in Egypt.

(4) *The Egyptian Caisse de la Dette*

The interests of bondholders had been carefully studied and serious guarantees would be offered. Technic alquestions were involved and Lord Lansdowne undertook to submit a detailed memorandum. Cambon tried to press for further information but Lansdowne refused to be drawn.

(5) *Support solicited by the British Government to obtain acceptance by the other Powers of agreements reached*

The Cabinet recognised that the initiative must come from Great Britain but would wish more from France than a simple engagement not to oppose. Backing was wanted.[1]

(6) *Duration of the reciprocal arrangements to be taken to ensure commercial liberty in Egypt and Morocco*

The Cabinet accepted a time limit but wished it to be a long one – at least 50 years with automatic renewal unless specifically renounced.

(7) *Position of French officials employed in Egypt*

The Cabinet believed that the Egyptian Government would show every consideration. Cambon asked for details and Lansdowne spoke of pensions on the British model. Cambon also insisted that some officials, in the archæological and museum

---

[1] In Lansdowne's version he assumes that this point has been accepted by the French. See *BD* ii, no. 380, p. 334.

services, who had always been French, ought to be maintained in office. Lansdowne agreed to this.

(8) *Article VIII of the 1888 Suez Canal Convention*

The Cabinet was still anxious to suppress this Article. Cambon tried to convince Lansdowne that it was not a matter of practical importance and that he would do well to consider whether it was worth grafting on to a *Caisse de la Dette* negotiation a matter connected with the neutralisation of the Suez Canal and one which would need to be negotiated with all the other Powers.

(9) *Newfoundland*

The Cabinet contested the importance of French rights and maintained that, if the fish were to return, then the British Government could cause serious embarrassment by compelling the French to adhere strictly to the Treaty.

The Cabinet absolutely refused to cede Gambia, even without the island of St Mary Bathurst; territorial compensation was admitted but only 'on a modest scale'. The Sokoto region was proposed on condition that the question of the Niger enclaves, which the French had promised to examine when their railway reached the Niger, was also included. 'I expressed to Lord Lansdowne', Cambon informed Delcassé, 'my regrets at the Cabinet's refusal to cede Gambia; it would notably have facilitated the whole negotiation. As for Sokoto, I said that it was of little value, and that the abandoning of a strip of territory south of the line established in 1898 would not be a sufficient compensation for Newfoundland and the Niger enclaves. Speaking purely personally, I said that our access to the Niger must be improved and I suggested the cession of Boussa, which had already been the subject of certain negotiations in 1898.'[1] From these remarks Lansdowne, as he confided to Monson, concluded that though Cambon 'deplored our refusal to give up Gambia he did not suggest that it was fatal'.[2] In fact Cambon's recommendation to Delcassé was 'to investigate everything which we can ask for in the region of the Niger'.[3]

During the course of these discussions Lansdowne took the opportunity to confide his anxieties over the situation in the Far

[1] Cambon to Delcassé, 11 Dec 1903, *DDF*, IV, no. 120, p. 175.
[2] Lansdowne to Monson, 11 Dec 1903, *BD* II, no. 380, p. 334.
[3] Cambon to Delcassé, 11 Dec 1903, *DDF*, IV, no. 120, p. 175.

East to Cambon.[1] Russian dilatoriness and Japanese impatience were causing him equal concern. He was now hoping, with French support, to attempt mediation in the dispute even if this implied bringing pressure on Japan. He still regarded eventual *rapprochement* with Russia as a desirable formula. The Cabinet, however, were in a very pessimistic mood and fear of giving any kind of offence to Japan was combined with gloomy over-estimates of Russian military power and the consequent problem of Indian defence. Endeavours to establish an Anglo-French approach to the Far Eastern problems therefore remained personal to the Foreign Secretary rather than part of any agreed policy. They were none the less important as an indication of the kind of relationship which had developed between Lansdowne and Cambon as a result of their protracted *Entente* deliberations.

While Delcassé pondered over the question of territorial compensation, Lansdowne now sought to meet lingering French misgivings over the Egyptian question. He was relieved to find that Cromer, via Gorst, was only too ready to try and find formulas of comfort for the French. On 24 December he was able to send the promised memorandum[2] to Cambon. It had in fact been drawn up by Gorst and opened by declaring that 'His Majesty's Government are prepared to do their utmost to meet Mr Delcassé's wishes in respect to the situation of the bondholders'.[3] The establishment of a special reserve fund and postponement for a period of five years of the proposed debt conversion were offered and 'in order to avoid the possibility of future misunderstandings, a Khedieval Decree was to be issued embodying the new arrangements and cancelling all past Decrees relating to the Egyptian Debt and *Caisse de la Dette*. The draft of this Decree would be submitted to the Government of the Republic, and should form an annex to any agreement at which the two Governments may arrive.'[4] With the communication of this memorandum the solution of the Egyptian question had been virtually achieved. French objections on form had been met while Cromer's substantive objectives were preserved. The French, however, were

---

[1] See Cambon to Delcassé, 11 Dec 1903, *DDF*, iv, no. 121, pp. 175, 176.
[2] See *BD* ii, no. 381, p. 335.
[3] Lansdowne Memorandum to Cambon, 24 Dec 1903, ibid.
[4] Ibid.

still searching for some kind of territorial compensation which, though theoretically bound up with Newfoundland, was really designed to balance the Egypt–Morocco bargain. It was precisely because agreement on these two major points had, with certain exceptions, been achieved and because other less important questions had failed to generate any dangerous heat that the question of territorial compensation was to loom so large during the remaining course of the negotiations. Lansdowne had led his Cabinet to believe that the bargain could be sealed without any serious sacrifice of African territory. Cambon was determined that, notwithstanding Delcassé's *grande idée* and the dangerous situation in the Far East, the bargain must not be sealed without some tangible token of compensation. The quest for territorial compensation began in earnest.

12

The Quest for Territorial Compensation

'I HAVE', wrote Cambon from Paris to Lansdowne on 27 December,

> consulted M. Delcassé about the territorial compensation which could be conceded to us as part of the settlement of the New-foundland question.
>
> He deeply regrets that you did not think you could give up Gambia and in seeking where we could find adequate satisfaction he has considered a rectification of our frontier on the Niger.
>
> During the 1898 negotiations we claimed access to the Niger below the Rapids; this was not granted and you conceded to us the two enclaves of Badjibo and Forcados. If you hand over the right bank of the Niger to us as far as the river Moussa, whose mouth is nearly opposite Badjibo, we would give up our enclaves, and M. Delcassé believes that he could get this com-pensation agreed by our Government and by Parliament; the Newfoundland question could thus be settled.[1]

To this new proposal Lansdowne replied in an uncompro-mising memorandum addressed to Cambon on 5 January.[2] He pointed out that the French were asking for a concession which

> comprises no less than 10,000 square miles of valuable territory, and contains several places notably Illo and Boussa, to which, as shown by the negotiations of 1898, His Majesty's Govern-ment attach great importance. By the Convention of 14 June

---

[1] Cambon to Lansdowne, 27 Dec 1903, *BD* II, no. 382, p. 336 [printed in the original French, my translation].

[2] See ibid., pp. 336, 337. In the meanwhile an article in *Le Temps* had appeared on 2 Jan stressing that French concessions in Egypt could only be sacrificed in return for major concessions. The article was no doubt directly inspired by Delcassé.

of that year, this territory was, after prolonged discussion, finally assigned to Great Britain. The boundaries have since then been marked out, the administration of the country has been organised, and the native inhabitants have been given assurances that they are to continue under British rule.[1]

Such a concession could not be defended in Parliament as an equivalent for the abandonment of French rights in Newfoundland. These rights were of a 'strictly limited kind' and had 'for some time past been declining steadily in value'. This point was baldly emphasised when Lansdowne insisted that the number of Frenchmen engaged in the fishing had declined to 258, that the gross value of the product was about £14,000 'against which must be set a considerable expenditure on account of bounties, and the cost of cruisers employed by the French Government'. Furthermore it was 'only by the indulgence of the British authorities in allowing French citizens to exercise privileges in regard to their buildings etc. in excess of their Treaty rights, that the French fishermen are able to carry on their profession at all. In the opinion of His Majesty's Government,' Lansdowne asserted, 'considering the fact that the French are not asked to give up the substantive right of participating in the Newfoundland fisheries, the case is not one in which, strictly speaking, any claim for territorial compensation should have been made. If such a claim is to be admitted at all, it must be moderate in point of extent, and should not affect any territory in which British administration had been definitely established.'[2] At most, Lansdowne concluded, he would be prepared to consider a revision of the boundary between the British and French West African possessions 'where it is formed by the arc of a circle drawn with a radius of 100 miles from Sokoto, so as to give a practicable route in French territory between the Niger and Zinder'.[3] As he explained he was repeating the offer which he had made to Delcassé on 7 July and which Delcassé had then seemed to regard 'favourably'.

This stiff memorandum[4] reached Cambon in Paris where he

[1] Memorandum by Lansdowne to Cambon, 5 Jan 1904, *BD* II, no. 383, p. 336.
[2] Ibid., p. 337.   [3] Ibid.
[4] In fact Gorst complained to Cromer in a letter written from Paris on 6 Jan that 'the spirit in which our Government and the Foreign Office are negotiating is much too stiff . . .'. See Zetland, *Cromer*, p. 280.

had been delayed on account of indisposition and was presumably in any case not in the most cheerful of moods. His irritation was obvious in the letter which he wrote to Cogordon on 7 January immediately after reading Lansdowne's memorandum. 'You will notice', he told Cogordon,

> that according to the Foreign Secretary, M. Delcassé seemed, during his London meeting, to have been content with a mere rectification of the Sokoto frontier.
>
> That is an error which must be rectified at once. The Minister could not have betrayed such an opinion because at that very time he was already asking for Gambia, and has never stopped doing so. It was in addition to Gambia that he was showing a desire to obtain a favourable delimitation of our Niger possessions.
>
> That proves that it is dangerous to appear too conciliatory.[1]

Cambon then recommended that he should be authorised to reply to Lansdowne (1) that the French were not prepared to discuss the value of the Fisheries and that they would not give up their rights without territorial compensation; (2) that having been invited to make a demand they had asked for Gambia, that when this was rejected they had asked for access to the Niger, that they could not ask for less and that they now must await offers; (3) that all the questions under discussion were related and that they could not usefully discuss Egypt until agreement was reached on territorial compensation for Newfoundland and on Morocco. These conditions Cambon proposed to transmit verbally. In three days, according to his doctor, he would be fit to travel and he would see Lansdowne once he got back to London; 'that will be quite soon enough', he somewhat acidly concluded.[2]

In fact it was not until 13 January that Cambon was able to visit Lansdowne. Early that morning he received a note from Delcassé asking him, in his agreed reply to Lansdowne, to add a specific protest about the allegation that French fishing establishments only existed by 'indulgence' of the British Government. It must be pointed out to Lansdowne that 'if these few buildings belonging to French fishermen must disappear, then the numerous

---

[1] Cambon to Cogordon, 7 Jan 1904, *DDF*, IV, no. 158, p. 225.
[2] Cambon to Cogordon, 7 Jan 1904, *DDF*, IV, no. 158, p. 226.

British buildings on the French Shore would have to disappear at the same time'.[1] With this addition to his brief he entered the lists against Lansdowne. After pointing out that, following the Gambia refusal, the French had sought access to the Lower Niger by asking for territories which had been the subject of negotiations in 1898, Cambon concluded somewhat sarcastically: 'You again refuse them because they have become British. And yet, if you do give us any territorial compensation it must surely consist of British possessions, for you can hardly offer us the property of anyone else. We have presented demands which seem acceptable to us; you reject them. We can find nothing else to ask you for, and we will wait for you to formulate an offer in your turn. I must warn you that it is important to reach agreement on this point before continuing our conversations on other questions; for it is useless to reach agreement on Egypt, for example, if the failure of our talks on Newfoundland prevents us from making any settlement.'[2] To Cambon it seemed that Lansdowne, in attempting to reply to this attack, was 'somewhat worried to have been obliged ... to submit two successive refusals'.[3] In Lansdowne's presentation of the Cabinet's case Cambon thought that he could detect 'the usual arguments of M. Broderick[4] and M. Austen Chamberlain'[5] and that Lansdowne himself would have preferred to be more supple.

In fact the discussion was conducted on very familiar lines. Lansdowne stressed the security of Britain's position in Egypt, and the value to France of her co-operation in Morocco; he pointed out that France would acquire a far more extensive sphere of influence in Siam and he made the usual remarks about Newfoundland. Cambon, with slightly more malice than usual, asked why, if the British were so secure in Egypt, Lord Cromer was in

[1] Delcassé to Cambon, 12 Jan 1904, *DDF*, IV, no. 170, p. 241.
[2] Cambon to Delcassé, 14 Jan 1904, *DDF*, IV, no. 178, pp. 248, 249.
[3] Ibid., p. 249.
[4] William St John Broderick, 1st Earl of Middleton (1856–1942).
[5] Cambon to Delcassé, 14 Jan 1904, *DDF*, IV, no. 178, pp. 248, 249. On 22 Jan 1904 Broderick wrote to Curzon: 'we are not yet at an agreement with France and I doubt whether any agreement will be regarded as very satisfactory in this country which would be accepted by Delcassé. In one respect conclusion of an agreement would be unfortunate, as it will add to the suspicion of and distrust for Germany and embitter the feelings between the two countries.' Quoted G. Monger, *The End of Isolation*, p. 135.

such a hurry to get French support for his financial reforms. He stressed all the difficulties which lay ahead for France in Morocco, argued that Britain's sphere in Siam, though less extensive, was of infinitely greater value and, in speaking of Newfoundland, raised the point added by Delcassé.[1] Believing perhaps that he had made some impression Cambon then asked Lansdowne to refer the last French proposals for territorial compensation back to the Cabinet. Lansdowne replied that the Cabinet had rejected them and that he did not believe there would be a change of mind. 'Then', according to Cambon,[2] 'Lansdowne opened out a map of Africa and, indicating a semi-circle around Sokoto, said that without being authorised to make a formal proposal, he considered that the Cabinet would agree to concede territory in this region.'[3] Cambon replied 'that this could not be regarded as territorial compensation of a substantial kind. The region in question consisted of what Lord Salisbury had once spoken of as "light land" and had no known value. Its importance from the French point of view, had, moreover, been much diminished by the discovery of water on the French side of the line, and wells had now been dug along the whole course of the route from Say to Zinder.'[4] Lansdowne rather hopefully enquired 'whether these wells would not require a good deal of watching', and pointed out that 'it must be of some importance to the French Government to avoid the long detour which the convoys now had to make in order to remain on their own side of the line'.[5] From Lansdowne's tone in making his offer Cambon gained the impression that he would have liked to be more generous than his colleagues. 'It was', Cambon noted, 'with a kind of sadness that he spoke of Sokoto, for he cannot think that we would be satisfied with that.[6] ... You will judge', he advised Delcassé, 'whether it would not be useful to request the Foreign Secretary to bring the Boussa question forward again to the Cabinet. We would thus gain time and Lord Cromer, who

[1] See p. 232.
[2] In Lansdowne's version Cambon pressed him to make an offer. See Lansdowne to Monson, 13 Jan 1904, *BD* II, no. 384, p. 338.
[3] Cambon to Delcassé, 14 Jan 1904, *DDF*, IV, no. 178, p. 251.
[4] Ibid.
[5] Lansdowne to Monson, 13 Jan 1904, *BD* II, no. 384, p. 338. Cambon did not mention Lansdowne's question and comment in his report to Delcassé.
[6] Cambon to Delcassé, 14 Jan 1904, *DDF*, IV, no. 178, p. 251.

would willingly give Gambia and Boussa for an Egyptian settlement, could be warned of the reason for the halt in the negotiations, and he could perhaps exercise a useful influence on his government.'[1] It is interesting to notice that at this stage in the negotiations Cambon should be able to speak of the advantage of 'gaining time' and that his advice, as will be seen, was in fact followed by Delcassé.

In spite of the threatening situation in the Far East, Cambon, with Delcassé's possibly somewhat grudging approval, was still trying to play the hand from strength. The success of the *Entente* continued to depend, in Cambon's opinion, on the demonstrable value of the bargain. The need for hurry was only to be invoked as a tactical weapon when French proposals were under consideration in England. A similar attitude and similar tactics guided British policy. It was only Cromer who consistently urged speed and who believed that, provided Egypt was settled to his own satisfaction, the bargain for Great Britain, whatever other concessions she might make, was a good one. Lansdowne, in his attempt to evade any major territorial concession, showed himself just as keen for the best bargain as Cambon. Towards the end of their conversation he reverted suddenly to Rabat and, insisting that his Cabinet colleagues were making difficulties about its exclusion from the neutral zone, he nevertheless indicated that, if his own Sokoto proposal was accepted, they might admit French influence to be extended to the heights above the right bank of the river Sebou.[2] This sweetener was duly transmitted by Cambon to Delcassé.[3]

In his account of the meeting Cambon did not, however, refer to one other important topic which was discussed. Lansdowne had in fact asked him 'whether he had considered the shape which, in the event of our coming to an Agreement about the different questions which we had discussed, that Agreement might take'.[4] According to Lansdowne, Cambon replied 'that he thought there would first have to be an exchange of notes citing generally the outline of the Agreement, and that after that "on devra régler

[1] Ibid.
[2] See Lansdowne to Monson, 13 Jan 1904, *BD* II, no. 384, p. 338.
[3] See Cambon to Delcassé, 14 Jan 1904, *DDF*, IV, no. 178, p. 251.
[4] Lansdowne to Monson, 13 Jan 1904, *BD* II, no. 385, p. 339.

chaque question pour soi" in the manner appropriate to each. Thus the Egyptian part of the Agreement would have to be embodied in a Khedival Decree, and the terms as to Morocco in notes to be exchanged between the two Governments, while Newfoundland would have to be dealt with by a Treaty.'[1] This was one of the very few occasions during the course of the negotiations when the question of final form was discussed. Possibly Lansdowne did so for tactical reasons. As he was unable to accept French demands he may have hoped, in this way, to indicate general goodwill. It was perhaps also significant that Cambon, who was still anxious to 'stiffen' Delcassé, should have omitted any reference to this part of the conversation.

On 14 January Monson visited Delcassé and enquired, presumably out of politeness, about the state of the negotiations. Delcassé summed up the story of British intransigence on the question of territorial compensation and concluded with the complaint: 'She [Great Britain] offers to cede us a few shreds of Sokoto, that is to say of those "sands" where Lord Salisbury used to say that the Gallic cock could scratch at ease.'[2] On 18 January Cambon, at his own request, visited Lansdowne and officially informed him that Delcassé 'found it absolutely impossible to accept Britain's offer of a Sokoto frontier rectification'.[3] Lansdowne expressed regret at this decision which seemed to bring negotiations 'to a deadlock'. At Cambon's suggestion[4] Lansdowne agreed to bring the French proposals regarding Boussa once more to the notice of the Cabinet but without holding out much hope of his 'colleagues changing their mind as to the territory on the right bank of the Niger'.[5]

Following a previous suggestion of Cambon's the French now tried to bring pressure on the British Government via Cromer. On 19 January Cogordon wired to de la Boulinière explaining the deadlock. 'It would be a good thing', he suggested, 'if you were to see Lord Cromer, to whom you would say, as if it were your personal opinion, that the fate of the projected arrangement concerning Egypt is subordinated to the compensation in

---

[1] Lansdowne to Monson, 13 Jan 1904, *BD* II, no. 385, p. 339.
[2] Delcassé to Cambon, 16 Jan 1904, *DDF*, IV, no. 184, pp. 257, 258.
[3] Lansdowne to Monson, 18 Jan 1904, *BD* II, no. 386, p. 339.
[4] See Cambon to Delcassé, 18 Jan 1904, *DDF*, IV, no. 196, p. 273.
[5] Lansdowne to Monson, 18 Jan 1904, *BD* II, no. 386, p. 339.

question.'[1] Accordingly on 20 January de la Boulinière saw Cromer
and conveyed the warning as instructed.[2] To de la Boulinière
Cromer replied that it was difficult for him to advise on matters
outside his competence but that he would do what he could; he also
suggested that Newfoundland might perhaps be left out of the
negotiations altogether.[3] Although obviously somewhat guarded
in his answer to de la Boulinière his reaction was in fact quite as
violent as the French had hoped. 'I have little doubt', he wired to
Lansdowne on 21 January, 'from what I hear on the spot that the
danger of a breakdown of the negotiations is serious. I venture to
urge most strongly the necessity either of making concessions
which will enable the Newfoundland question to be settled or of
dealing with Morocco and Egypt separately. The former is by
far the best solution but the latter is preferable to doing nothing.
To allow negotiations to break down now would in my opinion
be little short of a calamity whether from the general or the local
Egyptian point of view. Also I cannot but think that it would be
severely criticised by the public who already know more or less
what is going on.'[4] After this somewhat unkind reference to public
opinion in the light of the Government's increasing weakness and
unpopularity, Cromer insisted that French concessions in Egypt
were 'really far more valuable' than those being made to France
in Morocco. 'Further,' he argued, 'the recognition of the occupation removes what must otherwise always remain a source of
danger to peace. I cannot but think that this point, which appears
to me of the utmost importance, would be understood in England
and would serve as an adequate justification for some concessions
elsewhere.'[5]

Although French strategy was successful in moving Cromer
there is little evidence that Cromer's pressure, any more than the
rapidly deteriorating situation in the Far East, exercised any
decisive influence at this stage either on Lansdowne or on the
Cabinet. When Lansdowne received Cambon after a Cabinet
meeting on 23 January very little change in his attitude was
apparent. He told Cambon that the Cabinet had closely re-examined

[1] Cogordon to de la Boulinière, 19 Jan 1904, *DDF*, IV, no. 198, p. 274.
[2] See de la Boulinière to Delcassé, 20 Jan 1904, *DDF*, IV, no. 201, pp. 277, 278.
[3] Ibid., p.278.
[4] Cromer to Lansdowne, 21 Jan 1904, *BD* II, no. 387, pp. 339, 340.
[5] Ibid., p. 340.

France's Niger territory demands and had also reconsidered Gambia but that his colleagues 'remained strongly opposed to both of these proposals'.[1] He recapitulated the fate of previous proposals to cede Gambia and insisted that no government could face another attempt. 'It is', he told Cambon, 'if you like, a matter of sentiment.'[2] As far as the Niger territories were concerned Lansdowne said that the Cabinet wondered what exactly was France's objective, whether it was a trade route or just territory. To this Cambon replied that France needed tangible territorial compensation for Newfoundland. The Niger territories could be regarded in this light as well as providing a trade route, though that would be less important once the Dahomey railway was completed. The findings of the Anglo-French boundary commission in respect of these territories had not yet been ratified by the two Governments. Surely, therefore, Cambon argued, 'the question of sentiment raised relating to Gambia could not apply here and British opinion would have no pretext to be excited'.[3] Lansdowne rejoined that some people were always interested in exciting opinion. He added

> that the principle of territorial compensation was completely accepted and that, if the French wanted to obtain commercial facilities and some territory, he was authorised to make the following proposals:
>
> 1. A right of way between French possessions and the Niger below the rapids.
> 2. A rectification of the Gambian frontier to give access to the French to the river Gambia below the rapids.
> 3. A portion of territory included in the semicircle around Sokoto and, in the region of Lake Tchad, a rectification of the 1898 boundary so that the parallel established as a frontier south of Zinder would be extended to the Lake.[4]

Cambon agreed to pass these proposals on to Delcassé, but reminded Lansdowne that the Sokoto territories were regarded as valueless and that they would not constitute adequate territorial compensation. However, he did indicate that it was worth continuing the discussion. 'Yes', replied Lansdowne, 'discussion

[1] Lansdowne to Monson, 23 Jan 1904, *BD* II, no. 388, p. 340.
[2] Cambon to Delcassé, 24 Jan 1904, *DDF*, IV, no. 212, p. 287.
[3] Ibid.
[4] See Cambon to Delcassé, 24 Jan 1904, ibid.

must be kept open; for if we do not succeed in reaching agreement over Newfoundland, we could go no further. My colleagues still consider the abandonment of Morocco, where you are not established, as too important a compensation for the abandoning of some of your rights in Egypt, where England is already settled. They do not believe that public opinion would accept an agreement limited to settling the Egyptian and Moroccan questions and they consider it necessary to obtain satisfaction in Newfoundland.'[1] Cambon inevitably reaffirmed that territorial compensation must be adequate. It is interesting that, notwithstanding Cromer, the Cabinet should have regarded Newfoundland as vital to the negotiations. Thus each side was trying to use Newfoundland bargaining to balance the Egypt–Morocco deal. Small wonder that territorial compensation should have loomed so large.

Neither side wished to cut out a Newfoundland settlement. Without Newfoundland France could not make her territorial compensation claim. Without that claim the Egypt–Morocco deal was unacceptable to France while unless French rights in Newfoundland were abandoned it would not be acceptable to England. In fact Lansdowne's latest proposals, though not satisfactory to Cambon, represented just enough flexibility to suggest that the deadlock might be broken. At any rate it was clear that both sides wished to continue discussion. Perhaps to emphasise this point, and also to lighten his conscience, Lansdowne took the opportunity afforded by their latest meeting to ask Cambon 'whether he had had any further communications with the Spanish Government with regard to the negotiations'.[2] Cambon replied 'that there had been so many changes of administration in Spain that it was extremely difficult to do business with the Spanish Government. The situation had however been thoroughly explained to them as long ago as the Autumn of 1902', and that although agreement in principle had been established, 'the Spanish Government had never made any reply to the French communication'.[3] With this somewhat disingenuous reply Lansdowne seems

---

[1] Cambon to Delcassé, 24 Jan 1904, ibid., p. 288. In his account to Monson Lansdowne makes no mention of this. See Lansdowne to Monson, 23 Jan 1904, *BD* II, no. 388, pp. 340–1.
[2] Lansdowne to Monson, 23 Jan 1904, ibid., p. 341.
[3] Ibid.

to have been satisfied, merely commenting that he 'thought it most important that the Spanish Government, which naturally watched the progress of events in Morocco with an anxious eye, should not be taken by surprise'.[1] According to his own account Cambon took advantage of the occasion to remind Lansdowne of the decision already reached that, should the present negotiations succeed, Spain would be invited to join the provisions concerning Morocco but that the fate of the Anglo-French agreements would not depend on Spanish adherence and that, if that adherence were too long delayed, they would go ahead none the less.[2] Thus, almost casually, Cambon succeeded in establishing what was to prove an important point.

For the present, however, in spite of threats direct and indirect to break off the negotiations, Delcassé could detect little sign of weakening in Lansdowne's attitude towards territorial compensation. Nevertheless he decided, but without committing himself to any final comment on Lansdowne's latest offer, to instruct Cambon to seek clarification on the points mentioned in it and at the same time to demand the cession of 'the Los Islands opposite Konakry in French New Guinea'.[3] Provided satisfaction on these points was obtained and provided his new demand was accepted Delcassé now seemed disposed to make the best of a job and to quibble no longer about the terms offered.

Acting on Delcassé's brief Cambon had a long discussion, which he did not report to Delcassé, with Lansdowne on 27 January. The British proposals and French comments upon them were examined in considerable detail. Lansdowne's reactions, after consultation with his cabinet colleagues, were conveyed to Cambon in a formal letter of reply dated 5 February 1904.[4] 'Our conversation', he reminded Cambon, 'had reference to five points:

    1. The question of facilities for navigation on the Gambia.
    2. The question of similar facilities on the River Niger.
    3. The rectification of the frontier in the neighbourhood of Sokoto.

---

[1] Lansdowne to Monson, 23 Jan 1904, *BD* II, no. 388, p. 341.
[2] See Cambon to Delcassé, 24 Jan 1904, *DDF*, IV, no. 212, p. 288. Lansdowne made no mention of this in his account to Monson.
[3] Delcassé to Cambon, 26 Jan 1904, *DDF*, IV, no. 217, p. 295.
[4] See Lansdowne to Cambon, 5 Feb 1904, *BD* II, no. 389, p. 341.

4. The rectification of the frontier where it impinges on
Lake [T]Chad; and
5. The Isles de Los.[1]

On these five points he then offered his observations. The river
Gambia was, he maintained, navigable 'to a point about one mile
above Yarbutenda, even during the dry season'. He was, therefore, prepared to 'readjust the frontier so as to include the town of
Yarbutenda in French territory'.[2] He disputed the French conten-
tion that the river was not navigable above the Isle des Biches
(Deer Island) and in any case refused to 'entertain a proposal to
draw the frontier so low down the river . . .'.

With reference to the navigation of the Niger he explained that
his proposal concerned, not the right of passage to which Cambon
had pointed out the French were already entitled, but to 'facilities
for landing goods at certain places on the river above the enclave,
and for their transport by land round the rocks and rapids which
impede the navigation of the river'. He then gave details of those
facilities.

Turning to the French Government's request that the new
Sokoto frontier 'should leave the Niger at Gomba and follow the
course of the river . . . so as to give Maradi to France' and also
'the small triangle on the opposite, or right, bank of the Niger,
including Gomba and Ilo', he declared it 'inadmissible'.[3] 'The
region between the Sokoto River and the Anglo-French frontier'
he argued, 'contains districts which have been for some years
under British administration, and the inhabitants of them have
been assured that they are to remain British subjects.'[4] In addition
to this difficulty the river boundary proposed passed far too close
to the town of Sokoto and it had been previously agreed that 'a
certain amount of territory round Sokoto was for us a necessity'.
'If there is to be a rectification of the frontier', he continued:

> all we can offer is that it should leave the existing line at a point
> on the arc 15 kilom. due north of Matankari, and that it should
> be drawn thence in a direct line to a point 20 kilom. due north

---

[1] Lansdowne to Monson, 5 Feb 1904, *BD* II, no. 389, p. 341.
[2] Ibid.   [3] Ibid., p. 342.
[4] Ibid. In fact these territories had been 'conquered' as recently as May 1903
and had provided a splendid opportunity for the artists of the *Illustrated London
News* to give their impressions of the campaign.

of Konni [Birni N'Konni], thence in a direct line to a point 15 kilom. due south of Maradi, and thence direct to the point of intersection of the parallel of 13° 20′ north latitude with the meridian through a point of 70 miles east of the second intersection of the 14th degree of north latitude and the Sokoto arc. Such a rectification would afford a practicable route to Zinder, and about 9750 square miles of territory, some of which is of considerable value.[1]

On the Lake Tchad boundary rectification question, Lansdowne was 'not unwilling' to entertain the French proposal provided agreement on other points was reached. 'But', he pointed out, 'we should lose control of the important trade route running through Kabi, Buddam, and Maini Zumber and . . . part of a very valuable salt district from which we expect to obtain revenue derived by Excise duties, and which attracts a large trade from south and west.' Furthermore, even with one modification which he detailed, 'the proposed concession involves a further surrender of no less than 7000 square miles of territory, making altogether with the Sokoto concession between 16,000 and 17,000 square miles'.[2] Surely this, he argued, was 'amply sufficient compensation for the surrender of the French rights of using the Treaty Shore, which are not, strictly speaking, territorial rights at all'.[3]

However the French Government, he noted, was now anxious also 'to obtain possession of the group of islands known as the Isles de Los opposite Konakry. These islands lying at the door of French Guinea, and distant about 5 miles from the capital of that colony, must obviously be of considerable value to France. The Admiralty point out that any state holding these islands would have a convenient deep-water port considerably nearer to Sierra Leone than any now possessed by a European nation. They are admirably adapted for a coaling station, and whenever the question of their cession has been discussed it has been deprecated. We are not prepared to throw in these islands as a makeweight unless the French Government on its side will add something on our side of the scale.'[4] That something, Lansdowne proposed, should be a settlement of the New Hebrides question which would permit

---

[1] Lansdowne to Monson, 5 Feb 1904, *BD* ii, no. 389, pp. 342, 343.

[2] Ibid., p. 343.

[3] Ibid.   [4] Ibid.

Great Britain to establish her Protectorate over the whole group of islands.

This relatively uncompromising reply to Delcassé's proposals was prepared when the outbreak of war between Russia and Japan seemed virtually inevitable.[1] In spite of this and in spite of Cromer's insistent pleading there were no signs, on Lansdowne's part, of any scuttle to reach a settlement. On the contrary, he was still striving for agreement with a minimum of sacrifice and quite prepared to accept delay. Even though he might have wished some of his Cabinet colleagues to have proved more accommodating, he was willing to insist on their terms.

At this testing time Cambon also kept his nerve. In forwarding Lansdowne's reply to Delcassé on 5 February he confined himself to the comment that 'the offers . . . seem little satisfying; it remains for us to discuss them'.[2] Meeting Lansdowne again on 10 February Cambon told him that Delcassé was examining the British proposals but that 'his impressions were not favourable'.[3] In Delcassé's name, and obviously trying to make an emotional appeal, he added: 'At the moment when the *Entente Cordiale* is *à l'ordre du jour* M. Delcassé is surprised that you should set aside the moderate demands which he has addressed to you. He has not instructed me to make any communication on this subject, but I know his feelings. He regrets, above all in this time of crisis,[4] that the British Government should be adopting an attitude which will make any agreement impossible.'[5] There was, according to Cambon, a note of sadness in Lansdowne's admission that 'an agreement between us at this time would have great significance: we must try to reach it and not tire of seeking means of doing so'.[6]

Having thus matched Cambon's emotional appeal Lansdowne at once returned to more familiar ground by referring to the diminishing value of French fishing rights in Newfoundland and

[1] News of the Japanese naval attack which began the war was received on 9 Feb 1904. For Lansdowne's last tentative efforts towards mediation which he abandoned, in deference to the Cabinet, on 7 Feb 1904, see G. Monger, *The End of Isolation* pp. 154–5.

[2] Cambon to Delcassé, 5 Feb 1904, *DDF*, IV, no. 240, p. 320.

[3] Ibid., 11 Feb 1904, *DDF*, IV, no. 263, p. 343.

[4] The outbreak of the Russo-Japanese War.

[5] Cambon to Delcassé, 11 Feb 1904, *DDF*, IV, no. 263, pp. 343, 344.

[6] Ibid., p. 344.

by stressing the value of his proposed concessions: 'access to the Niger' and 'nine thousand square miles of Sokoto plus seven thousand square miles in the region of Tchad'.[1] Cambon could not refrain from rejoining that the right of access had already been guaranteed in 1898, that its importance would disappear when the Dahomey railway was completed and that the Sokoto and Tchad territories were valueless deserts which could not satisfy France. He added that Delcassé 'was chiefly struck by the rejection of his request for the Los Islands and that the resistance of the Admiralty on this point seemed quite excessive'.[2] Thus after an attempt by Cambon, which Lansdowne neatly turned, to use the Far Eastern crisis as a means of bringing pressure, the discussion ended by sticking in the accustomed groove.

Delcassé's official reply to Lansdowne's proposals of 5 February was conveyed by letter from Cambon to Lansdowne on 18 February.[3] Regarding the navigability of the river Gambia there was obviously a difference of opinion. Verification was necessary. Regarding access to the Niger no new advantages were being proposed. Lansdowne's suggestions were inherent in Article 29 of the 1885 Berlin Act and this had already been pointed out in a note of 24 October 1903. As for Sokoto and Lake Tchad the offer was a very reduced one. 'It was not, strictly speaking, a territorial compensation which was being proposed, but only a right of way.' The offer in no way corresponded to what had been expected. In the region of Zinder, Delcassé had not been able 'even with the aid of War Office maps published last year, to identify the right of way proposed via Kabi, Buddam and Maini Zumber, nor the Salt District to which reference had also been made'.[4] As far as the Lake Tchad territories were concerned Delcassé was only interested in improving French communications and he therefore proposed an alternative boundary formula which might be presumed to secure this. Regarding Sokoto, however, he hoped that re-examination would permit Lansdowne to make an offer which could be regarded as a serious element in territorial compensation. Over these various points it did not seem to him

[1] Cambon to Delcassé, 11 Feb 1904, *DDF*, IV, no. 263, p. 344.
[2] Ibid.
[3] See *DDF*, IV, no. 287, pp. 372–5, and *BD* II, no. 390, pp. 343–5.
[4] Cambon to Lansdowne, 18 Feb 1904, *BD* II, no. 390, p. 344.

that there was any very serious practical divergence of views. Concerning the Los Islands, however, Delcassé expressed surprise. He 'feared that in certain branches of the British Government there was not enough of the same spirit of *entente cordiale* which has allowed him to discuss Newfoundland'.[1] Sentiment had been invoked to justify the refusal of Gambia. Surely there could be no question of sentiment about the Los Islands. They were 'the residue of negotiations now closed and territorial pretensions now abandoned. Britain was making no use of them and could not exploit them.'[2] It seemed strange to Delcassé that there should be resistance on this point which could have no other objective than to reserve for the British Admiralty the possibility of building a naval base which would nullify Konakry. When efforts were being made 'to close sources of conflict and obliterate points of friction', the Admiralty seemed 'to be anxious to retain the Los Islands like a reserve hook on which some future difficulty could fasten'.[3] 'Nowadays', Delcassé pursued, 'when homogeneous groupings have been substituted for the former scattering of European trading centres on the coast of Western Africa the gap which Gambia makes in our possessions is already abnormal; but as for the Los Islands it would be truly excessive to refuse them to us.'[4] Although not estimating the value of the Islands highly Delcassé argued that 'a moral element' was at stake, 'a tangible manifestation of the actual dispositions of the two governments'[5] and that, for this reason, he must insist on obtaining them. On the other hand he totally rejected Lansdowne's suggestion that the British should be allowed to establish a New Hebrides protectorate in return. Although the tone of Delcassé's reply, as transmitted by Cambon, was reproving and at times peremptory, this fact covered a fairly substantial retreat. The insistence on Los Islands was not so much a major claim as a measure of the failure of previous higher bids.

On 25 February Cambon and Lansdowne met twice.[6] At the first meeting Lansdowne enquired whether there had been any developments in the French attitude and Cambon referred back

---

[1] Ibid., p. 345.   [2] Ibid.
[3] Ibid.   [4] Ibid.   [5] Ibid.
[6] See Cambon to Delcassé, 25 Feb 1904, *DDF*, iv, no. 316, pp. 417–19, for an account of both meetings and Lansdowne to Monson, 25 Feb 1904, *BD* ii, no. 391, p. 346, for an account of the second.

to Delcassé's views as stated on 18 February. Lansdowne murmured that the Admiralty were being awkward over the Los Islands and added that the Cabinet did not like the notion of sacrificing territory for fishing rights. Cambon suggested that the Cabinet was being unfair because not only had territorial compensation been agreed, but the French in fact were also sacrificing territorial rights in Newfoundland. Lansdowne endeavoured to reopen the New Hebrides issue but Cambon countered by arguing that the French had a better claim to the New Hebrides than the British. Lansdowne disputed this. He then sought to explore a totally new avenue by asking whether the French would be prepared to give up their rights in the Sultanate of Muscat.[1] Cambon replied evasively. For, as he explained to Delcassé: 'It did not seem in fact wise to me to get involved over Muscat at a moment when the Persian Gulf question is at issue between Russia and England. We would seem to be handing over to the British an excellent base at the outlet of the Gulf. It might be wise to consider giving up our rights in Muscat some day in return for good compensation, but the moment is not opportune.'[2] Lansdowne's efforts to get something in exchange for sacrificing the Los Islands had failed and he resigned himself to seek cabinet approval for abandoning them without any specific return. After a cabinet meeting and a session at the House of Lords Lansdowne again received Cambon and announced that he now had cabinet consent to offer the Los Islands.[3] On the other hand as far as the Sokoto and Tchad boundary questions were concerned he reported that the Cabinet was not willing to improve on previous offers.[4] He proposed that there should be a meeting on 27 February with a Colonial Office representative to fix a definite line for the Tchad concessions.[5] Leaving that point aside for the moment Cambon turned to Sokoto where he required that the frontier should be drawn closer to the river Goulbi. Lansdowne replied 'that this concession had been rejected because the towns of Matankari

---

[1] Anglo-French agreements of 10 Mar 1862 and 5 Aug 1890 had guaranteed the independence of Muscat. In consequence of these agreements the French had acquired various rights in the Sultanate.

[2] Cambon to Delcassé, 25 Feb 1904, *DDF*, iv, no. 316, p. 418.

[3] See Lansdowne to Monson, 25 Feb 1904, *BD* ii, no. 391, p. 346.

[4] Ibid.

[5] As a result of this meeting decisions acceptable to Delcassé were in fact reached.

and Birni N'Konni belonged to the Sultanate of Sokoto and that a division of the Sultan's possessions seemed impracticable'.[1] Cambon warned Lansdowne that he would not be surprised if Delcassé insisted on obtaining more territory in this region. As regards the river Gambia, Lansdowne remarked that the Admiralty still maintained that it was navigable to Yarbutenda but agreed to investigate further although, according to Cambon, he added that Britain would in any case be unwilling to cede territory as far as Deer Island.[2]

With the prospect of agreement over territorial compensation now in sight Lansdowne once again raised the question of Spain. 'We were', he said, 'particularly anxious' that Spain should not be able to say 'that an arrangement which she would regard as vitally affecting her interests' had been reached 'behind her back'.[3] Cambon granted 'the force' of Lansdowne's observations and suggested that, once England and France had come to terms, 'the nature of the arrangement contemplated might be made known to Spain'.[4] He urged that it would not be wise to consult Spain at an earlier stage. Lansdowne was apparently satisfied with this reply and on 27 February he spoke reassuringly to the Spanish Ambassador, concluding with a somewhat disingenuous promise that 'should we see our way to a settlement with France affecting the status of Morocco, Spain would certainly be taken into our confidence'.[5] In fact dealings with Spain were to be left to France and Lansdowne had implicitly recognised that Spain should be kept in the dark until Anglo-French agreement was not merely in sight but actually concluded.

On 1 March Lansdowne and Cambon met again. Lansdowne confirmed that the Cabinet had approved the concessions arising out of the conversations held on 27 February relating to the Lake Tchad territories.[6] The Cabinet was also prepared to agree that 'the line running westwards from Konni to the Sokoto arc should be drawn further to the South'. In return for these 'extensions' of territorial compensation Lansdowne said that the British would

---

[1] Cambon to Delcassé, 25 Feb 1904, *DDF*, IV, no. 316, p. 419.

[2] See Cambon to Delcassé, 25 Feb 1904, ibid. In fact at the meeting held on 27 Feb 1903 (see p. 246). Lansdowne withdrew this limitation.

[3] Lansdowne to Monson, 25 Feb 1904, *BD* II, no. 391, p. 346.

[4] Ibid.   [5] Lansdowne to Egerton, 27 Feb 1904, *BD* II, no. 392, p. 347.

[6] See Lansdowne to Monson, 1 Mar 1904, *BD* II, no. 393, p. 347.

'expect the French Government to offer no objection to the proposal . . . that a British Consul should be appointed at St-Pierre'.[1] Cambon said that he hoped to receive Delcassé's reply to these proposals on the following day.

In fact, however, when they met again on 2 March Cambon announced that he had not yet received instructions from Delcassé.[2] On the other hand he had received a series of enquiries arising from Delcassé's conversation with the French Colonial Minister. Because of Delcassé's 'extreme anxiety that the secrecy of the negotiations should be maintained' he had not, up to this point, taken the Colonial Minister into his confidence.[3] While allowing for Delcassé's well known reticence where his colleagues were concerned, it may be suggested that these matters had not hitherto been thoroughly investigated by the French Colonial Office, not so much because they were unaware of these British offers as because Delcassé had not, until relatively recently, been willing to accept them seriously as territorial compensation. Now he was anxious to present them in the best possible light and therefore eager to press any incidental advantages which the Colonial Office might assist him to include. According to Cambon the following enquiries and suggestions had in fact emerged from consultation with the Colonial Minister:

1. In 1899–1900 the French Government had made Treaties with various sultans ruling the region adjoining the frontiers. Amongst these Treaties were one with the Sultan of Tessawa and Maradi, a second with the Sultan of Zinder and a third with the Sultan of Gummel. The latter place proving to be entirely within British territory, the Treaty had not been ratified. The other two Treaties had, however, been ratified by the President. The French Government . . . were extremely anxious that . . . the whole of the territory belong to the Sultan of Tessawa-Maradi should remain on the French side of the line. . . . Similarly the Sultan of Zinder was believed to rule over a small extent of territory to the south of the degree of latitude which was to form the frontier at this point. The French Government would therefore like the line to be deflected so as to throw the whole of Zinder on the French side.

---

[1] See Lansdowne to Monson, 1 Mar 1904, *BD* ii, no. 393, p. 347.
[2] Ibid., 2 Mar 1904, *BD* ii, no. 394, pp. 347–9.
[3] Ibid., p. 348.

2. Passing to Lake Tchad, His Excellency pointed out that
the eastern boundary of Bornu had, in the map which accompanied the Convention of 1898, been drawn so as apparently
to intersect the middle of Lake Tchad, the idea presumably
being that the French should be given facilities for crossing by
water. . . . It had now been discovered that a great part of what
was shown as water belonging to the Lake . . . was, in reality,
marsh and sandbank, and therefore, not navigable. In these circumstances it was suggested that the line should be drawn in
such a manner as to give the French access across the Lake from
their northern to their southern possessions.[1]

Lansdowne was obviously somewhat disconcerted and he told
Cambon that it would be very awkward, after the difficulties
which he had already experienced with his colleagues, 'to apply
to them for still further concessions'. He added 'that if these concessions were to be made on the ground that it was inconvenient
to divide tribal territory', the same principle would have to be
applied 'throughout the whole extent of the line' and this might
operate 'at other points to the disadvantage of the French'.[2]
Cambon seemed to sympathise with Lansdowne's difficulty and
then turned the discussion to the navigability of the river Gambia.
He explained that the French were anxious for access which would
be suitable for sea-going ships and not merely river-craft. Lansdowne agreed to refer all these suggestions to the Colonial Office
but pointed out once again 'the inconvenience of opening up
these new questions at the last moment'.[3] While Cambon once
more made sympathetic noises Lansdowne pressed his demand
for permission to appoint a British Consul at St-Pierre. Cambon
guaranteed, on his own authority, 'that no objection would be
raised to this proposal'.[4]

On 3 March Lansdowne wrote to Cambon stating that he had
referred to the Colonial Office the French suggestion 'that the
boundary line in the region of Sokoto and Lake Tchad should be
drawn so as to give you the whole of the possessions of the Sultan
of Tessawa-Maradi as well as everything belonging to the Sultan
of Zinder'.[5] As a result he had been informed that 'we have no
information whatever as to the territorial limits of either of these

[1] Ibid. [2] Lansdowne to Monson, ibid.
[3] Ibid., p. 349. [4] Ibid.
[5] Lansdowne to Cambon, 3 Mar 1904, *BD* ii, no. 395, p. 349.

Sultanates nor should we be likely to obtain any until we have received the report of the Delimitation Commission now at work'.[1] The report was not expected for some time and in the meanwhile Lansdowne considered that it would be impossible 'to discuss in complete ignorance of the local conditions these suggestions for the alteration of the boundary upon ethnological or other grounds'.[2] Lansdowne therefore proposed to adhere to the line as originally settled with the proviso that it should be 'subject to modification with the consent of both parties in order to make it accord so far as possible with tribal or other acknowledged divisions'. He was also prepared to agree 'that the line where it intersects Lake Tchad from north to south should be drawn so as to give the French access by water from their possessions on the north to their possessions on the south of the Lake'.[3]

On the following day Cambon replied at length to Lansdowne.[4] After a recapitulation of the steps in the quest for territorial compensation which had led to the present situation he turned to the points now at issue.

There remains [he wrote] to settle the question of delimitation between the region of the Niger and that of Lake Tchad. The line drawn in 1898 on paper, without any previous reconnaissance, is only a theoretic one, which does not become definitive until after a revision to be operated by an Anglo-French Commission; it is an indication, a geometric figure, and nothing more.

It has been seen since then that if the line were definitive we would have no means of communication between our Nigerian and Tchad possessions. However, the intention of the authors of the Arrangement of 1898 was surely to guarantee to both countries the peaceful enjoyment of their possessions and to avert the misunderstandings and conflicts which always result from incursions into neighbour's territory. That was the principle and the raison d'être of the Convention of 1898, and you know as well as I do, by the reiterated requests which I have addressed to you for passage for our food convoys, that it is essential to modify the line drawn by that convention, so that we may have a practicable route.

Convinced like us of this necessity, the British Government has agreed, at your suggestion to adopt in the region of Sokoto

[1] Lansdowne to Cambon, 3 Mar 1904, *BD* 11, no. 359, p. 349.
[2] Ibid., *BD* 11, no. 395, p. 349.   [3] Ibid., *BD* 11, no. 359, p. 349.
[4] See Cambon to Lansdowne, 4 Mar 1904, *BD* 11, no. 396, pp. 349–51.

and in that adjoining Lake Tchad a line which would give us free use of the routes followed by our caravans. But between these two regions the delimitation of 1898 was fixed at 13° 20′, so as to leave us possession of Zinder and of Tessawa.

However it was not then known that the Sultanate of Zinder stretches somewhat to the South of parallel 13° 20′; and that it includes the territory called Damaguerrem by the natives; nor was it known that the Sultan of Tessawa held some of the region of Maradi.

If this had been known, it is obvious that it would have been stipulated that the line should include all the territories belonging to Zinder and Tessawa in the French zone.

On this last point the line which you kindly proposed in the last report to M. Delcassé to guarantee our communications between French Nigeria and Zinder leaves Maradi to the North and coincides roughly with the boundaries of the Sultanate of Tessawa. If there is an adjustment to be made, it is not of great importance, and the Anglo-French Boundary Commission can easily fulfil this task. The same is not true of the Damaguerrem country. Its boundaries are easy enough to fix because it is bordered in the south by the small Sultanate of Goumel and in the south-east by Bornou. Our explorers had made a treaty with the Chief of Goumel, but as the territory is entirely in your zone, my Government did not ratify it; as for Bornou it is yours.

Therefore all that is now necessary is to give the Boundary Commission instructions to follow a line which would leave Damaguerrem, that is to say the whole of the Sultanate of Zinder, in the French zone.

That is what M. Delcassé wishes and he is obliged to insist on obtaining it because the Newfoundland question is to be settled by a Treaty; because that Treaty will have to be ratified by our Parliament, and because that ratification would be rejected in the case of an arrangement which did not contain definite and precise stipulations.

In your letter of yesterday, 3 March, you expressed the opinion that the line of 1898 ought to be maintained but that the Boundary Commission could be authorised to modify it with the consent of both Governments, so as to respect as far as possible the divisions of tribes or other frontiers which might be discovered.

That formula more or less corresponds to M. Delcassé's demand, but it has the disadvantage of being vague and of leaving a hovering doubt over the future fate of the southern part of the Sultanate of Zinder. You were kind enough to tell me this morning that you wanted to treat this matter as far as possible as a mere delimitation of boundaries and I promised you that I would try to find a formula which could reconcile your point of view with M. Delcassé's. It seems that we might say this:

'As it emerges from certain information, whose accuracy it has not yet been possible to verify, that certain territories belonging to the Sultanates of Tessawa-Maradi and of Zinder may be situated south of the present line, the Commissioners entrusted respectively with the task of delimitation should, if necessary, establish the frontier line so as to include these territories in the French zone.'[1]

'I will not attempt to follow you', wisely replied Lord Lansdowne on 5 March, 'in your review of the negotiations which have led up to the point at which we have now arrived. Each side', he sensibly observed, 'will probably remain of opinion that the other is driving too hard a bargain.'[2] On the two latest points outstanding Lansdowne commented that no question 'concerning this portion of the (Tchad) frontier' had until the last moment been raised. However he did not anticipate difficulty in meeting Delcassé's wishes. As for the other boundary question, in the absence of any detailed information of the geography of the region, he felt unable to commit himself entirely to Cambon's proposal.[3] 'It must', he added, 'moreover be borne in mind that these tribal limits are of the most uncertain and elastic description. A tribe belongs to one petty ruler at one moment, and to another petty ruler at another. We cannot, therefore, attribute to such boundaries the sanctity of well-established limits. There is, moreover, this consideration of which we cannot lose sight – that if the line is to be corrected at one point in order to prevent the division of a French-protected tribe, we shall have to insist upon analogous deflections for the purpose of preserving the integrity of tribes enjoying our protection.[4] ... Any arrangement for the correction of the frontier', Lansdowne insisted, must have 'a bilateral character,' with the qualification that, where agreed trade routes for the French were concerned, that consideration would then

---

[1] Cambon to Lansdowne, 4 Mar 1904, *BD* II, no. 396, pp. 349–51.
[2] Lansdowne to Cambon, 5 Mar 1904, *BD* II, no. 397, p. 351.
[3] See Lansdowne to Cambon, 5 Mar 1904, ibid., p. 352.
[4] Ibid.

have priority. Consequently he proposed that 'when the Commissions now engaged in delimiting the conventional frontier return in the course of this spring, and can be consulted, the two Governments will, except as to those regions where the position of the frontier is governed by that of the trade routes, be prepared to consider any diversions of the conventional line which may seem desirable in order to avoid inconvenience to either party by interference with well recognised and established tribal limits.'[1] This formula, he hoped, would sufficiently provide for the Sultanate of Zinder.

In fact, Cambon reverted to his previous suggestion in which Tessawa-Maradi and Zinder were specifically mentioned.[2] Lansdowne then accepted this formula with the addition that tribes depending on British Sultanates should as far as possible be included in the British zone.[3] That amendment was accepted by Delcassé[4] and the long and arduous French quest for territorial compensation was finally completed.

[1] Ibid.
[2] See Lansdowne to Monson, 11 Mar 1904, *BD* ii, no. 398, p. 353.
[3] Ibid.
[4] Ibid., 13 Mar 1904, *BD* ii, no. 399, p. 354.

13

The Final Bargaining

AFTER consultations in Paris with Delcassé Cambon returned to London on 10 March and called on Lansdowne on the following day. He at once told Lansdowne that 'subject to the adjustment of one or two points of detail, M. Delcassé saw no reason why the negotiations . . . should not now be satisfactorily concluded'.[1] He then went on to explain that Delcassé considered that there would have to be a convention for Newfoundland but that other matters could be dealt with by an exchange of declarations.[2] During the long wrangle over territorial compensation the form and timing of the proposed agreements had very much dropped out of sight. Cambon pointed out that Delcassé was anxious to conclude the agreements before Easter.[3] Lansdowne was concerned that there should be no public communication until after the reassembly of Parliament. He considered it dangerous to abandon the agreements 'to the polemics of the press' and quoted the example of the recent Baghdad Railway negotiations which had been subjected to so much ill-informed criticism in the absence of Parliament that they had had to be abandoned.[4] Cambon then reminded Lansdowne that there had been no definite answer yet about the question of Rabat and the neutralised zone; Lansdowne indicated that this would not present a problem.[5] Finally Cambon asked Lansdowne whether in his opinion France could now safely go forward with a loan to Morocco: Lansdowne answered that he could see no objection.[6] This was in answer to a previous enquiry from Delcassé, which Cambon had at first

---

[1] Lansdowne to Monson, 11 Mar 1904, *BD* II, no. 308, p. 353.
[2] See Cambon to Delcassé, 11 Mar 1904, *DDF*, IV, no. 341, p. 449.
[3] Ibid. Easter fell on 3 April.
[4] Ibid.   [5] Ibid.   [6] Ibid.

misunderstood,[1] about whether negotiations were close enough
to successful conclusion to assume that the French would not
meet with British obstruction over the loan. When these matters,
as well as remaining points relating to the territorial compensation
issue, had been canvassed, the meeting adjourned so that Lansdowne could attend the Cabinet. He returned with some problems
and some answers.[2] On Rabat he could confirm acceptance of
French wishes. On territorial compensation a formula which
satisfied Delcassé was devised. Lansdowne was also able to promise
that Gorst would be in Paris on 14 March to concert final details
of the Egyptian financial measures proposed.

Timing of announcements was, however, likely to prove
difficult. The British Parliament was due to meet again between
the 15 and 20 of April. The French Chambers, so Cambon
reported, would not reassemble until 15 May. Lansdowne felt
this might be awkward because he and his colleagues would be
bound to answer questions in Parliament for a whole month
before Delcassé was able to do so. The alternatives seemed to be
to conclude as soon as possible and to try and keep the agreements secret until both Parliaments were in session or to give
them immediate publicity. Lansdowne doubted whether secrecy
could be maintained and on the whole came round to the opinion
that publicity should be given to the agreements as soon as
possible. His chief concern, however, was that Delcassé seemed
to think that the declarations could remain private. He himself
was quite certain that the House of Commons would insist on
having concrete information. It was this consideration which led
him to make a suggestion which was to have very important consequences and which was also, incidentally, to create problems of
final drafting. 'If', he proposed to Cambon, 'we needed to agree
on a certain disposition affecting, for instance, the end of the
status quo in Morocco, we could add to our agreement a secret
article.'[3] But, he insisted, some document must be available for
communication to Parliament. Lansdowne then raised the question of Spain indicating that he intended to speak to the Spanish
Ambassador and noting that Cambon would communicate with

[1] See *DDF*, IV, no. 333, p. 436.
[2] See Cambon to Delcassé, 11 Mar 1904, *DDF*, IV, no. 342, pp. 450, 451.
[3] Cambon to Delcassé, 11 Mar 1904, ibid., p. 451.

Delcassé at once about this. Cambon also told Lansdowne that Delcassé intended to get in touch with the German Ambassador at an opportune moment and confirm to him the guarantees of commercial liberty in Morocco which were being made to Britain. In reporting this discussion to Delcassé Cambon said that he hoped final agreement could be reached within a week and that communications, if necessary, could therefore be made in Parliament before the recess.[1]

Delcassé replied to Cambon on 12 March, agreeing with Lansdowne that it would be awkward to make an announcement before Easter.[2] A final draft was bound to take time to achieve, particularly since Lansdowne insisted on publishing the declarations. On the one hand France's position in Morocco must be made absolutely clear and on the other hand nothing must be said which would arouse Moroccan susceptibilities and thus make France's eventual task more difficult. The part of the arrangement relating to Spain also represented a problem as far as publication was concerned. Delcassé felt that 25 March was the earliest date by which an agreed draft could be prepared; that moment, he judged, would be the right time to communicate with Spain.

On 13 March Cambon discussed the contents of Delcassé's letter with Lansdowne.[3] He stressed Delcassé's fears of the difficulty of preparing any papers which could be submitted to Parliament before Easter and suggested 'that it might be desirable to postpone this'. Lansdowne answered that 'if we were in a position to sign we should . . . also be in a position to present the papers to Parliament. There might be one or two points which we should have to deal with in secret notes, but the greater part of the arrangement would have to be embodied in papers which it would be impossible for us to withhold from our Parliament.'[4] Apart from matters of form and timing, there now seemed to be no barriers in the way of successful conclusion. 'The French negotiations,' Lansdowne informed Cromer, 'after sticking in all sorts of ignoble ruts, suddenly began to travel at the rate of an express train.'[5]

[1] See Cambon to Delcassé, 11 Mar 1904, *DDF*, IV, no. 342, p. 451.
[2] See Delcassé to Cambon, 12 Mar 1904, *DDF*, IV, no. 343, p. 452.
[3] See Lansdowne to Monson, 13 Mar 1904, *BD* II, no. 399, p. 354.
[4] Lansdowne to Monson, 13 Mar 1904, ibid.
[5] Lansdowne to Cromer, 14 Mar 1904, quoted Zetland: *Lord Cromer*, p. 281.

In the meanwhile in Cairo, however, Cromer was becoming increasingly nervous about the possibility of opposition from other Powers to his proposed financial revolution and he telegraphed to Lansdowne: 'The most important point of all in the Egyptian Arrangement seems to me to make it quite clear that the French Government agree to give us a completely free hand to act as the occasion may require in the event of it being impossible to obtain consent of the other Powers.'[1] 'We are almost sure', he added, 'to have much difficulty with Germany.'[2] On Cromer's fears of encountering German opposition has been built a theory that Cromer foresaw the danger of pursuing a policy which might fatally estrange Germany and wished to give a warning to this effect.[3] In fact it seems probable that Cromer was more concerned with countering practical opposition from Germany than worried about a more remote future. It was fear that Germany might sabotage the Egyptian settlement rather than anxiety about other German reactions to Anglo-French *rapprochement* which chiefly concerned Cromer. As for Lansdowne, he firmly and perhaps blindly refused to speculate about the future of Anglo-German relations. The *Entente* seemed to him sufficiently valuable in itself and sufficiently important in relation to the Far East to warrant taking a chance on German attitudes. In his conception the *Entente* was not directed against Germany. Even if the Germans chose so to interpret it, he was not prepared to be deflected from his chosen course. Nor, on the other hand, was he willing at this stage to be guided by Cromer. He did not wish to make any additional demands on France for support against possible opposition from Germany.[4] That aspect of the bargaining, as far as he was concerned, was complete.

On 13 March Gorst arrived in Paris for discussions on matters of detail concerning the Egyptian settlement.[5] The British draft proposals dated 14 and 16 March were sent directly to him and he passed them on to Delcassé.[6] After consultation with Gorst Delcassé prepared the French counter-proposals and forwarded

---

[1] Cromer to Lansdowne, 14 Mar 1904, *BD* II, no. 400, p. 354.
[2] Ibid., p. 355.
[3] See G. Monger, *The End of Isolation*, p. 145.
[4] See Lansdowne to Cromer, 25 Mar 1904, *BD* II, no. 402, pp. 355, 356.
[5] See *DDF*, IV, p. 465, n. (2).
[6] See Delcassé to Cambon, 20 Mar 1904, *DDF*, IV, no. 354, p. 465.

them to Cambon on 20 March;[1] Cambon transmitted them to
Lansdowne on 21 March.[2] In doing so he told Lansdowne that
he did not consider that there was any fundamental difference
between the French and British drafts.[3] He added that Delcassé
'did not like' the British proposal that Article VIII of the Suez
Canal Convention of 1888 should not be brought into operation.[4]
His reservations only applied to the first clause. On 22 March
Cambon and Lansdowne met and discussed the French draft
proposals in detail. Cambon reported fully on this meeting to
Delcassé, giving first of all his general impression of Lansdowne's
attitude and then Lansdowne's specific comments together with
his own replies.[5] Concerning Egypt, Morocco and Newfoundland, Cambon judged that 'the points of difference are numerous
and some of them rather serious'.[6] As for Egypt and Morocco
Cambon rightly noted that Lansdowne was concerned 'to show
the public that he was not conceding anything without compensation and that Great Britain's situation in the Nile Valley would
henceforth be secure from any questioning' from France. 'Hence
his wish to suppress the secret articles and to leave us in a most
embarrassing position *vis-à-vis* the Sultan of Morocco.'[7] Cambon
advised that France should remain firm on this point. Lansdowne
seemed to him 'very anxious to conclude'.[8] 'The indiscretions of
the press', Cambon explained, 'and the general belief that the conclusion of an agreement simply depended on minor drafting details
are forcing him to hurry.'[9] Cambon added, 'I know that the King
is pressing him and he told me himself that the Prince of Wales
had expressed surprise that the matter was not yet settled.'[10]

Success was in fact vitally important to the Cabinet. The negotiations had been used to disarm criticism and Parliament, on
reassembly, was likely to indicate displeasure if they had not by
then been concluded.[11] Power to do so, Cambon assumed, now
must lie only with Lansdowne and Balfour as there would be no
further Cabinet meetings before Easter. Indeed Lansdowne had

---

[1] See Delcassé to Cambon, 20 Mar 1904, *DDF*, IV, no. 354, pp. 465–72.
[2] See Lansdowne to Monson, 21 Mar 1904, *BD* II, no. 401, p. 355.
[3] Ibid.   [4] Ibid.
[5] See Cambon to Delcassé, 23 Mar 1904, *DDF*, IV, no. 359, pp. 477–94.
[6] Cambon to Delcassé, 23 Mar 1904, ibid., p. 478.
[7] Ibid.   [8] Ibid.   [9] Ibid.
[10] Ibid.   [11] See Cambon to Delcassé, ibid.

explained that, even if they could not sign before Easter, he and the Prime Minister would remain close to London so that discussions could continue. 'Therefore', concluded Cambon, 'they don't need to consult their colleagues any further.'[1] Drawing confidence from this Cambon advised Delcassé against any surrender on Article I of the Egypt–Morocco declaration.[2] The point at issue was whether there should be any explicit French recognition of the British occupation of Egypt or whether, as Cambon and Delcassé still hoped, actual mention of the occupation could be avoided. 'It is only', Cambon counselled, 'if faced with an absolute certainty that the negotiations would be broken off that we could consent to some more or less vague reference about the time limit of occupation.'[3]

In fact Lansdowne was quite determined that satisfaction on this point must be obtained, and he indicated his views firmly to Cambon. But Cambon, relying on his own assessment of the situation, refused to be impressed.

In the meanwhile the British Press was beginning to take a lively interest.[4] On 22 March Lansdowne had spoken to Cambon of indiscretions and had declared them inevitable. There was, he had argued, some advantage in this kind of publicity: 'it prepared the public to appreciate the value of advantages gained and sacrifices accepted; it disposed the public to consent to concessions without which a bargain could not be struck'.[5] Cambon wrote,

> There is no paper which does not testify, in the most cordial manner, to the wish that as complete as possible an *Entente* should be established between France and Great Britain. Opinion is unanimous in hoping that all the causes of misunderstanding between the two countries will be removed. But the Englishman is above all a business man, and when calculations are made of what England will give and what she will receive, objections arise. They centre mainly on the concessions made to us in Morocco.[6]

Cambon then quoted Press extracts to illustrate the point and

[1] Cambon to Delcassé, 23 Mar 1904, ibid., p. 479.
[2] See Cambon to Delcassé, 23 Mar 1904, ibid.
[3] Cambon to Delcassé, 23 Mar 1904, ibid. This sentence was sent in cipher.
[4] See Cambon to Delcassé, 24 Mar 1904, *DDF*, IV, no. 362, pp. 497–9.
[5] Cambon to Delcassé, 24 Mar 1904, ibid., p. 498.
[6] Ibid.

A Mutual Sacrifice, 30 March 1904

added: 'Our French newspapers are too inclined to say that in England the concessions made to us are regarded as of little value. This is not correct, and there might be an interest in making it known.'[1] Reflection and reading of the British Press had perhaps brought Cambon round to the view that his recent advice to Delcassé had been somewhat precipitate and that the way must be paved for some slight retreat.

It was, at any rate, in a more compromising mood that he called on Lansdowne late during the evening of 24 March. Lansdowne had just ended a meeting with Balfour, Gorst and Sanderson. He told Cambon that Balfour had studied the French proposals very carefully and that 'he had shown considerable surprise at their unfavourable aspect. According to him the British Parliament would never ratify an agreement abandoning Morocco to France without obvious advantages in Egypt.'[2] Lansdowne then insisted that the French draft of Article I must be modified. Cambon, while continuing to reject the British version, abandoned his previous position and proposed 'speaking personally' to recommend to Delcassé the inclusion of a statement to the effect that France 'would not insist on fixing a date for the evacuation or a time limit for the occupation [of Egypt]'.[3] Lansdowne agreed that this proposal, which in fact Delcassé had previously put forward to Cambon, was worth consideration. Lansdowne, in turn, then accepted to modify his draft proposals referring to the promise of French support in gaining the adherence of the Sultan and of the Powers to the projected Khedival Decree so that support against opposition would not be implied. Lansdowne insisted that some mention of French backing must, however, be included in the published declaration.[4] Cambon explained to Delcassé that Balfour was adamant on these points and that he could not be shifted. The Cabinet was in too weak a position to be able to impose the agreement without serious debate in Parliament. Reference to the occupation, on the lines Cambon now proposed, would probably prove acceptable to Lansdowne and would have to be included in the public declaration. 'I know', added Cambon, 'that this is the sensitive point for French public

---

[1] Cambon to Delcassé, 24 Mar 1904, *DDF*, IV, no. 362, p. 499.
[2] Ibid., 25 Mar 1904, *DDF*, IV, no. 364, p. 501.   [3] Ibid., p. 502.
[4] See Cambon to Delcassé, ibid.

opinion; but unless we renounce for ever the hope of drawing some compensation for British establishment in Egypt we must resolve to recognise their right to be there.'[1] This was, of course, plain common sense but it did represent a withdrawal from the position which Cambon had until recently been trying to defend. As for the question of French backing for the Khedival Decree, Cambon considered that this was less difficult to promise. By adhering to the Khedival Decree France recognised its usefulness and there was no reason to make difficulties about letting her opinion be known to other Powers; 'We remain judges', Cambon pointed out, 'of the form we would give to our support and we could measure at our own free will the extent of our activity.'[2] He recommended that British wishes, as modified by Lansdowne, should be met.

Further discussion between Cambon and Lansdowne covered a variety of points of detail. In reporting on these Cambon refrained, with one exception, from making any specific comments. The exception arose over Lansdowne's proposal that an Article should be included in the Egypt–Morocco declaration about maintenance of the *status quo* as far as islands adjacent to the coast of Morocco were concerned.[3] Cambon enquired whether Lansdowne had intended to include the Canary Islands. Lansdowne obviously had had no intention of doing so and explained this to Cambon. Cambon however seemed to detect a sudden interest on Lansdowne's part.[4] He therefore suggested to Delcassé that it might be worth considering the advantages of an Anglo-French guarantee of neutralisation which would include not only the Canary Islands but the Balearic Islands as well. This could be important as far as French long-term prospects in Morocco were concerned.[5] Lansdowne, in the meanwhile, was aware that, by failing to insist on an open promise by the French that they would support any consequent unilateral British action in the event of refusal by the Sultan and by the Powers to adhere to the Khedival Decree, he had disappointed Cromer. On the other hand he had no doubts about the wisdom of his own decision. 'There would', he explained to Cromer,

---

[1] Cambon to Delcassé, 25 Mar 1904, *DDF*, iv, no. 364, p. 502.　　[2] Ibid., p. 503.

[3] See Cambon to Delcassé, 25 Mar 1904, ibid.

[4] Ibid.　　　　　　　　　　　　　　　　　[5] Ibid., p. 504.

in my belief be no prospect of obtaining consent of the French Government to such a clause, and I do not see how we can expect them to proclaim their intention of encouraging us to violate Treaty engagements to which both they and we are parties. From our point of view objection to this course would be not less strong. We have always professed respect for international obligations and denounced the conduct of those who ignored them. We may at any moment be confronted with questions raising this principle, e.g. that of egress of Russian Black Sea Fleet.

An open announcement that we had gone over to the side of international law-breakers would strike a fatal blow at our reputation.

Finally it seems obvious that public announcement of our intention to override opposition of other Powers would scarcely fail to increase our difficulties in dealing with them. . . .

What I am asking for is that France should publicly agree

(1) to support us in procuring adhesion of other Powers
(2) in the meanwhile, not to thwart or oppose us in our conduct of Egyptian business.

As to this, I think we could probably get private promise that French representatives would always act with ours on Caisse and on Railway Board.[1]

Cromer replied on 27 March.[2] He conceded that 'objections to publicity are certainly very strong' and he claimed that he himself had been about to propose 'a secret agreement in the sense of that which Lansdowne had adopted.' But he urged that this should be insisted upon 'as otherwise we shall be wholly at the mercy not only of the other Powers but also of the French. Their help', he cynically, and in the event unfairly, concluded, 'to get Decree accepted will presumably be half-hearted.' He himself relied on the hope that the other Powers would 'get an inkling of the Secret Agreement and that, if they once feel that we are fully determined to carry the thing through with or without their consent, they will probably come to terms'.[3] Cromer was here being unduly suspicious of the French and making exaggeratedly heavy weather of future prospects. However, from Lansdowne's point of view, it was satisfactory that he was not protesting too violently against the sensible compromises which had been reached.

---

[1] Lansdowne to Cromer, 25 Mar 1904, *BD* II, no. 402, pp. 355, 356.
[2] See Cromer to Lansdowne, 27 Mar 1904, *BD* II, no. 403, p. 356.
[3] Cromer to Lansdowne, 27 Mar 1904, ibid.

In Paris Delcassé was provided by the German Ambassador with an opportunity to speak of the Anglo-French negotiations now in train.[1] On the basis of this conversation he claimed, subsequently, that Germany had been informed about the projected agreement and had not raised any objections. 'Is it true', asked Radolin,[2] 'that an agreement has been signed or is on the point of signature between France and England?' 'Nothing', Delcassé replied, 'is signed nor on the point of being signed. But we have been talking for some time with the British Cabinet about a friendly settlement of questions interesting our two countries; the *Entente* has been recognised as possible and it is probable that it will end by being achieved.'[3] To Radolin's further questions Delcassé admitted that Newfoundland and Morocco were under discussion. Concerning Morocco he added:

But you know our point of view on this subject; and I have already repeated to you what I said in the Chamber of Deputies and in the Senate. We want to maintain the present political and territorial situation in Morocco as long as possible; but that situation, in order to last, must obviously be supported and improved. Last year alone Morocco offered us by repeated aggressions powerful and legitimate excuses for intervention. I resisted, but each time with greater difficulty, the natural pressures of those who wanted to seek in Morocco itself guarantees for our Algerian frontier and peace for neighbouring populations. We had to reinforce our posts and to establish new ones at considerable expense, which can only be reduced by an improvement in the situation in Morocco. The Sultan has already had a chance to be convinced of the efficiency of our help on matters where he has requested it. We now must continue that help. But it will be given to him so that all the world can benefit, particularly where commercial transactions are concerned because these are bound to benefit from the establishment of security which is one of Morocco's greatest needs. I do not need to add that, under whatever form we may be led to assist the Sultan, commercial liberty will be rigorously and absolutely maintained.[4]

'And Spain?', asked Radolin. 'Spain', replied Delcassé, 'I said

---

[1] See Delcassé to Bihourd, 27 Mar 1904, *DDF*, IV, no. 368, pp. 509, 510.

[2] Prince Hugo von Radolin, German Ambassador in Paris (1900–10).

[3] Delcassé to Bihourd, 27 Mar 1904, *DDF*, IV, no. 368, p. 509.

[4] Ibid.

formerly in Parliament that she knows we are her friend and that she can only expect friendly attitudes from us. It is not I who will misunderstand her positive interests and legitimate aspirations.'[1] According to Delcassé, Radolin found these declarations natural and perfectly reasonable.[2] The underlying assumption was that the fate of Morocco, provided commercial liberty was respected, would be decided without any reference to Germany. It was obviously with satisfaction that Delcassé observed that the point, for the present, was not being queried.

In London Lansdowne and Cambon met again on 28 March. Almost as a formality Cambon reiterated Delcassé's objections to any public reference to the British occupation of Egypt and spoke of the danger of awkward reactions in the Chamber of Deputies. Lansdowne said that he could appreciate parliamentary difficulties better than anyone, but, after the most careful study of the question with Balfour and his Cabinet colleagues, they must insist on specific mention.[3] Indeed he warned that 'If silence were kept on the most important point as far as British public opinion was concerned, it would not be possible to ratify the arrangements.'[4] Cambon then retreated to ground which had been prepared and reverted to the proposal which he had already indicated. He showed Lansdowne a draft and said that he would not submit it officially unless sure of its acceptance. Lansdowne agreed to submit the proposal to Balfour and intimated that he thought it would meet the case.[5] On the question of French support for obtaining the agreement of the Sultan and of the Powers to the projected Khedival Decree, Cambon submitted to Lansdowne Delcassé's proposal that there should be a mutual promise of diplomatic support 'to obtain the execution of the clauses of the present Declaration regarding Egypt and Morocco'.[6] Lansdowne seemed satisfied with this formula and agreed to submit it to Balfour. Over Article II, in which Great Britain recognised French rights to preserve order and to promote reforms in Morocco, a significant quibble over words arose. Cambon insisted that the French

---

[1] Ibid.
[2] See Delcassé to Bihourd, 27 Mar 1904, ibid., p. 510.
[3] See Cambon to Delcassé, 28 Mar 1904, *DDF*, IV, no. 370, p. 512.
[4] Cambon to Delcassé, 28 Mar 1904, ibid.
[5] See Cambon to Delcassé, 28 Mar 1904, ibid.
[6] Cambon to Delcassé, 28 Mar 1904, ibid., p. 513.

draft which contained the words 'it appertains *exclusively* to France' must be maintained, whereas Lansdowne was only prepared to accept '*especially*'.[1] Lansdowne agreed, however, to refer the French demand to his colleagues. On the remaining articles of the declaration to be published no important difference emerged although Lansdowne made a reservation concerning Article VI (Neutralisation of the Suez Canal).[2] Cambon supposed that this was because Lansdowne was still awaiting an opinion from Cromer, and in fact Delcassé's latest draft was eventually agreed on. Lansdowne also spoke of his proposed Article VIII relating to the maintenance of the *status quo* in Morocco and in the adjacent islands. Cambon pointed out that the maintenance of the *status quo* in Morocco was already covered by a previous article and that the islands did not seem sufficiently important to warrant a special mention. 'There are also the Canary Islands', remarked Lansdowne, thus confirming Cambon's previous impression that his interest had been aroused.[3] Cambon then suggested that, as the Canary Islands only indirectly touched the Moroccan question and as a special *entente* with Spain would be needed for neutralisation or other guarantees, it would be best to tackle this question separately. In mentioning the matter to Delcassé, as he had agreed with Lansdowne to do, Cambon remarked: 'Your Excellency will appreciate whether it would be useful to turn discussion in this direction. Perhaps it would be worth giving a bit of body to our negotiations with Madrid by introducing the question of the Canary Islands; it touches M. León Castillo closely as he is a native of Las Palmas.'[4] As far as the immediate problem was concerned, Lansdowne took no further interest in the article which he had proposed and it was dropped from the draft.

Discussion then turned to the proposed secret articles. Earlier in the discussion Lansdowne had argued in favour of the publication of Article II and had suggested that, if there were difficulties concerning the references to Morocco, those relating to Egypt might at any rate be published. Inevitably Cambon objected and Lansdowne seemed willing to concede.[5] Now he was anxious about secret Article V where it was stipulated that, should the

[1] See Cambon to Delcassé, 28 Mar 1904, *DDF*, iv, no. 370, p. 513.
[2] Ibid., p. 514; and see p. 258.   [3] Ibid., p. 515.
[4] Cambon to Delcassé, 28 Mar 1904, ibid.
[5] See Cambon to Delcassé, 28 Mar 1904, ibid., p. 514.

Sultan and the Powers reject the Khedival Decree, France would not oppose eventual debt conversions. Cambon was ready to accept this provided that the conversions did not take place before 15 July 1910, which was the date already stipulated in the projected Khedival Decree.[1] With that proviso, agreement on the wording of the article was reached.

On Newfoundland Cambon explained that he was expecting further instructions from Delcassé but that, as freedom to purchase bait was the vital point, he believed that Delcassé was likely to insist on his draft. Lansdowne replied that the Colonial Office had been corresponding for months with the Government of Newfoundland on this matter and that they were quite inflexible.[2] Although the long meeting thus ended on a note of difficulty it was obvious that much progress towards agreement on a final draft had been made.

'Thanks to your efforts', Delcassé wrote to Cambon on 29 March, 'the gap is clearly diminishing between the pretensions of the British negotiators and the concessions which you had decided we must not exceed.'[3] He then urged Cambon to remain firm on retaining the word 'exclusively' for the exercise of French influence in Morocco and on the necessity of keeping the whole of secret Article II within the secret part of the agreement.[4] In the meanwhile he gave formal approval to Lansdowne's draft of Article VII relating to Spain.[5] The question of the Canary Islands, he judged, could not be tackled immediately.[6] On the bait question he pointed out that he was under pressure from French fishing interests. Now that British grievances in Newfoundland were being met would it not be possible, he suggested to Cambon, to induce the British to abandon restriction in the sale of bait. It had, he added, only been instigated as a reprisal.[7]

On 29 and 30 March Lansdowne and Cambon met again and, although the discussions were lengthy, Lansdowne was mainly concerned about interpretations of the meaning of French

[1] Ibid., p. 515. When Cambon made this condition he had not yet received a telegram from Delcassé (see ibid., p. 508, n. 2) instructing him in the same sense.
[2] See Cambon to Delcassé, 28 Mar 1904, ibid., p. 515.
[3] Delcassé to Cambon, 29 Mar 1904, *DDF*, IV, no. 372, p. 517.
[4] See Delcassé to Cambon, 29 Mar 1904, ibid.
[5] See Delcassé to Cambon, 29 Mar 1904, *DDF*, IV, no. 372, p. 517.
[6] Ibid., p. 518.
[7] Ibid.

diplomatic support (Article IX) in giving effect to the present agreements and of the secret article concerning debt conversions in the event of opposition to the Khedival Decree. Cambon's verbal reassurances proved convincing.[1]

On 30 March Monson and Delcassé met in Paris and Monson wired to Lansdowne that Delcassé could not give way on the 'bait' question.[2] Lansdowne wired back in some annoyance insisting that 'we shall certainly break off the negotiations if the demand is pressed'.[3] Without making this threat explicit Monson advised Delcassé on 31 March that Lansdowne was adamant on the 'bait' question.[4] Delcassé accepted this point but, in return, proposed a redrafting of Article I of the Egypt–Morocco declaration.[5] Monson, who revealed by this how far out of touch he was in spite of copious information from Lansdowne with details of the negotiations, suggested that Delcassé's modification might prove acceptable.[6]

Before the confusion which Monson's intervention threatened had taken effect, Lansdowne and Cambon met again on 31 March.[7] Cambon indicated that Delcassé was ready to surrender on the 'bait' question and pressed for retention of the word 'exclusively' in return.[8] After their meeting Cambon received news from Delcassé of his latest conversation with Monson. Now Cambon wrote to Lansdowne proposing Delcassé's amendment of Article I.[9] Lansdowne totally rejected this possibility on 1 April.[10] On the other hand, provided 'other questions could be satisfactorily disposed of', he was prepared to take up Delcassé's latest suggestion that the exercise of French influence in Morocco should not be qualified either by the word 'exclusively' as the French desired or by the word 'especially' as the British wished.[11]

On 6 April Cambon made a last effort to use Delcassé's con-

[1] See Lansdowne to Monson, 30 Mar 1904, *BD* II, no. 404, p. 357.
[2] See Monson to Lansdowne, 31 Mar 1904, *BD* II, no. 405, p. 357.
[3] Lansdowne to Monson, 30 Mar 1904, *BD* II, no. 406, p. 358.
[4] See Monson to Lansdowne, 31 Mar 1904, *BD* II, no. 409, pp. 360, 361.
[5] Omitting the reference to British occupation; see p. 261.
[6] See Monson to Lansdowne, 31 Mar 1904, *BD* II, no. 409, p. 361.
[7] See Lansdowne to Monson, 31 Mar 1904, *BD* II, no. 408, pp. 359, 360.
[8] Ibid., p. 360.
[9] See Cambon to Lansdowne, 31 Mar 1904, *BD* II, no. 410, p. 361.
[10] See Lansdowne to Cambon, 1 Apr 1904, *BD* II, no. 411, pp. 361, 362.
[11] Ibid., p. 362.

cessions on the 'bait' question and on the word 'exclusively' to obtain a new and minor modification of Article I.[1] Lansdowne was able to brush this attempt aside with little difficulty.[2] Cambon now seems to have lost interest in the controversy over the word 'exclusively' and Lansdowne's latest proposal 'more particularly' was quietly accepted. After the failure of last minute endeavours to find any satisfactory formula of agreement over the New Hebrides problem, the draft texts of the agreements were finally approved.[3] A telegram from Cromer on 7 April, proposing yet another draft of Article I which he thought might placate the French and yet give him the substance of what he desired, may have caused amusement to Lansdowne but was otherwise no longer of any practical significance.[4]

On 8 April the Convention between the United Kingdom and France respecting Newfoundland and West and Central Africa, the Declaration between the United Kingdom and France respecting Egypt and Morocco, the five Secret Articles appended to that Declaration and the Declaration between the United Kingdom and France concerning Siam, Madagascar and the New Hebrides, were signed by Lansdowne and Cambon.[5]

The more the course of the laborious negotiations which led to these signatures is studied, the less easy it becomes to establish any direct connection between their progress and extraneous influences. The bargaining on both sides was keen throughout. Although both sides were obviously anxious to conclude, they only advocated speed when pressing a point of advantage. Cambon rightly concluded that the experience of the Boer War, the failure of Anglo-German negotiations and the situation in the Far East made the moment opportune for Anglo-French *rapprochement*. But, as he also knew, there was a long legacy both of quarrels

[1] See Lansdowne to Monson, 6 Apr 1904, *BD* 11, no. 413, p. 363. The new proposal was: 'On its part the Government of the Republic declares that it will not obstruct the action of Great Britain in that country [Egypt] by taking the initiative in asking that a limit of time be fixed for the British occupation'. 'Taking the initiative' was the new phrase to which Lansdowne objected as a weakening of the previous agreed formula.

[2] See Lansdowne to Monson, 5th Apr 1904, *BD* 11, no. 413, p. 363.

[3] Ibid.

[4] See Cromer to Lansdowne, 7 Apr 1904, *BD* 11, no. 415, p. 364.

[5] See *BD* 11, no. 417, pp. 373–98, for the final texts of the agreements, the British draft of 16 Mar 1904 and the French draft of 21 Mar 1904, are printed in parallel columns beside the final text.

and of abortive negotiations. On this occasion he himself had carefully explored and prepared the ground. Patience and attention to detail were obviously important. The deliberations belonged too much to the past to be hurried along by moods of the present. They needed also to be conducted in secret. Even though prompted, at any rate on the British side, by public opinion, there were matters at stake which demanded a certain privacy of bargaining. Lansdowne and Cambon, mainly because of their own attitudes and personalities, were able to achieve this. They bargained furiously, but quietly. It was, of course, important that there were concrete questions to bargain about. Quite apart from the general desirability of an Anglo-French *entente*, the settlement of particular questions at issue could provide mutual advantage. One of the difficulties about previous Anglo-German negotiations was that there were no particular questions at issue between England and Germany; agreement could only have been reached on matters of vague general policy. Cambon rightly diagnosed that this kind of alliance was not popular in England. The settlement of specific disputes, and these abounded between England and France, represented a far more hopeful basis for future co-operation. It was because there were direct questions at issue between England and France that their settlement appealed to Lansdowne, as it would have done to any British Foreign Secretary. Delcassé, with Cambon's full understanding, was more calculating. But, without a good bargain in prospect, even Delcassé would not have contemplated a diplomatic revolution.

14

The Entente Cordiale and the Origins of the First World War

THE signing of the agreements was greeted with enthusiastic approval on both sides of the Channel.[1] In England, where *rapprochement* had clearly been sponsored by public opinion, the applause was loudest. It was reflected in *The Times*, the *Mail*, the *Daily Telegraph*, the *Standard*, the *Westminster Gazette* and the *Daily News*. The *Morning Post*, the *Saturday Review* and the *Daily Chronicle*, taking their cue from Rosebery,[2] who was almost alone among leading politicians to criticise, offered some adverse comment but no categoric condemnation. In Parliament the agreements were approved without a division. It was left to Moussa Aflalo, a British citizen of Moroccan origin, to make the most bitter, but obviously personal, protest in a monograph published in August 1904 and entitled *The Truth about Morocco*. Apart from the narrowest of sectional interests and the awkwardness of Rosebery the verdict in favour of 'the most auspicious event of the twentieth century'[3] was virtually unanimous.

In France Press reactions, though less cordial, were favourable enough. *Le Temps*, *Le Journal des Débats*, *Le Siàcle*, *Le Figaro*, *Le Gaulois*, *L'Éclair*, *La Republique française* and *Le Petit Journal* all expressed satisfaction. A minority of the colonial group, who had

---

[1] For a study of Press reactions see J. J. Mathews, *Egypt and the Formation of the Anglo-French Entente of 1904*, pp. 106–12.

[2] For Rosebery's 'solitary opposition' see R. R. James, *Rosebery*, p. 449.

[3] As described by Dr Dillon in the *Contemporary Review*. 'France and England', he added, 'have settled their outstanding accounts just when the Central European Press, whose wish was father to their thought, were busiest saying they could not possibly do anything of the kind so long as the war lasted.'

not evolved with Étienne, lashed out in anger. In the Chamber,
436 deputies voted in favour and 94 against. Of these, some twenty
represented maritime constituences where resentment over the
Newfoundland settlement was strongest. For the majority of
Frenchmen, however, the most bitter pill to swallow was recognition of British supremacy in Egypt. But the prescription was
sugar-coated with Moroccan gloss and it had been endorsed by
leading colonialists. In these circumstances the welcome for
Entente Cordiale, though tinged with asperity, was solid enough.[1]

It now remained to be seen whether the agreements, thus backed
by public sentiment, would, as claimed, eliminate or at least
reduce previous sources of friction. Bargains can as easily promote
new bickering as they can dispel old quarrels. Cromer had constantly feared this. In fact he soon found that French hostility to
his programme of Egyptian financial reform was satisfactorily
suspended. His suspicions that France would prove lukewarm in
encouraging the adherence of the other Powers to the Khedival
Decree proved quite unfounded. At least as far as the French
were concerned he had a free hand in Egypt. One of the consequences was that Egyptian nationalists, deprived of any hope
of French support, began to learn to stand more firmly on their
own feet. New seeds of Anglo-Egyptian conflict were sown.
Although Egypt ceased to be a thorn in the side of Anglo-French
relations the Egyptian question remained a major problem for
British governments. Ironically Cromer's policy, which probably
was of more benefit to Egypt than to England, finally established
the British as *the* enemy in the eyes of most Egyptian nationalists.
But to all outward appearances the value of *Entente Cordiale* was
enhanced.

In return for recognising Britain's right to govern Egypt the
French had gained an option to embark on a similar policy in
Morocco. They were to have no cause for complaint with Britain's
interpretation of the agreement. But the Moroccans, abandoned
by the British, were reluctant to submit without a struggle. They
grasped eagerly at German promises of support. When these
eventually failed they fell back upon their own resources. The

----

[1] As *Punch* (11 May 1903) observed: 'the *Entente* continues to grow. A distinguished
French journalist denies that the English are a Germanic race, and declares that the
French are our real cousins. This must be Love.'

French conquest of Morocco was to prove a major and very costly military operation. Internationally, however, France enjoyed the full benefit of British diplomatic support and there is little doubt that it was this support which gave the French a free hand to subdue Moroccan resistance at leisure. However costly and dubious the benefit, Morocco figured for France on the credit side of the *Entente Cordiale*.

In West Africa the territorial adjustments were not so much important in themselves as symbolic of a final settlement. Even though the agreed demarcation lines often crossed territories as yet uncharted, the era of rivalry, and above all of uncertainty, was effectively ended. West African territories, which had been regarded as bargaining counters, in any case no longer seemed so significant once the main Egypt–Morocco bargain had been struck. Both England and France could now somewhat ruefully face the local problems of administering their vast African empires without reference to a wider struggle. In the absence of the excitement engendered by rivalry much of the glamour of Empire vanished. The reality of expensive civilising missions remained.

For the rest the Siamese compromise, already in working operation, presented no new problems. The Newfoundland settlement, while leaving a trail of local bitterness, successfully eliminated disputes from Foreign Office agendas. In general the claim that the agreements would remove causes of friction proved more than justified.

There was, however, a more positive element in the calculations, not only of Delcassé, but even of Lansdowne. Delcassé hoped gradually to develop links with England which would provide additional security against Germany. The *Entente Cordiale* was to become a corollary of the Dual Alliance. In this sense, although he was compelled to resign in June 1905, his hopes were in the long run completely fulfilled. On the other hand it is questionable whether the agreements themselves would have led to this result unless other factors, at the time quite incalculable, had pressed England in the same direction. There is, however, no doubt that the swing was thereby facilitated. For Lansdowne accommodation with Russia constituted the further objective of agreement with France. That objective was clearly out of reach during the Russo-Japanese War. But, on the other hand, in the delicate state of Anglo-Russian relations France could play a useful role in support of minor bargains and in the prevention of major disputes. This role France amply fulfilled. Russia adhered to the Khedival Decree.[1] British reassurances to the Russians about Tibet were, after much misunderstanding, accepted.[2] The Dogger Bank crisis was surmounted.[3] In all these matters French cooperation was in line with Lansdowne's expectations of *Entente Cordiale*.

When the Anglo-Russian *Entente* was achieved in 1907 other factors, incalculable in 1904, were no doubt decisive. On the other hand once again, *Entente Cordiale* surely facilitated the process.

The solidification of the *Entente Cordiale* which Delcassé had desired and the Anglo-Russian accommodation which Lansdowne had envisaged, though facilitated by the agreements of 1904, were in fact caused by German reactions to them. German policy was based on the assumption that Anglo-French and Anglo-Russian differences could never be satisfactorily resolved. The signing of the Anglo-French agreements in 1904, in spite of the long preparatory negotiations, came as a shock. The conclusion drawn was that what had been done could be undone. The Russo-Japanese War seemed to provide an immediate occasion. Germany was prodigal in declarations of support for Russia. France, it seemed, must either become embroiled in a quarrel with England as Japan's ally or forfeit her Russian Alliance. When these alternative hopes failed, Germany turned her attention towards Morocco. Here the *Entente Cordiale* could be tested. By blocking the forward policy which was postulated Germany could destroy the *Entente*. With Russia involved in a disastrous war against Japan circumstances seemed to be favourable. Germany's first attentions were concentrated on Spain. When Spain capitulated to French pressure and accepted her share of the bargain proposed in the Anglo-

---

[1] It was signed by the Khedive on 28 Nov 1904.

[2] Curzon's forward policy, demonstrated by Younghusband's occupation of Lhasa on 7 Sep 1904, was disavowed by the Cabinet and Lansdowne was eventually able to define British policy in a memorandum which calmed Russian irritation.

[3] During the night of 21 Oct 1904 the Russian Baltic Fleet, on its way to the Far East, fired on Hull fishing boats and caused a number of casualties. Delcassé played an important part in securing agreement to refer the incident to an International Court of Enquiry and in establishing its terms of reference as finalised on 25 Nov

French agreement[1] Germany turned towards Morocco itself. By visiting Tangier[2] the Kaiser proclaimed himself Morocco's protector. By his attitudes and in speeches he threatened France with war. England's friendship was to be revealed as valueless and France, abandoning *Entente Cordiale*, was ultimately to receive Morocco as a gift from Germany. Initially at any rate German pressure played into the hands of Delcassé. Lansdowne, impressed by the popularity of the *Entente Cordiale* at home and increasingly suspicious of German designs, was anxious to emphasise British backing. Bertie[3] and a growing group in the Foreign Office[4] and in the Service Departments, who regarded Germany as the prime menace to British security, were prepared to go much further in unofficial encouragement. Delcassé was convinced that Germany's war threats were no more than bluff and his diagnosis of British reactions encouraged him to call that bluff. The rest of the French Cabinet were less sanguine. They concentrated on the military realities of the situation. France seemed defenceless and British encouragement, in the circumstances, more dangerous than helpful. Rouvier, the Prime Minister, favoured a deal with Germany and it was Delcassé, isolated in the Cabinet, who resigned. *Entente Cordiale* was at its lowest premium.

Rouvier's hopes of appeasing Germany by sacrificing Delcassé and playing down Anglo-French *rapprochement* foundered in the face of German attempts to exploit success. Over Morocco Germany continued to insist on the necessity of an international conference. The private deal on which Rouvier had counted remained unattainable. Furthermore, although American arbitration promised to bring the Russo-Japanese War to an end, Rouvier now was faced with what seemed like the most serious German threat to the Franco-Russian Alliance itself. The Björkö meeting on 23 July 1905 between the Kaiser and the Tsar filled him with apprehension. 'What have those two Emperors plotted against us?', he grumbled. 'William II will soon make me as Germanophobe as Delcassé.'[5] 'What a responsibility', he confided to

---

[1] The resultant Franco-Spanish Convention was signed on 3 Oct 1904.

[2] On 1 Apr 1904.

[3] See p. 119.

[4] For a study of this transformation see Zara Steiner, 'The Last Years of the Old Foreign Office 1898–1905', *The Historical Journal*, VI, 1 (1963) 59–90.

[5] M. Paléologue, *Un Grand Tournant de la Politique Mondiale*, p. 392.

Révoil,[1] 'I would carry in history if Germany destroyed the Franco-Russian Alliance while I was Minister.'[2] Even though the Björkö 'plot' failed Rouvier's suspicions and fears were not allayed. It seemed as though Germany was determined to take advantage of French weakness, while her Russian ally remained prostrate, to inflict at least diplomatic and perhaps military humiliation on France. Even if Germany intended no more than an exercise in brinkmanship Rouvier's confidence in the efficacy of appeasing tactics was severely shaken. Although he eventually capitulated to Germany's demand for a conference over Morocco he did so in a mood of resentment and suspicion. Having criticised Delcassé for provoking Germany by stressing French links with Great Britain, he now devoted his energies to strengthening those links. Grey,[3] who had succeeded Lansdowne at the Foreign Office after Balfour's resignation but before the elections which were to produce a Liberal landslide, accepted the *Entente Cordiale* as a cornerstone of British foreign policy. The popularity of the *Entente*, which had proved the only recent successful measure of the moribund Conservative administration, made him anxious to defend it. He was sensitive to Conservative taunts that Liberal governments were not competent to conduct foreign policy. The preservation of the *Entente Cordiale* seemed to constitute an immediate and direct challenge. Furthermore he was impressed by the attitude of the new school in the Foreign Service where *Entente Cordiale* had already become an article of faith. Anxiety about the growth of the German Navy, which had been confined to narrow circles within the Admiralty and to the navalist Press, had now taken root in Foreign Office calculations. If Germany had come to represent the main threat to British security then Britain, for her safety, depended not only on her Navy but on the armies of France, and France must be backed in any confrontation with Germany. It was these considerations which induced Grey to countenance Staff conversations. The tentative contacts established when Lansdowne had been Foreign Secretary developed into detailed plans for military co-operation in the

[1] See p. 130. Révoil was now attached to the French Foreign Office with the rank of Minister and he was subsequently to represent France at the Algeciras Conference.

[2] M. Paléologue, *Un Grand Tournant de la Politique Mondiale,* p. 392.

[3] See p. 62.

event of a German attack through Belgium on France.[1] Henceforth all British war games were based on the assumption that Germany was the only possible enemy and that France was the essential ally.

In these circumstances it is not surprising that Grey should have been anxious, not only to afford diplomatic support to France at the Algeciras Conference, but also for it to be obviously seen by the French that such support was forthcoming. Though Grey was less than candid with the Cabinet he did succeed in his own objectives: the prevention of French capitulation to Germany and the preservation and strengthening of the *Entente Cordiale*. The *Entente* now emerged, quite contrary to Lansdowne's intention but much as Delcassé had planned, as an anti-German alignment. This consummation was largely due to clumsy German efforts at prevention. German resentment, in spite of the measure of German responsibility, was none the less acute.

Once Great Britain began to envisage the possibility of military co-operation with France against Germany the desirability of *rapprochement* with Russia assumed a new meaning. It was now not merely a question of reducing Far Eastern tension and of simplifying the defence of India but of a revolutionary European alignment. The point struck Nicolson[2] forcibly at the Algeciras Conference. As Ambassador-designate to St Petersburg he became convinced that it must be his mission to achieve an Anglo-Russian *entente*. German attitudes at the conference, even if he may have misinterpreted them, left him with the impression that the main objective of British foreign policy must be to conjure the threat from Germany. Accommodation with France's Russian ally was, in these circumstances, mandatory.

In reaching this conclusion Nicolson was in line with the current development of Foreign Office thinking. He was, however, quite out of step with public sentiment where traditional mistrust of Russia on the one hand, and liberal disapproval of the Tsar's autocracy on the other, combined to prevent any enthusiasm for Russian *rapprochement*. Even Grey, although he accepted the

[1] For a valuable reappraisal of the origins and progress of the Staff conversations see G. Monger, *The End of Isolation*, chap. 9, pp. 237–56.

[2] See p. 128. He was now Ambassador at Madrid and Britain's representative at the conference.

reasoning, was dubious, after the Tsar's dismissal of the Duma, as to whether the negotiations which Nicolson had quickly opened with Izvolski[1] should continue to be pursued. But he allowed himself to be convinced by Nicolson's pertinacity.[2] The Anglo-Russian Convention which emerged and which ostensibly settled questions at issue in Persia, Afghanistan and Tibet was in reality a diplomatic revolution. Under cover of pursuing a traditional objective Nicolson achieved a new and very different purpose. The decks were cleared to meet a German challenge.

With the making of the Anglo-Russian *entente* it could be argued that the encirclement which Germany feared had finally materialised. The rival power blocks now faced each other and, with little room for manœuvre, prepared for a struggle which, however much they might deplore, they could hardly hope to avoid. As an important step in that direction the making of the *Entente Cordiale* can be considered as a vital link in the chain of circumstances leading to war in 1914. But, in fact, the role of the *Entente Cordiale* was far less significant than this line of argument would suggest. The probability of an Anglo-French alignment against Germany was predetermined by factors which existed before the conclusion of the *Entente Cordiale*. The Schlieffen Plan,[3] although not completed until 1905, had been in preparation since 1892 when the decision to concentrate the bulk of the German armed forces on the Western Front was taken. From 1897 onwards all projects for deployment included passage over Belgian territory. Once the German General Staff had decided that the security of Germany could only be guaranteed by preparing, in the event of any European conflict, for a major attack against France, then France must remain *the* enemy. No real flexibility in German diplomacy was possible when all guns were pointed at France. The crisis of 1905, when French weakness in the face of possible German attack was so obviously stressed, merely demonstrated that, while the Schlieffen Plan remained the basis of German strategy, France could only preserve her independence as a nation as long as she was equipped to meet that

---

[1] Alexander Izvolski (1856–1919), succeeded Lamsdorf as Russian Foreign Minister in 1905.

[2] See H. Nicolson, *Lord Carnock*, pp. 223–4.

[3] See G. Ritter, *The Schlieffen Plan* (Munich, 1956, English translation 1958).

military challenge. The fact that the Schlieffen Plan entailed attack via Belgium meant, as the German General Staff clearly appreciated, that England would in the event of war have an obligation, as well as a possible interest, to support France. Germany's military calculation counted on French defeat before any effective British intervention.

If the Schlieffen Plan dominated Franco-German relations it was the Kaiser's endorsement of the Tirpitz naval programme which effectively determined Anglo-German relations. Even though the process whereby the building up of the German Navy was regarded as a direct and formidable threat to British security proved a gradual one, it was, none the less, conclusive. By 1906, and for this reason, Germany had become, in Foreign Office calculations, *the* enemy. It was this, rather than the existence of the *Entente Cordiale*, which tied Britain to France, and which lay behind the settlement with Russia. Undoubtedly the making of the *Entente Cordiale* facilitated the growth of new and stronger bonds with France and eventually the reconciliation with Russia. But the German Navy made these objectives seem essential. Although combined resistance to Germany was accepted as a basis of policy by the directors of foreign policy in England and in France the prospect of actual confrontation was viewed, on reflection, with little relish. As Britain lavishly prepared to meet the German naval menace she learned little by little to live more easily with knowledge of the existence of a German Navy. As the French began to dig their teeth into Morocco the possibility of a bargain with Germany over the final stages of absorption seemed worth exploring. In German councils brinkmanship tactics appeared to have been significantly discredited. During the crisis which followed Austria–Hungary's annexation of Bosnia and Hercegovina[1] Germany on the one hand and England and France on the other tried to restrain rather than stimulate the passions of their allies. In the last stages of the crisis Germany was unable to resist inflicting diplomatic humiliation on Russia but this move was only made when any serious risk of conflict had receded. Germany again tempted France with the prospect of a Moroccan bargain. It was these negotiations, however, which eventually led to the

[1] In Oct 1908.

fiasco of Agadir.[1] Great Britain's anxiety about the possibility of too great an improvement in Franco-German relations sharpened the crisis. Instead of a Franco-German *détente* there was a new pronouncement of Anglo-French solidarity.[2]

After the crisis, however, both England and France sought once again to live more amicably with Germany and Germany seemed ready to respond. During the Balkan Wars,[3] when conflict between the two great European power blocs seemed almost inevitable, Germany on the one hand and England and France on the other appeared fully to appreciate the danger and equally anxious to avert it. The system of alliances and alignments which the Anglo-Russian *Entente* had completed was not in itself doomed to generate war.

Indeed even in 1914 and after the murder of the Archduke Francis Ferdinand in Sarajevo on 28 June of that year, it was not the alliances and alignments but the rigid German military planning which proved decisive. Germany possessed no means of backing Austria–Hungary against Russian opposition save by all out military attack on France. She was not prepared for any other kind of war. At the last moment the Kaiser enquired of his Chief of Staff whether German armies could be moved to the Eastern front as a means of bringing pressure on Russia and in the hope that France would then join in trying to promote a settlement. He was told that the switch was impossible because it had not been planned. The invasion of France via Belgium was the only military move, or indeed threat, which Germany could make. It was not the crystallising of alliances and alignments but the inflexibility of the Schlieffen Plan which brought France and Germany to war. Similarly British involvement depended, not on the *Ententes* with France and Russia or even on their consequences, but on calculations based on the existence of the German Navy. Although advocates of a preventive naval war against Germany no longer commanded much respect it was accepted by the Foreign Office that if war in Europe came Great Britain could not afford to keep out. German victory would

[1] The German gunboat *Panther* arrived at Agadir on 1 Jul 1911, allegedly to protect German interests menaced by French expansion in Morocco.
[2] Significantly Delcassé was recalled to office as Navy Minister.
[3] Mar 1912 – Aug 1913.

imply German hegemony in Europe. Given the existence of a powerful German Navy that hegemony would represent a threat to Britain's security which British naval power could then no longer guarantee. But if against predictions France and Russia should, without British aid, emerge victorious, Britain's position would still be precarious. Russia's Indian appetite would be whetted and France herself would then be too powerful for English comfort. However much a European war was deprecated, if war came, England must play the part for which she had been preparing against Germany and on the side of Russia and France. This kind of logic, familiar in the Foreign Office and in the Service Departments, was understood but not relished by Grey. He shielded not only his more susceptible colleagues and the House of Commons, but even himself from its stark conclusions. By Germany's invasion of Belgium he was able to rally most of the Cabinet and public opinion to a war policy without admitting that he subscribed to the view that intervention was in any case essential. Cambon, who found these niceties exasperating, suffered agonies of mind while Great Britain went through the motions of seeming to reach a decision on what had in fact been long decided. Evaluation of British national interests whether rightly or wrongly construed, and not the making of *Ententes* with France or with Russia, determined England's entry into war against Germany.

On the other hand there is no doubt that the existence of the *Ententes* facilitated preparations for a confrontation which German policies had postulated. Russian and French resolutions were stiffened by the promise, which the *Ententes* symbolised, of British support. British public opinion, after ten years of *Entente Cordiale*, was tuned in sympathy with France. At the same time, by their very existence, the *Ententes* may have tempted Germany to cling to policies previously launched when otherwise they might more easily have been discarded. Would the Schlieffen Plan have remained the basis of German strategy, and German foreign policy its prisoner, unless German fears had been kept quickened by the making and maintenance of the *Ententes*? Only if that question could be answered would it be possible to estimate how far the *Entente Cordiale* can be regarded as a contributory cause of the First World War.

When the climax came it was fittingly dramatic that, of the three main authors of the *Entente*, Cambon should have been at his post to remind Britain of her obligations of honour, Delcassé should have returned amid popular acclaim on 28 August 1914 to the Quai d'Orsay, and Lansdowne[1] should eventually have made a courageous plea for a compromise peace.

[1] See p. 112.

Bibliography

As indicated in my Introduction, this study is based almost entirely on printed sources and these, save in the case of usual works of reference, are included below. For details of the most important available manuscript collections of official and private papers see the bibliographies of G. Monger, *The End of Isolation, British Foreign Policy 1900–1907* (1963), and C. M. Andrew, *Delcassé and the Making of the Entente Cordiale* (1968).

ABBAS, M., *The Sudan Question* (1952).

AFLALO, MOUSSA, *The Truth about Morocco; an indictment of the policy of the British Foreign Office with regard to the Anglo-French Agreement* (1904).

AHMED, JAMAL MOHAMMED, *The Intellectual Origins of Egyptian Nationalism* (1960).

ALBERTINI, L., *The Origins of the War of 1914*, 3 vols trans. L. M. Massey (1952–7).

AMERY, J., *The Life of Joseph Chamberlain*, vol. 4 (1951).

ANDERSON, E. N., *The First Moroccan Crisis (1904–6)* (Chicago, 1930; reprinted Hamden, Conn., 1966).

ANDERSON, M. S., *The Eastern Question 1774–1923* (1966).

ANDERSON, P., *The Background of Anti-British feeling in Germany* (1939).

ANDREW, C. M., 'German World Policy and the Reshaping of the Dual Alliance', *Journal of Contemporary History*, I, no. 3 (1966), 137–51.

— 'France and the Making of the Entente Cordiale', *Historical Journal*, X (1967), 89–105.

— *Delcassé and the Making of the Entente Cordiale* (1968).

ANSTEY, R. T., *Britain and the Congo in the Nineteenth Century* (Oxford, 1962).

ANTONIUS, G., *The Arab Awakening* (1938).

BALFOUR, M., *The Kaiser and his Times* (1964).

BARATIER, A. E. A., *Souvenirs de la Mission Marchand*, 3 vols (Paris, 1914–41).

BARCLAY, Sir THOMAS, 'A General Treaty of Arbitration between England and France', *Fortnightly Review*, LXXV (1901) 1022–9.

— *Thirty Years of Anglo-French Reminiscences, 1876–1906* (1914).

BARRÈRE, C., 'La Chute de Delcassé', *Revue des deux mondes* (1 Aug 1932) 602–18 and (1 Jan 1933) 123–33.

BARTLETT, C. J., *Castlereagh* (1966).

BENSON, E. F., *The Kaiser and English Relations* (1936).

BÉRARD, V., *L'Affaire marocaine* (Paris 1906).

BLAKE, R., *Disraeli* (1966).

BLAXLAND, G., *Objective: Egypt* (1966).

BOMPARD, M., *Mon Ambassade en Russie, 1903–7* (Paris 1937).

BRANDENBURG, E., *From Bismarck to the World War: A History of German Foreign Policy 1870–1914* (1927).

BRINTON, J. Y., *The Mixed Courts of Egypt* (New Haven, 1930).

British Documents on the Origins of the War, 1871–1914, ed. G. P. Gooch and H. Temperley (1926–38).

BROGAN, Sir DENIS W., *The Development of Modern France, 1870–1939* (1940; new and rev. ed., 1967).

BRUNSCHWIG, H., *L'Avènement de l'Afrique noir* (Paris, 1963).

BÜLOW, Prince VON, *Memoirs,* trans. F. A. Voigt, 4 vols (1931–2).

BURY, J. P. T., 'Gambetta and Overseas Problems', *English Historical Review,* LXXXII (1967) 277–95.

CAIX, R. DE, *Fashoda, La France et l'Angleterre* (Paris, 1899).

CAMBON, H., [Un Diplomate]: *Paul Cambon, Ambassadeur de France, 1843–1924* (Paris, 1937).

— 'Paul Cambon et les préliminaires de l'Entente Cordiale', *Revue de Paris,* XLIV (1937) 545–64.

CAMBON, P., *Correspondence 1870–1924,* ed. H. Cambon, 3 vols (Paris, 1940–6).

CARROLL, E. M., *French Public Opinion and Foreign Affairs, 1870–1914* (1930).

— *Germany and the Great Powers, 1866–1914: A Study in Public Opinion and Foreign Policy* (1939).

CATTAUI, R. and G., *Mohamed-Aly et l'Europe* (Paris, 1950).

CECIL, Lady GWENDOLEN, *Life of Robert, Marquis of Salisbury,* 4 vols (1922–32).

CHAPMAN, G., *The Dreyfus Case: a Reassessment* (1955).

— *The Third Republic in France. The First Phase, 1871–1914* (1962).

CHARLES-ROUX, FRANÇOIS, *Souvenirs diplomatiques d'un âge révolu* (Paris, 1956).

CHURCHILL, R. S., *Lord Derby 'King of Lancashire'* (1959).

COLLINS, R. O., *The Southern Sudan 1883–1898: A Struggle for Control* (New Haven, 1962).

COLVIN, Sir AUCKLAND, *The Making of Modern Egypt* (1906).

COMBARIEU, A., *Sept ans à l'Elysée avec le President Loubet: de l'affaire Dreyfus à la Conférence d'Algeciras, 1899–1906* (Paris, 1935).

COMBES, E., *Mon Ministère, 1902–5* (Paris, 1956).

CROMER, Earl of, *Modern Egypt* (1911).

— *Abbas II* (1915).

CROMWELL, V., 'Communication: Great Britain's European Treaty Obligations in March 1902', *Historical Journal,* VI, 2 (1963) 272–9.

CROUCHLEY, A. E., *The Economic Development of Modern Egypt* (1938).

CROWDER, M., *The Story of Nigeria* (1962).

CROWE, S. E., *The Berlin West African Conference 1884–5* (1942).

DAWSON, W. H., *Richard Cobden and Foreign Policy* (1926).

DELCASSÉ, T., *Alerte! Où allons-nous?* (Paris, 1882).

DENNETT, T., *Roosevelt and the Russo-Japanese War* (New York, 1925).

DICEY, Sir Edward, 'The Rival Empires', *The Nineteenth Century*, LIV (Dec 1903) 885–902.
— 'The Anglo-French Compact and Egypt', *Fortnightly Review*, LXXXI (1904) 778–88.
Die Grosse Politik der europäischen Kabinette, 1871–1914, ed. J. Lepsius, A. Mendelssohn-Bartholdy and F. Thimme (Berlin, 1922–7).
Documents Diplomatiques Français, 1871–1914, 1st and 2nd series (Paris, 1929–62).
DODWELL, H. H., *The Founder of Modern Egypt: Mohammed Ali* (1931).
DOUMER, PAUL, 'The Anglo-French Agreement', *The National Review* (Jun 1904).
DOUIN, G., *Histoire du Règne du Khedive Ismail*, 3 vols (Cairo, 1933–41).
DUCHENE, A., *La Politique coloniale de la France* (Paris, 1928).
DUGDALE, B. E. C., *Arthur James Balfour*, 2 vols (1936).
EARLE, E. M., *Turkey, The Great Powers and the Bagdad Railway* (New York, 1923).
ECKARDSTEIN, Baron VON, *Ten Years at the Court of St. James, 1895–1905*, trans. and ed. G. Young (1921).
EDWARDS, E. W., 'The Japanese Alliance and the Anglo-French Agreement of 1904', *History*, XLII (1957) 19–27.
EDWARDS, M., *The West in Asia, 1850–1914* (1967).
ELGOOD, P. G., *Bonaparte's Adventure in Egypt* (1931).
ENSOR, R. C. K., *England 1870–1914* (Oxford, 1936).
ESHER, Viscount, *The Influence of King Edward and Essays on other Subjects* (1915).
— *Journals and Letters*, ed. M. V. Brett and Oliver, Viscount Esher 4 vols (1934–8).
ÉTIENNE, E., 'The Colonial Controversies between France and England', *The National Review*, LXXXII (1 Jul 1903) 395–410.
— *Son œuvre coloniale, algérienne, et politique. Discours et écrits divers, 1881–1906*, 2 vols (Paris, 1907).
EUBANK, K., *Paul Cambon, Master Diplomatist* (Norman, Oklahoma, 1960).
— 'The Fashoda Crisis Re-examined', *The Historian*, XII (Feb 1960) 256–70.
EYCK, E., *Bismarck and the German Empire* (1950).
FAGE, J. D., *An Introduction to the History of West Africa*, 3rd ed. (1962).
— *An Atlas of African History* (1963).
FEIS, H., *Europe the World's Banker, 1870–1914* (New Haven, 1930).
FITZMAURICE, Lord E., *The Life of Granville George Leveson-Gower, Second Earl Granville, K.G., 1815–1891*, 2 vols (1905).
FLINT, J. E., *Sir George Goldie and the Making of Nigeria* (1960).
FOOT, M. R. D., *British Foreign Policy since 1898* (1956).
FRASER, P., *Joseph Chamberlain: Radicalism and Empire, 1868–1914* (1966).
FREYCINET, C., *La Question d'Égypte* (Paris, 1904).
GAILEY, H. A. Jr, *A History of the Gambia* (1964).
GARDINER, A. G., *Life of Sir William Harcourt*, 2 vols (1923).

GARVIN, J. L., *The Life of Joseph Chamberlain*, 3 vols (1932–4).

German Diplomatic Documents, 1871–1914, 4 vols. Selected and translated from *Die Grosse Politik* by E. T. S. Dugdale (1928–31).

GIFFEN, M. B., *Fashoda: The Incident and its Diplomatic Setting* (Chicago, 1930).

GIRARDET, R., *Le Nationalisme français, 1871–1914* (Paris, 1966).

GOBLET, R., 'L'Arrangement franco-anglais', *Revue politique et parlementaire*, XL (10 May 1904) 229–41.

GOLDBERG, H., *The Life of Jean Jaurès* (Madison, 1962).

GOOCH, G. P., *Before the War: Studies in Diplomacy*, 2 vols (1936).

— *Studies in Diplomacy and Statecraft* (1942).

GOODSWAARD, J. M., *Some Aspects of the End of Britain's 'Splendid Isolation'* (Rotterdam, 1952).

GOSSES, F., *The Management of British Foreign Policy before the First World War* (Leiden, 1948).

GRENVILLE, J. A. S., 'Lansdowne's abortive project of 12 March 1901 for a secret agreement with Germany', *Bulletin of the Institute of Historical Research*, XXVII (1954) 201–13.

— 'Goluchowski, Salisbury and the Mediterranean Agreements, 1895–1897', *Slavonic and East European Review*, XXXVI (1957–8) 340–69.

— *Lord Salisbury and Foreign Policy* (1964).

GREY OF FALLODON, Viscount, *Twenty-Five Years, 1892–1916*, 2 vols (1925).

HALE, O. J., *Germany and the Diplomatic Revolution, a Study in Diplomacy and the Press, 1904–6* (Philadelphia, 1931).

— *Publicity and Diplomacy, with Special Reference to England and Germany 1890–1914* (1940).

HALÉVY D., *La Fin des Notables* (1930).

— *La République des Comités, essai d'histoire contemporaine, 1895–1934* (1934).

— *La République des Ducs* (1937).

HALÉVY, E., *A History of the English People in the Nineteenth Century. Epilogue 1895–1914*, trans. E. I. Watkin and D. A. Barker, 2 vols (1934).

HALLBERG, C. W., *The Suez Canal; Its History and Diplomatic Importance* (New York, 1931).

HAMPDEN JACKSON, J., *Clemenceau and the Third Republic* (1946).

HANOTAUX, G., *Le Partage d'Afrique; Fashoda* (Paris, 1909).

— *L'Entente Cordiale* (Paris, 1912).

Hansard's Parliamentary Debates, 4th series, vol. CXXXV, 499–577; vol. CXLIII, 999–1047; vol. CXLIV, 460–564.

HARDINGE, Sir A., *Life of Henry, Fourth Earl of Carnavon*, 3 vols (1925).

HARDINGE OF PENSHURST, Baron, *Old Diplomacy* (1947).

HARDY, G., *Histoire de la Colonisation française* (Paris, 1947).

HARGREAVES, J. D., 'The origin of the Anglo-French Military Conversations in 1905', *History*, XXXVI (1951) 244–8.

— 'Entente Manquée; Anglo-French Relations, 1895–1896', *Cambridge Historical Journal*, XI (1953) 65–92.

— *Prelude to the Partition of West Africa* (1961).

HARRIS, W. B., *Morocco that Was* (1921).
HAYASHI, Viscount, *Secret Memoirs*, ed. A. M. Pooley (1915).
HEADLAM, C. (ed.), *The Milner Papers* (1931–3).
HEADLAM-MORLEY, J. W., *Studies in Diplomatic History* (1930).
HENDERSON, G. B., *Crimean War Diplomacy and other Historical Essays* (1947).
HILL, R. L., *Egypt in the Sudan, 1820–1881* (1959).
— *Slatin Pasha* (1965).
HINSLEY, F. H., *Power and the Pursuit of Peace* (Cambridge, 1963).
— 'Bismarck, Salisbury and the Mediterranean Agreements of 1887', *Historical Journal*, i (1958) 76–81.
HOLLAND, B., *The Life of Spencer Compton, Eighth Duke of Devonshire*, 2 vols (1911).
HOLT, P. M., *The Mahdist State in the Sudan, 1881–1898* (Oxford, Clarendon Press, 1958).
— *Egypt and the Fertile Crescent 1516–1922* (1966).
HOSKINS, H. L., *British Routes to India* (Philadelphia, 1928).
HOWARD, C. H. D., *Splendid Isolation* (1967).
HOWARD, J. E., *Parliament and Foreign Policy in France* (1948).
HUDSON, G. F., *The Far East in World Politics* (1939).
HURST, H. E., *The Nile* (1952).
ILAMS, T. M., *Dreyfus, Diplomatists and the Dual Alliance: Gabriel Hanotaux at the Quai d'Orsay*. (Geneva–Paris, 1962).
INGHAM, K., *The Making of Modern Uganda* (1958).
JAMES, R. R., *Lord Randolph Churchill* (1959).
— *Rosebery: A Biography of Archibald Philip, Fifth Earl of Rosebery* (1963).
JARAY, G. L., 'L'Opinion publique et le Rapprochement franco-anglais', *Questions diplomatiques et coloniales*, XVIII (1904) 593–609.
— 'Notre Accord avec l'Angleterre et la Politique franco-anglaise', *Revue politique et parlementaire*, XL (10 Jun 1904) 462–506.
JEFFERSON, M. M., 'Lord Salisbury and the Eastern Question, 1890–1898', *Slavonic and East European Review*, XXXIX (1960–1) 44–60.
JENKINS, R., *Sir Charles Dilke: A Victorian Tragedy* (1958).
JOHNSON, D. W. J., *France and the Dreyfus Affair* (1966).
— *Guizot: Aspects of French History, 1787–1874* (1963).
JOHNSON, F. A., *Defence by Committee: The British Committee of Imperial Defence 1885–1959* (1960).
JOLL, J. (ed.), *Britain and Europe. Pitt to Churchill, 1793–1940* (1950).
JULLIEN, E. L., *Notice sur la vie et les travaux de M. Paul Cambon* (Paris, 1926).
KAYSER, J., *Les Grandes Batailles du Radicalisme, 1820–1901* (Paris, 1962).
KENNEDY, A. L., *Salisbury, 1830–1903* (1953).
KURTZ, H., 'The Lansdowne Letter', *History Today*, XVIII, 2 (Feb 1968) 84–92.
LAMB, A., *Britain and the Chinese Central Asia: The Road to Lhasa, 1767–1905* (1950).
LANDES, D. S., *Bankers and Pashas: International Finance and Economic Imperialism in Egypt* (1958).

LANESSAN, J. L. de, *Histoire de l'Entente Cordiale anglo-française* (Paris, 1916).

LANGER, W. L., *The Franco-Russian Alliance, 1890–1894* (Cambridge, Mass., 1929).

— *European Alliances and Alignments, 1871–1890* (New York, 1931).

— *The Diplomacy of Imperialism*, 2nd ed. (New York, 1951).

LAROCHE, J., *Quinze Ans à Rome avec Camille Barrère* (Paris, 1943).

LEAMAN, B. R., 'The Influence of Domestic Policy on Foreign Affairs in France 1898–1905', *Journal of Modern History*, XIV (1942) 449–79.

LEE, Sir S., *King Edward VII*, 2 vols (1927).

LEES, F., 'Some Promoters of Anglo-French Amity', *Fortnightly Review*, LXXX (Jul 1903) 132–140.

LEWIS, S. E., 'Anglo-German Diplomatic Relations 1898–1902', *Bulletin of the Institute of Historical Research*, IX (1931–2) 123–7.

LIVERMORE, S. W., 'The American Navy as a Factor in World Politics, 1903–1913', *American Historical Review*, LXIII (Jul 1958) 863–79.

LLOYD, Lord, *Egypt since Cromer*, 2 vols (1933–4).

LONGFORD, E., *Victoria R.I.* (1964).

LOUIS, G., *Les Carnets de Georges Louis*, 2 vols (Paris, 1962).

LOWE, C. J., *Salisbury and the Mediterranean, 1886–1896* (1965).

LYALL, A. C., *The Life of the Marquis of Dufferin and Ava*, 2 vols (1905).

MAGNUS, Sir P., *Gladstone: A Biography* (1954).

— *Kitchener: Portrait of an Imperialist* (1958).

— *King Edward the Seventh* (1964).

MALZANOFF, A., *Russian Far Eastern Policy, 1881–1904* (University of California, 1958).

MANSERGH, N., *The Coming of the First World War 1878–1914* (1949).

MANTOUX, P., 'The Debut of M. Paul Cambon in England, 1899–1903', in *Studies in Anglo-French History*, ed. A. Coville and H. W. V. Temperley (Cambridge, 1935) 145–58.

MARDER, A. J., *British Naval Policy 1880–1905: The Anatomy of British Sea Power* (1940).

— (ed.), *Fear God and Dread Nought: the correspondence of Admiral Lord Fisher of Kilverstone*, 3 vols (1952–9).

— *From Dreadnoughts to Scapa Flow. The Royal Navy in the Fisher Era 1904–1919*, vol. I (1961).

MARLOWE, J., *Anglo-Egyptian Relations, 1800–1953* (1954).

— *The Making of the Suez Canal* (1964).

MATHEWS, J. J., *Egypt and the Formation of the Anglo-French Entente of 1904* (Philadelphia, 1939).

MAUROIS, A., *King Edward VII and his Times* (1933).

MAXWELL, Sir H., *The Life and Letters of George William Frederick, Fourth Earl of Clarendon, K.G., G.C.B.*, 2 vols (1913).

MEDLICOTT, W. N., *The Congress of Berlin and After* (1938).

MEVIL, A., *De la Paix de Francfort à la Conférence d'Algéciras* (Paris, 1909).

MICHON, G., *L'Alliance franco-russe, 1891–1917* (Paris, 1927).

MIÈGE, J. L., *Le Maroc et l'Europe (1830–1894)*, vol. 4: *Vers la Crise* (Paris, 1963).

MILLER, T. B., 'The Egyptian Question and British Foreign Policy, 1892–1894', *Journal of Modern History*, XXXII (Mar 1960) 1–15.

MILNER, Lord, *England in Egypt* (1905).

MONEYPENNY, W. F., and BUCKLE, G. E., *The Life of Benjamin Disraeli*, vols V, 1868–76, and VI, 1876–81 (1920).

MONGER, G., *The End of Isolation. British Foreign Policy 1900–1907* (1963).

MONTEIL, P. L., *Souvenirs reçus: quelques feuillets de l'histoire coloniale* (Paris, 1924).

MOON, P. T., *Imperialism and World Politics* (New York, 1926).

MOREL, E. D., *Morocco in Diplomacy* (1912).

MORLEY OF BLACKBURN, Viscount, *Recollections*, 2 vols (1917).

MORLEY, J., *Life of W. E. Gladstone*, 3 vols (1903).

NÉTON, A., *Delcassé, 1852–1923* (Paris, 1952).

NEWBURY, C. W., 'The Development of French Policy on the Lower and Upper Niger, 1880–1889', *Journal of Modern History*, XXXI (1959) 16–26.

NEWTON, Lord, *Lord Lansdowne* (1929).

NICOLSON, Sir H., *Sir Arthur Nicolson, Bart., First Lord Carnock. A Study in the Old Diplomacy* (1930).

NISH, I. H., *The Anglo-Japanese Alliance, 1894–1907* (1966).

NOEL, L., *Camille Barrère* (Bourges, 1948).

NOLDE, B., *L'Alliance franco-russe* (Paris, 1936).

OLIVER, R., *Sir Harry Johnston and the Scramble for Africa* (1956).

— and ATMORE, A., *Africa since 1800* (Cambridge, 1967).

— and FAGE, J. D., *A Short History of Africa* (1962).

ORMESSON, W. DE, 'Vergennes et Delcassé', from *Portraits d'hier et d'aujourd'hui* (Paris, 1925).

PALÉOLOGUE, M., 'Un prélude à l'invasion de Belgique', *Revue des deux mondes* (1 Oct 1932) 481–524.

— *Un Grand Tournant de la Politique Mondiale, 1904–6* (Paris, 1934).

— and BRUGÈRE, R., 'Le plan Schlieffen et le Vengeur', *Revue des deux mondes* (15 Nov 1932) 425–30.

PARR, J. F., *Théophile Delcassé and the Practice of the Franco-Russian Alliance, 1898–1905* (Moret-sur-Loing, 1952).

PENSON, L. M., 'The New Course in British Foreign Policy, 1892–1902', *Transactions of the Royal Historical Society* XXV, 4th series (1943) 121–38.

— *Foreign Affairs under the Third Marquis of Salisbury* (1962).

PERHAM, M., and BULL, M. (eds), *The Diaries of Lord Lugard. Nigeria 1894–5 and 1898*, vol 4 (1963).

PERHAM, M., *Lugard: The Years of Adventure, 1858–1898* (1956).

PETRIE, Sir C., *The Life and Letters of the Right Hon. Sir Austen Chamberlain, K.G., P.C., M.P.*, vol I (1939).

POINCARÉ, R., *Au service de la France*, 2 vols (Paris, 1926).

PONSONBY, Sir F., *Recollections of Three Reigns* (1951).

PORTER, C. W., *The Career of Théophile Delcassé* (Philadelphia, 1936).

PRIBRAM, A. F., *England and the International Policy of the European Great Powers, 1871–1914* (1931).

PURCELL, V., *The Boxer Uprising* (1963).

RECLUS, M., *La Troisième République de 1870 à 1918* (Paris, 1945).

RECOULY, R., 'Le Septennat de M. Delcassé', *Revue politique et parlementaire*, XLVI (10 Dec 1905), 532–46.

— *La Troisième République* (Paris, 1927).

— *De Bismarck à Poincaré: soixante ans de diplomatie républiquaine* (Paris, 1932).

RENOUVIN, P., '*La Crise européenne et la Grande Guerre, 1904–14*, 2 vols (Paris, 1934).

— *La Question d'Extrême Orient* (Paris, 1946).

— 'Les Origines de l'expedition de Fachoda', *Revue historique*, CC (1948) 180–97.

— (ed.), *Les Politiques d'expansion impérialiste* (Paris, 1949).

REYNALD, G., 'La Diplomatie française: l'œuvre de M. Delcassé', from *Pages d'Histoire, 1914–15* (Paris, 1915).

RICH, N., and FISHER, M. H. (eds), *The Holstein Papers*, 4 vols (Cambridge, 1955–63).

— *Friedrich von Holstein*, 2 vols (Cambridge, 1965).

RIFAAT, M. BEY, *The Awakening of Modern Egypt* (1947).

RITTER, G., *The Schlieffen Plan. Critique of a Myth*, trans. A. and E. Wilson (Wolff, 1958).

RIVIÈRES, E. SÉRÉ DE, *Histoire du Niger* (Paris, 1965).

ROBERTS, S. H., *History of French Colonial Policy, 1870–1925*, 2 vols (1929).

ROBINSON, R., and GALLAGHER, J., *Africa and the Victorians: The Official Mind of Imperialism* (1961).

RONALDSHAY, Earl of, *The Life of Lord Curzon*, 3 vols (1928).

SABRY, M., *Épisode de la question d'Afrique. L'Empire Égyptien sous Ismail et l'ingérence anglo-française, 1863–1879* (Paris, 1933).

SAINT-CHARLES, FLEURY DE; 'L'Accord franco-anglais et l'Europe', *Revue d'Histoire diplomatique*, XVIII (Jun 1904), 454–75.

SAINT-RENÉ TAILLANDIER, G., *Les Origines du Maroc français* (Paris, 1930).

SAMMARCO, A., *Histoire de l'Égypte moderne* (Cairo, 1937).

SANDERSON, G. N., *England, Europe and the Upper Nile, 1882–1899* (Edinburgh, 1965).

SCHMITT, B. E., *The Coming of the War: 1914*, 2 vols (1930).

SCHUMAN, F. L., *War and Diplomacy in the French Republic* (1921).

SETON-WATSON, H., *The Decline of Imperial Russia, 1855–1914* (1952).

SETON-WATSON, R. W., *Disraeli, Gladstone and the Eastern Question* (1935).

— *Britain in Europe, 1789–1914* (Cambridge, 1945).

SHAPIRO, D. (ed.), *The Right in France 1890–1919*, St Antony's Papers, no. 13 (1962).

SONTAGG, R. J., *Germany and England, Background of Conflict 1848–94* (1938).

SOUTHGATE, D., *The Most English Minister: The Policies and Politics of Palmerston* (1966).

SPRING RICE, Sir CECIL, *Letters and Friendships, a Record,* ed. S. Gwynn, 2 vols (1929).

STEED, H. W., *Through Thirty Years 1892–1922* (1924).

STEINBERG, J., *Yesterday's Deterrent* (1965).

STEINER, Z. S., 'Great Britain and the Creation of the Anglo-Japanese Alliance', *Journal of Modern History,* XXXI (1959), 27–36.

— 'The Last Years of the old Foreign Office', *Historical Journal,* VI (1963) 59–90.

STUART, G. H., *The International City of Tangier* (1931).

SUMNER, B. H., *Tsardom and Imperialism in the Far East and the Middle East 1880–1914* (1942).

TABOUIS, G., *Jules Cambon,* trans. C. F. Atkinson (1938).

TARDIEU, A., *France and the Alliances* (New York, 1908).

TAYLOR, A. J. P., *Germany's First Bid for Colonies 1884–1885. A Move in Bismarck's European Policy* (1938).

— 'Prelude to Fashoda: The Question of the Upper Nile, 1894–5', *English Historical Review,* LXV (1950) 52–80.

— 'British Policy in Morocco, 1886–1902', *English Historical Review,* LXVI (1951).

— *The Struggle for Mastery in Europe, 1848–1918* (Oxford, 1957).

TEMPERLEY, Sir H., *The Foreign Policy of George Canning* (1925).

— *England and the Near East. The Crimea* (1936).

— 'British Secret Diplomacy from Canning to Grey', *Cambridge Historical Journal,* VI (1938) 1–32.

— and PENSON, L., *Foundations of British Foreign Policy from Pitt to Salisbury* (Cambridge, 1938).

TERASSE, H., *Histoire du Maroc jusqu'au Protectorat français,* 2 vols (Paris, 1949–50).

THOMSON, D., *Democracy in France: The Third Republic* (1946).

TIGNOR, R., 'The Indianization of the Egyptian administration under British Rule', *American Historical Review* (1962) 636–61.

— *Modernization and British Colonial Rule in Egypt, 1882–1914* (1967).

—and COLLINS, R. O., *Egypt and the Sudan* (New York, 1967).

TINT, H., *The Decline of French Patriotism 1870–1940* (1964).

TREVELYAN, G. M., *Grey of Fallodon* (1937).

TRUHOS, P., *M. Delcassé et sa Politique* (Paris, 1910).

TUCHMAN, B. W., *August 1914* (1962).

TUGAY, EMINE FOAT, *Three Centuries. Family Chronicles of Turkey and Egypt* (1961).

VAILLE, E., *Le Cabinet noir* (Paris, 1950).

VANSITTART, Lord, *The Mist Procession* (1958).

VILLOT, R., *Eugène Étienne* (Oran, 1951).

WEBSTER, Sir C., *The Congress of Vienna* (1919).

— *The Foreign Policy of Castlereagh, 1815–1822* (1934).

— *The Foreign Policy of Palmerston, 1830–1841,* 2 vols (1951).

WHATES, H., *The Third Salisbury Administration, 1895–1900* (1901).

WHITE, J. A., *Diplomacy of the Russo-Japanese War* (1965).

WILLIAMS, B., *Cecil Rhodes* (1921).
WILLS, A. J., *An Introduction to the History of Central Africa* (1964).
WILSON, Sir A., *The Suez Canal, its past, present and future* (1939).
WODEHOUSE, C. M., *The Greek War of Independence* (1952).
WOLF, J. B., *The Diplomatic History of the Bagdad Railroad* (Columbia, 1936).
WOODWARD, Sir E. L., *Great Britain and the German Navy* (1935).
WRIGHT, G., *France in Modern Times* (1962).
ZETLAND, Marquis of, *Lord Cromer* (1932).

NEWSPAPERS AND PERIODICALS

The Daily Chronicle
The Daily Mail
The Fortnightly Review
The Illustrated London News
The Manchester Guardian
The Morning Post
The National Review
Punch
The Review of Reviews
The Spectator
The Sphere
The Standard
The Times
The Westminster Gazette
Bulletin du Comité de l'Afrique française
La Dépêche coloniale
La Dépêche de Toulouse
L'Echo de Paris
Le Figaro
Le Matin
La Revue des deux mondes
La Revue politique et parlementaire
Le Temps

Index

Malay Peninsula, the, 182–3
Malta, 15, 41
Manchester Guardian, 150
Manchuria, 107, 115, 116, 162, 168–9, 202, 214
Maradi, 241–2. *See also* Tessawa-Maradi
Marchand, Jean-Baptiste (1863–1934), and Marchand mission, 62, 65, 68–70, 72, 82, 85–90 *passim*
Massip, M., 77
Matacong, 33
Matankari, 241, 246
Matin, Le, 88
Mazagan, 141, 205–6
Mediterranean Agreements (Feb and Dec 1887), 52–3, 67
Meheddi, Sid Menebhi, 129, 131, 133, 221
Mekong valley, the, 65 n, 182–3
Melilla, 212
Méline, Jules Félix (1838–1925), 75, 80, 81
Mellacourie river, 23, 25
Menelik, Emperor of Abyssinia, 62
Metternich, Prince Clemens (1773–1859), 16
Metternich, Count Paul, 120
Miquelon, *see* St-Pierre and Miquelon
Mixed Tribunals, Egyptian, 29 n
Mohammed Ahmed of Dongola (1840–1885), the Mahdi, 45–6, 49
Mohammed Ali Pasha (1769–1849), ruler of Egypt 1805–49, 18, 19, 28, 45
Mohammed Said Pasha (1822–63), ruler of Egypt 1854–63, 21 n, 28 n
Mohammed Tewfik (1852–92), Khedive of Egypt 1879–92, 30, 31, 38, 39, 40, 46–7
Monroheim, Baron de, 95
Monson, Sir Edmund (1834–1909), 83–90 *passim*, 95, 100, 103–4, 106, 142, 148, 163, 165, 167, 208–9, 236, 268
Monteil, Parfait Louis (1855–1925), 61–62, 65
Moroccan seaboard, neutralisation of, 139, 152–3, 175, 182, 192, 195, 205–6, 217, 220, 223, 225, 254
Moroccan trade, freedom of, 139, 153, 175, 182, 187, 195–6, 205, 212, 224, 226, 256, 264
Morocco, 68, 81, 123, 125–42 *passim*, 145–8, 152–4, 169, 170, 175–6, 180–200 *passim*, 205–6, 208, 210–12, 215–

225 *passim*, 232–40 *passim*, 255–69 *passim*, 272–5, 279
Morocco lobby, 125
Mossi, 71
Moussa, river, 230
Muong Sing, 65 n
Muraviev, Count, 102, 106
Muscat, 100, 101, 246

Napoleon I, Napoleon Bonaparte (1769–1821), Emperor of the French 1801–1815, 15–17
Napoleon III, Charles-Louis-Bonaparte (1808–73), Emperor of the French 1852–70, 20–3
Napoleonic Wars, the, 15–17
National Africa Company, 37
National Review, The, 144, 155, 173
Navarino, battle of (Oct 1827), 18
Navy League, the, 144, 155
Nelson, Horatio, Viscount (1758–1805), 15 n
New Guinea, French, 240, 242
New Hebrides, the, 135, 175, 179, 183, 189–90, 192, 195, 197, 205, 207, 212–213, 242, 245–6, 269
Newfoundland, 14, 35, 97–8, 130, 133, 135, 140, 175, 179–80, 187, 189–90, 192, 195, 197, 205–7, 210, 212–13, 216, 219–24, 227, 229, 231–9 *passim*, 243, 245–6, 251, 254, 258, 267–9, 272–3
Newfoundland bait question, the, 179, 180, 206, 212, 219, 267–8
Newfoundland bounty question, the, 180, 187, 197, 207–8, 213, 216, 219
Newfoundland, French establishments, 219, 231–3
Newfoundland, French fishing rights, 14, 15, 179, 180, 206–7, 213, 219, 227, 231–2, 243, 246
Newfoundland French shore, 131, 180, 213, 219, 233, 242
Nice, 21
Nicholas II (1868–1918), Tsar of Russia 1894–1917, 275, 277–8
Nicolson, Sir Arthur, later Lord Carnock (1849–1928), 128–32 *passim*, 135, 277–8
Niger, river, 50, 51, 71, 213, 224, 227, 230–2, 236, 238, 240, 241, 244, 250
Niger Company, the Royal, 51, 56, 60
Niger enclaves, 207, 213, 227, 230
Niger, Lower, 37, 49, 60, 66, 233
Niger, Upper, 50, 56